SURVEY OF WORLD CULTURES

Editor, THOMAS FITZSIMMONS

JORDAN

its people   its society   its culture

George L. Harris _{Lawrence} ,1910 –

IN COLLABORATION WITH
Moukhtar Ani
Mildred C. Bigelow
John Cookson
Sheila C. Gillen
George A. Lipsky
Charles H. Royce
Alex H. Westfried
Percy Winner

HRAF PRESS *New Haven*

Already Published in this Series
I Poland

LIBRARY OF CONGRESS CATALOG CARD NUMBER: 58–12701

ⓒ COPYRIGHT 1958

HUMAN RELATIONS AREA FILES, INC.

NEW HAVEN, CONN.

PERHAPS at no other time in history has so much been written about the different peoples of the world. While there remain critical areas of ignorance about motivation and behavior, the dynamics of society, culture and its power, there do exist quantities of recorded observations and information, and of highly detailed analyses of this or that aspect of life as it is lived by given groups. Observations, information, analysis —all usually are scattered, available but separate. The books of this series represent an endeavor to gather and interpret the separate pieces. The series itself proceeds from an earlier group of studies—the Country Series—issued experimentally in limited quantity to discover what needs they might fill and how they might be improved. The need has been defined, it is enormous. The series will present works on representative societies in each major culture area of the world.

This, then, is a different kind of book in that it is concerned with the relationship of aspects usually studied separately. The focus of the book is a society as it functions, the interrelationship of its parts and of the parts to the whole. Emphasis is on the dynamics of that interplay, on constants of attitude and behavior, abiding values, the presence and impact of forces for change. Containing a great deal of information, and thus useful as a reference, it is not merely a collection of data. Covering the political, economic, and sociological aspects of a society, it presents no minute analysis of any element within these catagories. Asserting as valid only what has stood up to the simultaneous and systematic challenge of the various social science disciplines represented by the persons who wrote it, the book has no recourse to the citation of authorities.

Much that has remained implicit in previous separate studies is here made explicit, and should generate controversy. In the course of challenging the available materials, and consequent selection, generalization, and implication, many gaps in existing knowledge have been exposed. In some cases it has been possible to indicate the general outline and probable significance of such gaps, and this should be useful as a guide to further exploration. These are, in short, books out of which should come many questions. That there may also come some increased understanding of the seemingly endless and confusing diversity of ways by which men approach the experience of living with one another is the wish of all who have participated in the making of the series.

Thomas Fitzsimmons

Washington, D. C.

ACKNOWLEDGMENTS

PUBLICATION of this study, and of the series, is possible because many individuals gave unstintingly of time, talent, critical and creative energy. Review procedures designed to tap all the resources of the HRAF research staff as well as those of outside specialists were supervised by Dr. Herbert H. Vreeland, who read and commented upon each chapter as it was drafted. In addition to drafting several chapters, Mr. Percy Winner, of the senior staff, rendered especially valuable assistance to Dr. Vreeland and to the Editor.

The authors had at their disposal working papers prepared by Dr. Raphael Patai under a contract administered by Dropsie College. Miss Charlotte M. Morehouse, regional specialist, graciously read and criticized the completed draft. Mr. William Sands, Editor of *The Middle East Journal,* and Director of Publications at the Middle East Institute, provided valuable materials and advice.

While these and many others contributed to the Jordan study, whatever shortcomings it may have are the sole responsibility of its authors and the Editor.

THE HUMAN RELATIONS AREA FILES

THE HUMAN RELATIONS AREA FILES is a nonprofit research corporation affiliated with Yale University and sponsored and supported by its sixteen member universities. HRAF was established in 1949 "to collect, organize, and distribute information of significance to the natural and social sciences and the humanities." It has concentrated upon furthering a fresh approach to the study of societies, culture, and social behavior.

The files themselves contain carefully selected sources analyzed according to G. P. Murdock's *Outline of Cultural Materials.* Located at each of the member universities, they are a new kind of reference library in which basic information about nearly two hundred peoples can be consulted with ease and speed. Preparation of the present study was facilitated by the use of the Middle East File and the Jordan File.

MEMBER UNIVERSITIES

University of Chicago
University of Colorado
Cornell University
Harvard University
University of Hawaii
Indiana University
State University of Iowa
University of Michigan

University of North Carolina
University of Oklahoma
University of Pennsylvania
Princeton University
University of Southern California
University of Utah
University of Washington
Yale University

TABLE OF CONTENTS

Contents (*continued*)

THE CULTURE AND THE SOCIETY

JORDAN, AS AN INDEPENDENT POLITICAL ENTITY, WAS THE PROD-
uct of events which followed World Wars I and II. Not until after
the latter did the country acquire its present boundaries, population,
and full independence. For four hundred years before that, the present territory of Jordan was a tenuously held and lightly administered province of the Ottoman Empire. Still earlier it had been a
vaguely defined southern district of Syria under a succession of rulers
—Greek, Roman, and Arab. With no natural boundaries to set it off
from the territory around it, Jordan never stood alone, nor did it
occur to its few townsmen, isolated villagers, and scattered nomads to
think of themselves as "Jordanians."

The rule of a central government and the external pressures
converging on the new state were only beginning to create the conditions for the social integration that would have made of Jordan a
nation as well as a state when it joined the Arab Federation. Definitions used to distinguish the inhabitants of Jordan from their Arab
neighbors continue to be largely arbitrary and formally political.

Nationalism and Arabism

Jordan shares in a general scheme of social life which imparts a
degree of cultural unity to the Arab Middle East. Obvious among the
unifying factors that make it possible to speak of an "Arab world"
are the Moslem religion and the Arabic language. Despite sectarian
differences within Islam, the Moslem faith represents a shared body
of values and prescriptions for conduct which give a distinctive cast
to life. The Moslem religion, for all the local and regional differences
in the specifics of its content and in the intensity of its meaning for
its adherents, provides a framework within which men tend to identify
themselves as one people. For Jordanians and most other Arabs this

broadly integrating feature of Islam has in some degree worked to retard the development of the kind of national separateness implied by recently drawn political boundaries. Many West Bank Jordanians, looking across the fortified Israeli frontier at lands once their own, and embittered at what they regard as the temporizing policy of the Jordanian Government, have found it easy to accept the leadership, not of their own legal sovereign, but of the militant head of another Moslem state, President Nasser of Egypt.

Arabic in its written form provides a common medium of communication in the area despite differences among spoken dialects. Moreover, classical Arabic, the language of the Koran and of the whole Islamic literary tradition, has acquired a deeply felt social value which, for the illiterate majority as well as for the literate minority, gives intensity to a general sense of Arab identity.

In Jordan the vast majority is Moslem and Arabic-speaking; there is no serious problem of ethnic minorities to divide the country. There are, however, other deeply divisive factors; two of these are inherent in the pattern of social organization characteristic of the Middle East in general and of its Arab portion in particular: a form of kinship organization in which the family and its extensions mark the boundaries of the strongest loyalties of the individual, and a residence pattern within which most of the population lives in the relative isolation of scattered agricultural villages.

The Kinship Principle

The traditional Arab family is not merely a unit in which children are born, raised, and prepared for life in the larger community. Constructed on the principles of descent in the male line and the authority of the eldest male, it unites several generations in a tightly cohesive group whose members throughout life cooperate in securing a living, look to each other for aid and protection, and accept the discipline imposed by the family head. Kin ties do not end with this extended family but reach out in a widening ring of real or fictitious relationship through the lineage or clan, composed of a number of extended families, and in the case of the bedouins, to the tribe. It is these concentric circles of kinship—operating with varying degrees of strength in the town, the village, and the desert—that still give the Jordanian his primary identity, and not some civic concept of national citizenship. Wealth, education, and appointment to civil or military office can raise a man on the social ladder, but their acquisition, when it does not come directly through family connections, most often comes through family efforts. The effect of this system is to divide the society into many competing, only sometimes cooperating, kin-groups. These, rather than the community or the country at large, mark the limits of the individual's strongest allegiance.

Events of the last decade have brought about a sudden multiplication of Jordan's urban population, and western influence has presented the people with problems and opportunities which the unmodified family institution was unable to solve or grasp. The familial principle nevertheless remains strong, and family exclusiveness can be expected to yield only slowly to more inclusive patterns of community organization.

Local Exclusiveness

Kin exclusiveness is matched by the local exclusiveness of the villages in which live the rural two thirds of Jordan's settled population. The social horizons of the Jordanian peasant (fellah), tied to the arid land by poverty, historically have been limited to the village in which he is born and dies—at most, to a few adjacent villages and perhaps a nearby market town. Sometimes all the residents of a village belong to a single lineage, in which case kin and local ties coincide. Larger villages usually contain several lineages, but in all of them the village and its associated fields represent the only clear-cut territorial unit with which the inhabitants can readily identify themselves.

The Jordanian Moslem villager shares his religion, language, and basic social patterns with his fellows throughout Jordan, but these integrating factors mean little in a concrete way given the absence of any significant degree of conscious social interaction beyond the confines of his home village. Various forces are eroding the old isolation and self-sufficiency of the village: the operations of the central government, the pull of the growing towns, and the stimulus of the new needs and expectations created by these influences. Jordan's villages, nevertheless, continue in large measure to be what they have been for centuries, so many approximately complete and self-contained small societies—Arab but as yet only geographically "Jordanian."

East Bank–West Bank Division

The fragmentation of Jordanian society into kin-groups and local groups goes far back into history and is characteristic of the social landscape throughout the Arab world. Recent events, however, have introduced a new and more sharply drawn division, that which exists between the largely rural population of the Transjordanian East Bank and the relatively urbanized Palestinians of the West Bank territory annexed after the Arab-Israeli war of 1948. The West Bank, closer to the ports and population centers of the Mediterranean shore and under direct British rule for nearly three decades after World War I, was subjected to much stronger western influences than the East Bank. The Arab-Israeli conflict and the acquisition of the West Bank tripled Jordan's population, bringing in, as well as the 400,000 inhabitants of the annexed area, almost half a million refugees. Discontent and frustration among the refugees, most of whom after nearly ten years are still living in extreme hardship in camps supported by the United Nations, were inevitable.

The Palestinian Arabs had experienced great cultural changes under the British Mandate. Schools, hospitals, and industrial enterprises were established. Urban patterns were intensified; a middle class and an urban working class began to emerge. Many learned something of the principles of modern administration; many more began to develop a political consciousness which reached beyond the limits of village or even regional political experience. After the annexation Jordan had to absorb professional, social, and political elements which constituted a group much more westernized than any to be found within the boundaries of the original Transjordan.

The relatively urban and westernized elements in the Palestinian group tended to view the East Bank population as ignorant and backward and to resent the entrenched position and conservative policies of the East Bank leaders. Rivalries quickly developed between East and West Bank. East Bank Jordanians were stung by the superior attitude of the newcomers. The literacy and technical ability of the Palestinians made them strong claimants for positions on levels of prestige and authority which until then had been Transjordanian preserves; they were dissatisfied with the secondary role they were forced to play while Transjordanians remained entrenched in the key positions of political power. This division as yet shows no sign of disappearing, and there are indications that the rivalry may be, if anything, intensifying. The political potentialities of that rivalry were apparent in the crisis of the spring of 1957, when King Hussein mustered loyal East Bank bedouin military forces to counter a threat posed to his authority largely by disaffected West Bank elements.

Nomad, Villager, and Townsman

A final division, which is present throughout the Middle East, separates Jordan's population into three discrete and fundamental occupational sectors: pastoral nomads, village agriculturalists, and townsmen.

These three types of occupation and residence represent distinct modes of life which from early times have differentiated the populations of the Middle East. At all times the numerically dominant type has been the village peasantry engaged in sedentary agriculture, while the urban dwellers and the nomads have constituted small, but far more dynamic, minorities. Of Jordan's present population of nearly 1,500,-000, about 800,000 are village cultivators, upwards of 400,000 are urban dwellers, and hardly more than 200,000 are bedouin pastoralists, ranging from the purely nomadic camel-breeders of the desert to the partly sedentarized groups on the margin of the sown area who mix herding of sheep and goats with seasonal agriculture.

The early Arab conquests and the initial spread of Islam were carried out by bedouin armies, and the recollection of that spectacular burst of energy has persisted in both the Arab world and in the West. The actual elaboration of the Moslem religion and the specialized cultural developments associated with Islam, however, were the work, not of the nomadic tribesmen, but of the specialists of the towns. Meanwhile, the basic economic production which made these developments possible and the dominant way of life of the mass of the people continued, as it does today, to be centered in the villages. That observers in both the Middle East and the West have tended to give more attention to the nomads than to the villagers and townsmen reflects an historic interest rather than an actual assessment of the relative importance of the three types.

The integrating factors of religion, language, and the rule of a national government crosscut the social differences among nomad, peasant, and townsman, but do not transcend them. The profound cleavage among the three has been manifest not only in such obvious things as occupation, dress, shelter, and food but also in social values, outlook, expectations, and in the way in which the basic cultural materials of the Arab-Islamic tradition have been put to use.

For the pastoral nomads, social existence took meaning in terms of the value placed on independence, freedom, leisure, honor, pride in noble blood, bravery, generosity, hospitality, vengefulness, forgiveness, and loyalty to kin-group. Conflict between tribes was formerly the major type of competition; droughts, locusts, thirst, hunger, shame, dishonor, and the menace of demons and evil spirits are still main sources of fear and anxiety. The suppression of intertribal raiding has left the nomad with no avenue but service in the government forces for the demonstration of the military prowess so highly valued. The enforced tribal peace has produced new frustrations while the old anxieties remain.

The two thirds of Jordan's population who live in the country's agricultural villages have been strongly influenced by nomadic ideals, but the conditions of village life have produced important differences in value and outlook. The nomadic preoccupation with independence and freedom, for example, is little developed in a settled peasantry, disciplined in the hard labor of the fields and accustomed to the controls of the settled community. Important as kinship ties and the compulsions of family authority are among the nomads, they have gripped the peasant even harder.

The towns differ more from the villages than the villages from the nomadic encampment. The towns dilute the intensity of personal relationships, which are so striking a feature of life in the village and the bedouin tribe. Urban occupational diversity and class differentiation contrast with the relative social homogeneity of the village and the tribe. The townsman, historically cosmopolitan in contrast to the population of the countryside, has been subjected to a generation of western influence, and new notions of the rights of the individual compete with the waning claims of the authority of the traditional family. Political ideals of independence and freedom are at work and they take on special meaning in the context of actual or imagined interference of outside powers. There is a growing awareness of the world beyond Jordan's boundaries, even though this may be seen largely in the slogans turning on the subject of "imperialism" and "colonialism." The townsman still shares a large body of traditional values with the villager and the nomad, but, in the increasingly impersonal environment of the changing town, his fears and anxieties concerning his personal economic and social status, more familiar to the western observer, are becoming dominant.

Intergroup Attitudes

Traditional Arab culture at the height of its development during the medieval period was an extremely well-integrated complex of behavior and belief. Its educational and socializing methods and aims were well adjusted to the values and goals dominating adult life in general. Its religious doctrines, moral precepts, and ritual observances combined to make economic and social inequalties appear not only bearable but natural. The knowledge that beyond all the tribulations of this world there is a divine reward made for endurance in the face of hardship and poverty. Folk customs, arts, and rites made life "worth living" in spite of the poor material rewards and monotony of the agricultural labor in which most Jordanians engaged.

For villager, urban dweller, and nomad alike, the close circle of kin-group provided a sense of security and a small arena within which the conforming individual could count on achieving a place of honor and dignity. Where many died young, old age was honored, and to become old carried its own reward.

Within this general framework of shared feeling there were, however, major disharmonies among the three main sectors of Arab society, each being pitted against the others in particular ways. These disharmonies continue to be apparent in Jordanian life. More and more nomads, for example, are being transformed into village cultivators by the social and economic pressures of the present day, but nomadic contempt for the settled population still persists. The recognition of the strength in wealth and numbers of the settled sectors of the society no doubt tinctures with helpless anger the nomad's disdain for townsman and villager. To the extent that the government can be identified with domination by the settled people it loses prestige in the eyes of the nomads. When King Hussein in the spring of 1957 called upon the bedouins for assistance against disruptive forces in towns and villages they responded to the opportunity to strike at the sedentary enemy. The bedouin sheikhs assisted the King, not so much in his modern role as chief of state, but in his traditional role of paramount tribal sheikh.

The Jordanian villager—when he is not himself a recently sedentarized nomad—has traditionally regarded both nomads and townsmen with fear and dislike. The nomads formerly raided and robbed the villages and have only recently been restrained from doing so by the police power of the government. Another kind of exploitation, in the form of rents, dues, and taxes, came from the officialdom and the well-to-do of the towns. Although the villagers over the centuries learned submissiveness, hatred for their oppressors did not lie far below the surface. Today, as the villager becomes more aware of the possibilities for improvement of his physical lot, his old resentments acquire a much more explosive political potential. The ways of the nomads have always been distasteful to the villager, and the newly acquired manners, behavior, and appearance of the modern townsmen at once attract and repel him. It is the villager who is most conscious of the heritage of Islam and who clings to the forms of his traditional religion with the greatest determination.

In the eyes of the urban dweller, both nomads and villagers are backward, primitive, and ignorant. Western influence has been felt most strongly in the towns and its acceptance there has involved one degree or another of modification or rejection of the traditional culture. In human terms the process is not an easy one, for the old ways are often discarded or lose force before the new patterns can be assimilated and adapted. The consequence for many is a kind of cultural rootlessness which finds one of its expressions in the violent twists and turns of Jordanian urban politics. The break with the past, however, is never complete, even among the most westernized, and there is an evident and ambivalent nostalgia in the pains taken by the townsman to trace his lineage back to a noble tribe, thereby tacitly conceding the claims of the bedouins that they are the fundamental source and protectors of the Arab tradition.

Each of the three large sectors of Jordanian society shows a vertical stratification of wealth and power based upon its peculiar economic arrangements and social values. The gap between highest and lowest is widest in the towns, narrowest in the bedouin tribe. With their new sources of wealth and new forms of political power, the towns are in the ascendancy in the country as a whole. Nomadic influence, however, cannot be discounted, as was seen in the political crisis of 1957. The villagers, as so often in the past, are caught in between; their effect upon national policies is still felt largely through the sheer weight of their numbers and in the economic problem they present to Jordan's leaders. There is a growing official concern for the difficulties of the peasant, but he remains a passive rather than an active force in the life of the country.

Economic Factors

Transjordan in 1948, though still exhibiting a clear nomad-agricultural dichotomy, had long been witnessing the eastward expansion of the cultivated area and the slow transformation of the nomads into settled agriculturalists. Modern developments are hastening this process. Motor transport has reduced the importance of the camel; governmental authority has reached into territories which once knew only tribal controls; and the relative wealth and power of the settled area is borne in upon the nomads as it had not been in the past. All of these factors combine to exert a sedentarizing pressure on the nomads, who increasingly are yielding by turning from camels to sheep, from sheep to part-time cultivation, from part-time cultivation to the full status of settled villagers.

Industry played very little part in the country until 1948 and it has even now only begun to affect the lives of the people. Economic self-sufficiency, though at a very low level, has been characteristic of the village economy, which as long as wants were few produced practically everything the villagers consumed. The introduction of commercial farming and the influx of factory products have brought increasing dependence upon the town and the outside world. This evolution, which had gone further in Palestine than in Transjordan, was greatly accelerated by the annexation of the West Bank. The sudden growth of Jordan's capital city, Amman, from a population of 30,000 to nearly 200,000 in five years strikingly reflects the speed of the economic and social change taking place.

Modernization and industrialization are shifting the ownership and the distribution of wealth. The traditional Middle Eastern pattern of a small minority group of landed proprietors and a large impoverished mass has existed in a less exaggerated form in Jordan than in some other countries of the area. Today the pattern is being modified by the appearance of a small but growing urban middle class, which appears as a direct product of the new economic and intellectual currents flowing into Jordan from the West.

Direction of Change

The changes which are remaking Jordanian life are most rapid in the towns, slower in the villages and among the nomads. None of these social segments is being affected in precisely the same way, but certain broad effects are evident throughout. Technological innovation is not restricted to the urban centers but is present in the irrigation projects and the modern methods which are beginning to benefit some rural communities. A few of the wealthier bedouin tribes are using modern agricultural machinery and supervised peasant labor on their domains. New political ideologies are competing for the allegiance of people whose political activity until recently was restricted to the control processes of kinship group and local community.

In the Moslem Arab tradition the past was an age of glory, and Arab greatness reached its height in the time of the Abbasside Caliphate. Still earlier Mohammed and his contemporaries had witnessed the last and final revelation of the Divine Will and had taken up the sword and carried God's word across the world. Succeeding generations moved farther and farther from the early spirituality and grace and it became the task of later religious leaders to try to reconstruct what was done and said by Mohammed as a guide to life. The revivalistic movements from the eighteenth century onward, when Islam began to feel the impact of the forces generated in the West, invariably stressed a return to the ideal of Islam in its "pure" form. In secular terms, of course, this traditionalist affirmation had a political aspect in its appeal as a means of preserving the old order.

More recently there has been an effort to reconcile the old

Islamic tenets with the changed conditions and the demands of the present day, but on the whole there is a drift away from orthodox religion, and the concerns of the present and hopes for the future are replacing preoccupation with the past. Traditionalism in Jordan and elsewhere in the Arab world, however, has its extreme protagonists, and these stand in fanatic opposition to the no less determined modernists. The clash is a new and gravely disturbing factor in Arab society. The position of the more youthful, energetic, and aggressive modernists is complicated by the fact that they are divided among themselves by the competing ideological choices with which the West has presented them. The conservatives, confronted with the inevitability of change, range from those who blindly resist the new forces to those who seek to fit them into the pattern of the past. The pressures of this struggle bear most strongly upon the urban population, in particular its small intellectual segment.

Jordan today is thus caught up in a crisis which grips the entire Middle East. Jordan's difficulties, however, are perhaps more acute than those of some of its Arab neighbors. Its long common frontier with Israel gives the general Arab-Israeli antagonism a special reality for Jordanians. Scanty resources and a large refugee population place the country in a position of economic dependence which even the most vigorous efforts cannot soon alter. Politically, Jordan has been pulled between the policies of Egypt, which aspires to leadership of the Middle East, and reliance upon the West, which can provide the economic support it must have. Whether the country can, within the framework of the Federation, construct among its people the basic forms of unity which will enable it to preserve its identity remains to be seen.

The growth of cities, the introduction of western ideas and technology, and the inducements and dangers which confront the country in the international arena are creating conditions for internal unity as well as for division. The bedouins, threatened by urban power, see a protector in the throne and are reinforced in their traditional loyalty to the royal family; among the townsmen and villagers, those who have begun to profit by economic developments—halting and uncertain as they are—are acquiring a vested interest in the preservation of the country and a felt loyalty to the nation.

HISTORICAL SETTING

THE HASHEMITE KINGDOM OF JORDAN WAS CONSTITUTED IN 1949 with the annexation (formalized in 1950) by the Kingdom of Transjordan of a portion of Arab Palestine west of the Jordan River. The country is not only new, it is in a sense an accidental creation, stemming more out of a confluence of external forces and events than from any historical sense of nationhood. Jordan's recently acquired West Bank and its East Bank are separated by more than the short river, the Jordan, which empties into the salt waters of the Dead Sea. The West Bank with its towns and settled agriculture has experienced for more than a generation the westernizing influences that reached it when it was part of the British Palestinian Mandate. The East Bank, until World War I a feebly administered part of the Turkish province, Syria, has for centuries been an isolated zone of marginal agriculture and nomadic pastoralism. The sedentary patterns and the modern influences which make possible the idea of nationality and necessitate the development of complex political institutions have only begun to touch Jordan's original East Bank population, approximately one third of the total population. This one third and the Palestinian majority—half of whom are refugees—make uneasy compatriots in a state which has not had time to become a nation.

Jordan is not without a history, but all except the last pages of that record, written in this generation, are not the history of the Kingdom of Jordan but of a vaguely defined territory. Against that blurred background the bedouins, except for their more sophisticated leaders, have little or no conception of state or national boundaries. · Sheikh, family, clan, tribe, and the larger identity of Arabic and the Moslem religion mark the human boundaries within which they move and the points on which center their loyalties. The peasants, more accessible than the nomads to the control of central government, are somewhat more aware of political processes in the modern sense, but their horizons are still largely those of kin-group and village. It is among the Palestinians that the clearest notions of nationality have developed; yet even here these notions have meant a kind of generalized "Arabism" rather than any loyalty to the Hashemite throne, which their most articulate leaders continue to denounce as pro-West and "soft" toward the archenemy, Israel. Recent events, however, have generated a motivation to bolster the present and shape the future by reference to a common past, and out of this may come a Jordanian interpretation of history in national terms.

Jordanian Palestine has a history much marked in the story of Christian civilization, for the territories annexed to the kingdom in 1950 embrace Bethlehem, the old city of Jerusalem, and other places of Christian pilgrimage.

The larger area to the east of the Jordan River is essentially an arid region flanked by population centers which have been foci of civilization and power since ancient times. It has been invaded and fought over many times as an object of conquest itself or in the ebb and flow of other campaigns. On occasion, it has known nominal independence, maintained by one or another outside power needing a buffer against competitors. After the Arab conquest (633–636 A.D.) the territory was often employed as a base by groups interested in exploiting their ability to interfere with pilgrimages to Mecca. At other times local forces have gained strength enough to assert temporary hegemony over the area and to maintain a brief independence against outsiders. For four centuries under Turkish rule the land was administered as part of the historic territory, Syria, and some Jordanians today still refer to themselves as "Syrians" or "south Syrians" and view with equanimity or actively support projects for political union with Syria. The approval with which even official Jordanian circles have in the past considered plans for federation with Syria and Egypt as well as Iraq is a further expression of the absence of a compelling sense of Jordanian historical continuity.

Early History

In Biblical times, the area of Transjordan was roughly covered by the small states of Gilead, Ammon, Moab, and Edom. Echoes of Ammon sound in the name of the present capital Amman. The West Bank encompasses the old districts of Samaria and Judaea, which for a time were included in the Hebrew monarchy. During the period prior to the Greek conquest the area was successively dominated by Assyrians, Chaldeans, and Persians. The Seleucids, successors of Alexander the Great, who conquered the area in 333 to

332 B.C., firmly controlled the northern part of the area, but the south was at times occupied by the Ptolemies of Egypt. One of the latter, Philadelphus (285–246 B.C.), beautified Rabbath Ammon and renamed it Philadelphia, but its ancient Semitic name reasserted itself in modern Amman. Philadelphia was one of the league of ten Greek-speaking cities, the so-called Decapolis (Matthew 4:25).

Gerasa, another of the ten cities, is the present-day Jerash, whose Roman ruins attract tourists from all over the world. These and other remains indicate that the East Bank was more densely populated under the Romans than today. The Roman period was ushered in with the conquest of the region by Pompey in 64 to 63 B.C. In the last pre-Christian centuries the Arab Nabataeans, whose capital was the rock-hewn caravan city of Petra, achieved prosperity and power and extended their empire northward to Damascus and eastward to the Euphrates, with spheres of influence on the Sinai Peninsula and in northern Arabia. The multicolored ruins of Petra are among the archaeological beauty spots of this part of the world. Strabo speaks of the Nabataeans as an energetic and active people, adding that there were no slaves nor poor among them. Nabataean ascendancy in the area was destroyed by the Romans in 106 A.D.

The Qudaa and the Ghassanids also settled in Jordan at a very early date—certainly long before the advent of Islam. During an early time, too, other Arab tribes such as the Koreish (as is mentioned in the Koran) made regular commercial expeditions to Syria and Jordan. (Mohammed, himself a member of the Koreish, participated in more than one of these expeditions before he embarked on his religious mission.)

After the conversion of the Emperor Constantine in 313 A.D. brought an end to the persecution of Christianity, the new faith spread widely in the area. There is concrete evidence for this in the ruins of churches and monasteries—at Hubras, Umm Al Jimal, Amman, Jerash, and Qilwa—that were built after Constantine's time. When Islam emerged in Arabia, Christianity had been accepted not only by the settled inhabitants but even by the bedouins, notable among whom were the Ghassanids, centered at Busra Eski Sham in the Hauran.

Arab Conquest

From the standpoint of Jordan's present position, the conquest of the area by Arab Moslems in 633 to 636 may be considered the most significant development in the country's history. As with other conquered territories, the Jordanian area was subsequently absorbed in the great Moslem Caliphate under the first Caliph, Abu Bakr; some-time later it came under the Ommiad Dynasty with its center in Damascus, then under the Abbassides with Baghdad as their capital, and then the Fatimids in Cairo. With the subsequent breakup of the Arab empire, Transjordan fell under the rule of various successor states. During the years of the Arab Caliphate the people of Palestine and Transjordan were almost totally Islamized and Arabicized, so that today Islam is the prevailing religion and Arabic the predominant language. Memories of older traditions or cultures, Semitic or Greco-Roman, are practically forgotten.

In the early days of Islam, before Mecca became the principal Moslem holy place, Mohammed and his followers turned in prayer to Jerusalem. As the stopping place of the Prophet on his nocturnal journey heavenward, Jerusalem was (and is) sacred, and it became the object of further veneration when the two Ommiad Caliphs of Damascus, Abd al-Malik (685–705) and al-Walid (705–715), under whom the Moslem empire reached unprecedented heights, chose it as a site for the Dome of the Rock (called Omar Mosque) and the Aqsa Mosque, considered the most sacred places of worship in Islam after the sanctuaries of Mecca and Medina.

The Crusades, which saw the establishment of the Latin Kingdom of Jerusalem by the Christian invaders, focused Arab attention on the Palestinian area. Moslem writers, calling for a counter-Crusade, tended to exaggerate the sanctity of Jerusalem and other Moslem centers threatened or held by the infidel. Then as later, however, the region was less important in itself than for its position on the communications line between the Arab centers of power in Syria and Arabia.

Turkish Conquest

In 1516–1517 the Ottoman Turks conquered Syria and Egypt. During this period Syria, with its western frontier at the Jordan River, extended southward to the Gulf of Aqaba and included the area of Transjordan. The area east of the Jordan River (later known as Transjordan) achieved special importance as a pilgrimage route between Turkey and Hejaz. It was the responsibility of those in control here to see to it that the pilgrim caravans passed unhindered and unharmed. Perhaps the most important means of assuring safe passage was the payment of subsidies to the local bedouins.

Down through the nineteenth century there were frequent outbursts of warfare and rebellion in the area, but by the beginning of the twentieth century the Ottoman government had succeeded in establishing calm. Though Ottoman rule lasted four centuries, the region retained its Arab character, receiving few colonists from the ruling state. There is relatively little Turkish admixture in the population.

Evolution of the Kingdom

The Arab Revolt

Following negotiation and agreement with the British during World War I, the Arabs of Hejaz under the leadership of Sherif Hussein of Mecca (later King of Hejaz) revolted, June 1916, against Turkish rule. Arab troops attacked Turkish garrisons in Hejaz; Sherif Faisal (son of Sherif Hussein and later King of Iraq) attacked and captured Aqaba, after which Turkish communications with Hejaz could be destroyed and the Turkish left flank in Palestine attacked. The Arab assault northward was based on Aqaba and had as its immediate objective the isolation of the Turkish forces in Hejaz. The campaign was successful, and eventually all of Transjordan and Syria was conquered by combined British and Arab troops. The whole territory was included in a kingdom under Sherif Faisal, with Damascus as its capital. The Arabs, however, were disappointed in their assumption that the Allies meant to establish a large, independent Syria. A French mandate was imposed upon the part of the region that has since become the republics of Syria and Lebanon; Palestine and Transjordan were brought under British mandate.

The Emergence of Transjordan

Transjordan—later to be enlarged into the present Hashemite Kingdom of Jordan—came into being in 1921. Hussein's second son, Abdullah, the eventual ruler, appeared in Amman in February of that year with the purpose of launching a campaign against the French to restore the rule of his brother in Syria. He was dissuaded from this project in a series of conferences in Jerusalem with Winston Churchill, then Secretary of State for Colonies. The understanding provided that Britain would use its good offices to influence the French to restore an Arab government in Syria with Abdullah at its head. In the meantime, Abdullah accepted the rule of Transjordan under the general supervision of the British High Commissioner for Palestine, who represented the mandatory power. Abdullah had earlier been offered the royal authority in Iraq, but the Iraqi throne went to Faisal and Abdullah had to content himself with Transjordan, which had originally been included in Faisal's Syrian kingdom. The solution was acceptable to Abdullah and the British obtained an Arab administration as a buffer against raiding bedouins.

Although Abdullah, as Emir, began in April 1921 to set up a central administration in Transjordan to replace the local autonomous political entities that had appeared following the overthrow of Faisal in Syria, his government as an autonomous power under mandatory jurisdiction was first explicitly announced on May 26, 1923. The Emirate included all of the territory of the present Hashemite Kingdom of Jordan, except the West Bank (formally annexed in 1950). The *de facto* retention of Maan and Aqaba by Transjordan was accepted by Saudi Arabia in the Treaty of Jidda with Great Britain in May 1927.

A statement of the Palestine High Commissioner in April 1923 had made Transjordan's new semi-independent status conditional upon the establishment of a constitutional government and the conclusion of a treaty confirming Britain's rights and obligations. The treaty was negotiated in February 1928; the Emirate of Transjordan was recognized as independent, Britain retaining military and some financial powers, and an Organic Law that year provided for an elected Legislative Council. The ratifications of the treaty were exchanged in Amman in October 1929. These events brought to a close the period of Abdullah's direct rule through an Executive Council and inaugurated the slow evolution of constitutional political processes, on the western model, that placed some limitations upon the royal authority. The 1928 treaty, amended in 1934 and again in 1941, was superseded in 1946 by a treaty in which Britain recognized Transjordan's full independence, and in 1948 by a treaty of preferential alliance.

Abdullah's government was faced at the outset with the problem of bringing under control the bedouins and other local forces in the area; in the early years several rebellions had to be put down. To meet this initial resistance and to maintain the peace, the Arab Legion (al-Jaysh al-Arabi), a regular military force officered in large part by British personnel and supported by annual British grants-in-aid, was established. Under the leadership first of F. G. Peake Pasha and later John Bagot Glubb Pasha, the Legion became known as the most efficient military force in the Arab world. Assisted by local tribes, in particular the Beni Sakhr, and the Royal Air Force, the Legion proved its effectiveness, not only in the early internal troubles but also against the Wahhabi invasions from Nejd, one of which penetrated to within a few miles of Amman.

Transjordan in World War II

At the beginning of World War II, Transjordan placed the Arab Legion at the disposal of Britain and offered any assistance within its power. It strongly supported the British against the pro-Axis officers who seized power in Iraq in May 1941 and opened fire on the British at Lake Habbaniyah. It was also effective in assisting the British against the Vichy French authorities, who, under a German Armistice Commission, had come into control in Syria and Lebanon. Legion forces also did service in guarding vital centers in the Middle East.

Establishment of the Kingdom

In March 1946, Britain, in the Treaty of London, recognized Transjordan as a fully independent state; on May 25, Abdullah was proclaimed King and a Constitution replaced the Organic Law of 1928. In 1948 the Arab Legion, together with other military forces of the League of Arab States, took part in the Arab-Israeli war and occupied a considerable portion of Palestine. Three Palestinians were added to the Cabinet, and Transjordan adopted as its official name "The Hashemite Kingdom of Jordan"—after the name of the ruling dynasty descending from the grandfather of Mohammed. An armistice agreement between Jordan and Israel was signed in April 1949 through the good offices of the United Nations Mediator in Palestine. Jordan was left in control of central Palestine (including the part of Jerusalem known as the Old City).

The formal act of union of the East and West Banks took place on April 24, 1950, following a general election for a new Council of Representatives in which the Palestinians were to have the same number of seats as the Transjordanians. The first act of the new Council was to approve the unification of the two territories, already acted upon by Parliament in 1948.

Recent Years

Jordan's recent past has been studded with problems and crises. These have been compounded of forces generated by four main factors: (1) the establishment of the state of Israel and the entry into Jordan after the Arab-Israeli war of nearly a half million destitute and embittered refugees, determined somehow to revenge themselves on Israel and return to their homes; (2) the growth of Arab self-awareness at a time when the ideological alternatives of the new countries of Asia are being presented in the hard relief of the cold war; (3) scanty resources and dependence on outside economic aid to sustain its people; (4) the strategic location of the kingdom, making it an object of the ambitions of surrounding powers.

King Abdullah's annexation of the Palestinian West Bank left him vulnerable to the charge that he had accepted the permanent existence of Israel—a damaging indictment in the League of Arab States, of which Jordan is a member, and most especially in the eyes of many of his new Palestinian refugee subjects. Abdullah's assassination in June 1951 by a follower of the ex-Mufti of Jerusalem represented an extremist translation of this feeling into action. The strong personality of Abdullah having been removed, the West Bank forces found it easier to contend with royal authority. Abdullah's successor, his son Talal, proved mentally incompetent and the precedent of executive decision by the Cabinet operating independently of the royal authority began to be established. With the accession of Talal's son, sixteen-year-old Hussein, in 1952, power remained centered in the Cabinet, drawing strength from powerful forces in the Parliament, through which the trend toward West Bank domination of Jordanian politics was continued. The adoption of a new Constitution in 1952 made it still easier to circumscribe the royal authority (see chap. 8).

West Bank elements after September 1945 were further incited by the open encouragement of Egypt and Syria, whose governments were promoting a Pan-Arabism dedicated to the physical extermination of Israel and committed to policies at once damaging to the West and favorable to the Soviet bloc (see chap. 10). Hussein, by dismissing the British commander of the Arab Legion, Glubb Pasha, in March 1956, seemed to signalize his own accord with these developments; this step and the subsequent termination of the 1948 Anglo-Jordanian treaty of preferential alliance went considerably beyond what the ailing Talal had done in signing the Collective Security Pact of the League of Arab States. Thereafter, events moved rapidly and, with the disaffected West Bank street mobs daily growing more restive, King and Cabinet found themselves in fundamental conflict during a series of political crises in the spring of 1957. In April the King took decisive action—dismissing the Cabinet, abolishing all political parties, and declaring a state of emergency. Whatever the future might bring, the young monarch's stand marked a dramatic turn in the course of Jordanian politics; it presaged the emergence of a new alignment in the Middle East, with Jordan and Iraq ranged against Egypt's ambitions to set the course of the Arab world.

GEOGRAPHY AND POPULATION

THE NAME JORDAN IS DERIVED FROM THE HEBREW YORDAN (IN Arabic *urdunn*), meaning "descender." The river is aptly named; issuing from its sources in Syria at an altitude of 1,000 feet, it flows south through Lake Hula and Lake Tiberias (Sea of Galilee) to the Dead Sea over a course of about 200 miles; for two thirds of the way the river is below sea level.

The area of Jordan is approximately 37,000 square miles, about the same as that of Indiana. Lying between latitudes 29 and 33 degrees north—on a line with northern Florida—and roughly bisected by the 37-degree meridian of longitude, Jordan has only one point of access to the sea at the small, underdeveloped Red Sea port of Aqaba. Very limited in agricultural and industrial resources, this largely desert region which was once the southern section of the Ottoman vilayet (province) of Syria first became a political entity, arbitrarily created, after World War I, when it was awarded to Abdullah, son of King Hussein of Hejaz (see chap. 2).

To the east and south the Jordanian desert merges imperceptibly into Iraq and Saudi Arabia; the northern (Syrian) boundary is demarcated in its western half because of the relatively high concentration of population in the border area, but to the east the border with Syria is open desert country. The torturous 350-mile border with Israel is marked with barbed wire and heavily patrolled.

The dominant topographical feature of Jordan is its division by the depression of the Jordan River into distinct eastern and western zones. The depression itself, some 65 miles in length and 3 to 14 in width, is the hottest and most forbidding area in the Fertile Crescent. Throughout history it has been a barrier between Palestine on the west and Transjordan on the east. This geological rift also initially divided the two distinct groups among Jordan's 1,440,000 people— the relatively urban and westernized Palestinians of the West Bank,

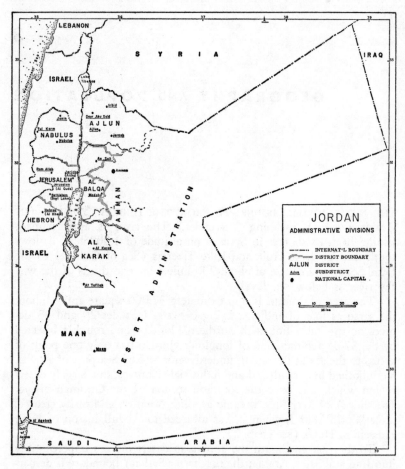

and the more isolated and conservative inhabitants of the East Bank. Today, however, Palestinians are to be found throughout the country. The two populations are not amalgamating easily, and the effort to bring them together in a single national entity continues to involve friction and unrest.

East Bank and Central Depression

More than four fifths of Jordan's East Bank region is geographically and climatologically part of the Syrian or North Arabian Desert. Rainfall—less than five inches as an annual average—is concentrated in the short cool season from December to March. The long, hot, rainless summer, which lasts from April to November, is marked by great day-to-night temperature differences: the days are hot, nights cool, often cold. Spring and fall, as known in more temperate climates, can hardly be said to exist in Jordan; the transition from "winter" to the heat of summer is swift.

The average elevation of East Bank Jordan is about 1,650 feet; some areas rise to more than 3,000 feet above sea level. Agriculture, even the most primitive dry farming, is impossible in most of the region and only pastoral nomadic tribes can find subsistence. Toward the northwest, however, rainfall gradually increases, and in the corner bounded by the Jordan River and its principal tributary the Yarmuk to the west and the north and by the Damascus-Amman (Hejaz) railroad in the east, it is sufficient (in some places over 10 inches annually) to make cultivation possible. (A minimum of 8 inches of rainfall enables the Jordanian peasant to engage in marginal farming; over 15 is sufficient for normal cultivation.)

Both the Jordan and the Yarmuk flow too far below the land level of the surrounding areas to permit irrigation without costly pumping machinery. It was estimated in 1946 that only about 5 percent of the total territory of the East Bank was under cultivation; with the uncertain political conditions that have existed ever since, it is unlikely that this fraction has increased to any marked extent.

Nearer the western borders of the East Bank the desert level becomes gradually higher, eventually giving way to the sparsely populated steppe country of the Jordanian highlands—high limestone plateaus, with an average elevation of 3,000 feet, and hills which rise to more than 4,000 feet in the north and 5,400 feet in the south. The western edge of the plateaus forms an escarpment over the Jordan Valley-Dead Sea rift. The rift continues southward, though in a less accentuated form, to the head of the Gulf of Aqaba. At the northern end of the rift are the headwaters of the Jordan and of the Yarmuk. The Yarmuk forms part of the boundaries of Syria, Israel, and Jordan. Inside Jordanian territory the Jordan River winds and twists its way through dense scrub toward the Dead Sea.

The Jordan Valley is characterized by warm, short winters, with a rainfall varying from 10 to 15 inches, and by very hot, dry, and long summers. A hot dry wind, the khamsin, is common in the spring and may also come, rarely and mildly, in the fall. During the khamsin days, which are felt as far west as the Mediterranean shore, a high wind blows from the east, bringing with it fine desert dust and frequently raising the temperature to 120 degrees Fahrenheit or above.

The Dead Sea, 1,000 feet deep in some places, occupies the central part of the rift. More than 1,200 feet below sea level at its surface, it lies in the deepest depression on the land surface of the earth. The completely barren Lisan Peninsula divides it into a larger and deeper northern basin and a very shallow southern basin, the average depth of which is about 10 feet. The total length of the Dead Sea is about 55 miles, its maximum width from east to west about 10 miles. An inland salt lake without outlet, its water level is maintained by the balance between the inflowing water of the Jordan—and its tributary wadis (watercourses)—and an evaporation loss of 5.5 million tons a day. Rainfall over the Dead Sea is negligible, and excessive evaporation has left so great a concentration of minerals in the water that no animal or plant life can exist there. The soil of the narrow plain at the northern end of the Dead Sea is saturated with salt to such a degree that it supports practically no natural vegetation and its cultivation is possible only after a costly process of washing down the salt content of the topsoil with sweet water.

West Bank

The West Bank, constituting only 6 percent of the total area of Jordan, is divided by the Jerusalem corridor into a larger northern bulge—roughly comprising historical Samaria—and the smaller southern area of Judaea. Central Samaria is a deeply dissected region with altitudes as high as 3,000 feet and with foothills falling eastward into the Jordan Valley and westward into the Sharon Plain (in Israel). Springs are not numerous; settlement is confined to the larger valleys, and the uplands are utilized only as pasture. Judaea, on the other hand, is an unbroken upland plateau with few diversifying elements. Bare rocky surfaces strewn with boulders and stones defy cultivation. The few small depressions and valleys are often waterless; vegetation is rarely more than patches of scrub and thorns.

The West Bank, however, contains most, though not the best, of Jordan's cultivable land. The mountain region in the northern bulge receives up to 30 inches of rain annually, making terraced farms and vineyards possible. The much smaller southern bulge receives sufficient rain only in the area west of Jerusalem and Hebron; to the east lies the Judaean desert, a bare, dusty region, practically uninhabited, where even nomads can subsist only with difficulty. An occasional oasis is found, as in the area of Jericho, where springs supply enough water for the irrigation of small, intensively cultivated patches.

Population

The population of Jordan in June 1956 was estimated at about 1,440,-000, including some 476,00 Palestinian Arab refugees. With an area of just over 37,000 square miles, the average population density was

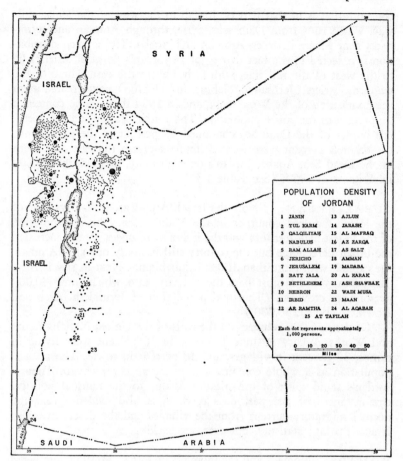

POPULATION DENSITY
OF JORDAN

1	JANIN	13	AJLUN
2	TUL KARM	14	JARASH
3	QALQILIYAH	15	AL MAFRAQ
4	NABULUS	16	AZ ZARQA
5	RAM ALLAH	17	AS SALT
6	JERICHO	18	AMMAN
7	JERUSALEM	19	MADABA
8	BAYT JALA	20	AL KARAK
9	BETHLEHEM	21	ASH SHAWBAK
10	HEBRON	22	WADI MUSA
11	IRBID	23	MAAN
12	AR RAMTHA	24	AL AQABAH
		25	AT TAFILAH

Each dot represents approximately
1,000 persons.

0 10 20 30 40 50
Miles

39 per square mile; since, however, the area under cultivation is considerably under 2,000 square miles (4.8 percent of the total), the density of the planted area was about 780 persons per square mile—a high density for an agrarian country. (See Map, Population Density.)

Distribution of the Population

The distribution of the population is determined by the rainfall pattern. In the north, the mountains are higher and the winds carry a fair amount of moisture from the Mediterranean; south of the Dead Sea, the elevation is less and the prevailing winds cross the hot, dry Sinai Peninsula, losing a great deal of their moisture on the way.

With the exception of the 200,000 nomadic tribesmen population concentration is in that part of Jordan to the west of the Hejaz railway, which runs from Damascus, Syria, through Amman and terminates near Maan, between Amman and Aqaba. The uneven distribution is reflected in the fact that eight of Jordan's political districts lie to the west of the rail line, with only one to the east. Three of the western districts (Jerusalem, Nablus, and Hebron) were created upon the annexation of the West Bank, and in 1954 these alone contained 56 percent of the entire population. The Jordan Valley and the northern border of the Dead Sea contained 36 percent of the population; the other 8 percent were located immediately to the east and south of the Dead Sea. Aqaba, Jordan's only port city, had less than 5,000 inhabitants in 1954. (See Table 1.)

RURAL-URBAN. Before the Israeli-Arab war, Jordan was one of the least urbanized countries in the Middle East. The incorporation of the Palestinian territory and the influx of refugees greatly increased the urban percentage but the country still has only one city, Amman, the capital, with more than 100,000 inhabitants. Next in size is Arab Jerusalem, for the most part the old city, into which some 80,000 persons are crowded. (The total population of Jerusalem, Arab and Israeli, is about 250,000.)

Of the 476,000 refugees on the rolls of the United Nations Relief and Works Agency in June 1953, some 30 percent were living in camps, 32 percent in villages, and 38 percent in towns. The refugee population as a whole contains a large urban complement. Though Jordan's rapid spurt of urbanization is due to the unusual political circumstances of the past decade, there is also evidence that the normal migratory current from the villages and the desert to towns is accelerating; statistics, however, are lacking.

NOMADS. Nomads and seminomads in Jordan in 1952 numbered some 200,000. They are divided into four principal tribal groupings—the Rwala, the Huwaytat, the Beni Sakhr, and the Sirhan—and a number of tribes of lesser importance with comparatively restricted ranges of movement. The Rwala is the only tribe that wanders across national boundaries; its incursions into Jordan, where pasture is scarce at the best of times, often signal a flare-up of feuding with the nomads whose territory is contained entirely within Jordan's boundaries. A traditional enmity also exists between the Beni Sakhr and the Huwaytat. All of these nomads, who count themselves Arab in the restricted sense of a camel-breeding nobility, are now experiencing hard times. With the advent of motor transport the camel has declined in commercial value and the economic base of tribal society has been seriously weakened. Scorning to become herders of sheep and goats —though this is still a profitable business—many nomads are now either living on government relief or reluctantly becoming sedentar-ized.

The lesser tribes are predominantly shepherds and goatherds, in varying stages of sedentarization. Because of the inability of their flocks to move far without water, they have a much narrower range of movement and remain as close as possible to the cultivated areas. Many of them live in permanent villages; during the winter rains they move to tented quarters on the plain, then return to the villages for the harvest.

On the lowest level are the vassal tribesmen. One such tribe is the Solubah, and that name in the course of time has come to be applied to all of the relatively small groups of tinkers, smiths, and artisans who attach themselves to the larger tribes (see chap. 6).

There are also in the Jordan Valley a number of small outcast tribes, often consisting of only a few families. Some show Sudanese or Ethiopian physical traits, being descended from slaves escaped from the larger tribes in the area or from Arabia or Egypt. Some engage in nomad pastoralism, moving their flocks on an annual cycle between summer and winter pastures. The remainder form a pool of cheap labor in the vicinity of the few towns. According to reports, their standard of living is extremely low, often inferior even to that of the refugees.

Population Growth

The recent population growth of Jordan, like that of most Middle Eastern countries, has been spectacular. The addition of the 400,000 West Bank inhabitants and 476,000 refugees has more than trebled Jordan's population since 1948.

BIRTH RATE. The 1954 birth rate in Jordan was reported as 38.4 per thousand. It was probably higher than that; the birth rate for Moslems in Palestine from 1943 to 1946 averaged 53.6, and most of the present population of Jordan consists of Palestinian Moslems —whose fertility is hardly likely to have changed markedly. Some births are not registered. The actual birth rate for the country as a whole may be in the neighborhood of 45 per thousand.

DEATH RATE. The reported number of deaths in Jordan per thou-sand population was 10.4 in 1954. The rate in the United States in the same year was 9.2. Even granting that the United States popula-tion has a considerably larger number of older people and that therefore the crude rate does not indicate the true difference in mortality, the Jordanian figure seems too low. This impression is strengthened by the considerable variation in death rates as reported from one sub-district to another. As with births, some deaths are not registered; the death rate is undoubtedly higher than that reported.

From 1943 through 1945 the Moslem death rate in Palestine averaged 17.6 per thousand. Although the rate was falling, the decline probably slowed or ceased with the health problems created by the Arab-Israeli war. This circumstance in conjunction with the fact that health conditions in East Jordan had not been as good as those in more urban Palestine suggests that the Jordanian death rate today may be at least 17.5 per thousand, if not higher.

NATURAL INCREASE. Taking the difference between the reported birth rate and the reported death rate, the rate of natural increase of Jordan's population would be 28 per thousand or 2.8 percent. If the birth and death rates, however, were in fact 45 and 17.5, the natural increase becomes 27.5 per thousand, or 2.75 percent. Either rate, if continued, would double the population in some 25 years. In any event, the official estimate which places the average yearly increase in population between 1950 and 1954 at 2.1 percent appears to be too low.

With the refugees have come acute difficulties of poverty and discontent, placing the entire country in a precarious position. The 476,000 refugees on the United Nations Relief and Works Agency rolls in 1953 constituted 35 percent of the entire population of the country. About 100,000 refugees with urban backgrounds concentrated in the towns, particularly Amman, and found places in the Jordanian economy as professional men, civil servants, skilled workers, or independent businessmen. The remainder—farmers or agricultural laborers lacking other skills and so far showing little evidence of adaptability—could not be absorbed into Jordan's meager agriculture. They continue to be officially classified as refugees dependent on relief for their support.

The country lacks the resources to support most of these people. There is the further problem of the many Jordanian villages that lost much of their agricultural land when the new border was established. UNRWA estimated that there were 111 Jordanian towns and villages in this category, with 181,000 inhabitants, of whom only 2,000 were self-supporting.

Relief work among the refugees is not confined to furnishing food but must also provide medical attention, sanitation, and education. The death rate in the camps has been kept reasonably low, and a high birth rate increases this huge block of unabsorbed people every year. The shortage of arable land keeps even those refugees with farming experience near the towns and cities, thus increasing urbanization to an extreme degree in a country with an almost completely agricultural economic base.

ETHNIC GROUPS AND LANGUAGES

THE DESERTS OF JORDAN, SYRIA, THE NORTHERN PART OF SAUDI Arabia, and the northeastern projection of Iraq form a geographic, and to a large degree an ethnic, continuum. The people of Jordan, whether town dwellers, villagers, or nomads, are, with the exception of small and comparatively recently arrived minorities, members of one or another of the closely related Arab groupings inhabiting the general area.

Arabic, the official language of Jordan, is the native tongue of almost the entire population. Arabic dialects have been spoken in the region that is now Jordan since as early as the sixth century B.C., but the language did not come into general use until the Arab conquest in the seventh century A.D., when it completely supplanted Aramaic, Syriac, and other locally spoken languages.

Minority languages in Jordan are numerically insignificant and are well on the way to disappearing altogether. Surviving at present are Cherkess, spoken by the older descendants of the Circassian groups who went to Transjordan in the 1870's, and the Persian of the small Bahai religious minority.

The great majority of the Jordanian Arabs are Sunni Moslems. The only non-Moslems are a minority of about 100,000 native Christians who belong principally to the Greek Orthodox, Greek Catholic, or Roman Catholic Church. Religious division has no ethnic significance (see chap. 5).

Physical Types

There exists in Jordan a high degree of physical homogeneity, with some European increment (probably dating from the Crusades), some Negroid characteristics reflecting a slave admixture, and some central Asian traits absorbed over the centuries. There is little if any marked difference in type between urban and village dwellers, but somewhat more difference between these and the desert Arabs, who have preserved with a minimum of deviation the physical characteristics of the early inhabitants of the area.

The typical desert Arab of the East Bank region of Jordan is slender, wiry, and about five foot four in height. The hair is coarse, dark brown or black, the beard is sparse. Skin color varies between a light brown and a deep red-brown. The face may be either the thin-featured, aquiline-nosed type popularly associated with the desert Arab, or it may be broader and coarser featured, with a fleshier, straight nose and thicker lips. The latter type predominates by about two to one.

In the cities, villages, and on the desert fringes (more especially on the West Bank) there are somewhat higher proportions of ethnic mixture than among the bedouins. Canaanites and Hebrews, Syrians and Greeks, Romans and Byzantines—all the peoples who invaded and occupied Palestine in the pre-Islamic period—and later, Europeans and Turks contributed to the composition of the West Bank population. Characteristics of the long-faced, beak-nosed (Irano-Afghan) type, the blue-eyed, red-haired Nordic, and the stocky, round-headed Alpine are all likely to appear in varying combinations but among a relatively small part of the Jordanian population as a whole. These minor physical variations are given little importance by Jordanians, and constitute negligible differentiations as compared to the divergent cultural experiences undergone by the people of the area since the disintegration of the Ottoman Empire.

The Ethnic Majority

Since there is little physical difference between the desert wanderer and the townsman, the surest identifying mark is dress. The basic piece of clothing of the bedouins of Jordan—and of the neighboring countries—is the aba, a square ankle-length cotton, woolen, or camel's-hair cloak with an open front and two holes at the sides for the arms. Its quality and the amount of embroidery on it vary according to a man's economic status. Though tribal traditions regarding ornamentation have to be adhered to, some latitude is given for individual taste in the matter of color. In summer abas of lighter material, sometimes silk, are worn by those who can afford them. Under the aba is worn a white, long-sleeved shirt (thawb) reaching the ankles. The head is covered with a four-foot square of white or checkered cotton cloth, the kaffiyyeh, folded into a triangle and worn with two points falling over the shoulders and the third hanging down the back. It is usually held in place by a black ropelike hoop, the agal.

The dress of bedouin women resembles that of the men. Under the thawb, however, they wear several long, loose robes (more than a yard longer than the height of the women), tucked up and held to the body by a broad, woven belt. In many groups, they wrap their heads with large (usually black) kerchiefs which cover the sides of the face and pass under the chin, leaving the front of the face uncovered. Sandals or shoes are worn only by the well-to-do, but every bedouin woman has some jewelry in the form of necklaces, earrings, bracelets, anklets, and, frequently, nose rings, which may be of any material from glass to silver or gold.

Both the girls and the young men of certain tribes dye their eyelids with black kohl (antimony powder), and women dye their palms and fingernails with henna; bridegrooms also dye the palms of their hands. Older women use henna as a hair dye.

The educated minority of city dwellers, some of whom have lived and been educated abroad, wear western dress almost exclusively. Among the older Moslem townsmen a form of dress similar to but much richer and more elaborately ornamented than that of the bedouins may often be seen, with the tarboosh perhaps substituted for the kaffiyyeh. The rank and file of the townspeople wear the simple thawb with either a kaffiyyeh, if they are of recent bedouin origin, or the tarboosh. Many elements of the population, and notably the lower middle classes, sometimes compromise by wearing a western suit jacket over the thawb.

Urban women of westernized, upper-class families wear western clothes both at home and in public. They are few in number, however; the majority of townswomen still live under the restrictions of the Moslem tradition. In the streets upper-class women may add the veil to their western dress. Women of the lower classes are rarely veiled, although the flowing head scarf often is pulled across the face when strangers are encountered.

Ethnic Minorities

About 12,000 Circassians, descendants of Sunni Moslem tribes who emigrated from the Caucasus after the conquest of that region by the Russians in the nineteenth century, constitute the largest non-Arab minority in Jordan. The Sultan of Turkey, as the protector of all Moslems, settled the Circassian refugees in the vicinity of Amman and at Al Qunaytra (now in Syria). Close contacts are still maintained between the Circassian groups in Jordan and Syria, and intermarriage is frequent. Cultivators for the most part, the Circassians may be distinguished from their Arab neighbors by their fair skins, their more methodical methods of farming, and until recently their distinctive Cossack-style dress. Circassian women are noted in the area for their beauty and in former times were much in demand by wealthy Arabs and Turks as wives or concubines.

Circassians put far greater stress on literacy than do the village Arabs, yet in recent years a tendency to assimilate to the Arabs has become noticeable. Arabic is displacing Cherkess, the dialect spoken by the Circassians, and intermarriage between Circassians and Arabs is becoming more common. Assimilation to European customs and modes of dress has also been noticeable, particularly among the young people.

Another Circassian tribal group, the Chechens, who are Shiah Moslems, came to Jordan about the same time as their Sunni compatriots, whom they closely resemble in occupational preferences and physical type. Today the Chechens are few in number and are settled in villages in the area of Amman.

A curious example of group survival is found at Nablus, where until recently there were some 200 Samaritan Jews. Their number, however, has been decreased as the result of recent migrations to Israel.

The Arabic Language

Arabic, a Semitic language related to Phoenician, Aramaic, Hebrew, and the Ethiopian languages, is spoken in various dialects by about fifty million people from the Persian Gulf to Morocco. It exists in two forms, the classical and the colloquial. The classical form is invariable and is understood to one degree or another throughout the Arab world. Colloquial Arabic differs from area to area and many of its dialects are mutually unintelligible. It departs from the classical in many ways, notably in vocabulary and in the absence of such features as the use of certain case endings and the dual form of verbs and adjectives. Much is made of the difficulties of learning Arabic: the colloquial is considered "very difficult for foreigners," while classical Arabic poses extreme difficulties to foreigners and native speakers alike. Speakers of Indo-European languages have considerable trouble with Arabic grammar.

Spoken and Written Usage

Certain social circumstances call for the use of classical Arabic; others call for colloquial. In general colloquial is spoken, rarely written; classical is usually written, less frequently spoken. Classical Arabic, for example, is used for all books, periodicals, personal letters, and official records, and for such purposes as street signs, movie subtitles, and train tickets.

The Arabic alphabet is written from right to left, and all books, newspapers, and magazines seem to the westerner to start from the back cover. The failure of the script to indicate vowels and the differences between classical and colloquial add to the difficulties of education, and undoubtedly contribute to low literacy rates.

The circumstances in which classical Arabic is spoken are few but important. All radio broadcasts, except at the lowest level of popular entertainment, are announced and delivered in classical Arabic. Formal occasions and public speeches usually, though not always, call for the classical form. Sermons in the more important mosques are usually delivered in the classical form, but colloquial is often heard in the small mosques where the imam (prayer leader) may have little classical learning. For reading purposes, the trend now is toward an amalgam of the classical and colloquial forms such as is found in the newspapers.

The Classical Ideal

Poorly understood by the vast majority, classical Arabic is nevertheless regarded with reverence by all Arabs, whether or not they are able to use it. Even the illiterate refer to it as "our language," and most Arabs will declare that colloquial Arabic should be abandoned and classical used everywhere; as noted, the actual trend is toward a wider use of colloquial. Nevertheless, colloquial Arabic is looked upon, not as a separate language in itself, but as a corruption of classical Arabic. Classical Arabic is "correct"; colloquial Arabic is "incorrect"—and anyone who openly advocated the use of colloquial rather than classical would be considered at best an eccentric and at worst an enemy of religious and Arab unity.

The status of classical Arabic is in part due to its religious significance. Moslems believe that the Koran is God's word in form as well as substance: the words of the Koran are believed—with certain sectarian differences as to detail—to be the very words of God's revelation to Mohammed through the angel Gabriel. God chose Arabic above all other languages for its perfection; consequently the language of the Koran represents an a priori standard, and deviation from it can only fall short of the pinnacle of linguistic beauty. The continued loving preservation of classical prose and poetry has also done much to keep the classical form alive and valued.

The tradition of philological studies among the Arabs is preserved at the Arabic academies in Cairo, Damascus, and Baghdad. Attention is, however, devoted exclusively to the classical language and to traditional methods of study; modern scientific linguistic techniques are not taken into account. Grammar and composition are emphasized, and calligraphy is considered an important art form. Classical and colloquial proverbs, and religious quotations of various sorts are popular literary devices, the ability to use them appropriately being considered a social asset.

Colloquial Arabic in Jordan

Colloquial speech in Jordan varies with locality; there are also minor differences between Moslem and native Christian usage. The greatest contrast exists between the colloquial of the nomads and that of the townsmen and villagers.

No Jordanian dialect carries more general prestige than another, but each dialect group believes its speech to be nearer to the classical than others and therefore more deserving of prestige.

Colloquial Arabic is the exclusive language of conversation, no matter how serious and formal. Today court proceedings are in colloquial Arabic, although the records of the proceedings are written in classical Arabic. The circumstances in which colloquial Arabic is written, however, are still very rare, and the few examples of colloquial journalism and cartoon captions which appear are usually of Egyptian or Lebanese origin and can hardly be interpreted as indicative even of the beginning of a trend.

There is a common misconception that colloquial Arabic "has no rules" and that "one may speak as one wishes." Although considered "incorrect," it clearly contains standards of correctness to which people adhere even though they may be unconscious of them. Classical Arabic is weighted with formal and highly complex rules; the Jordanian in studying it—and learning it only with arduous and lengthy effort—sees that the colloquial differs from the classical and hears these differences stigmatized by his teacher as "errors." Considered unworthy of scholarly investigation, colloquial Arabic has been studied only by foreign linguists and a few westernized Arabs.

The Use of Language

There is an extensive and many-sided Arabic literature on which the Jordanians, like other Arabs, may draw. Listening to folk tales and poetry is a favorite pastime of the illiterate people of the nomadic tribes, agricultural villages, and to a lesser extent the towns.

A conversation in Arabic invariably begins with set forms of mutual greeting, a pattern which is apt to strike the westerner as time-consuming. Used by Moslems and native Christians alike, these linguistic formulas are rigidly prescribed by tradition, and their omission on the appropriate social occasions by anyone expected to know them would be construed as an insult and might even lead to feuding. It is customary, for example, to hail an older man as "my uncle," a younger boy as "my son." A woman of the same age as one's self is addressed as "sister," a younger woman as "my daughter." Any serious student of Arabic must acquaint himself with the social circumstances requiring the use of such formulas.

For an orator the established patterns of usage are not merely a convention but the materials of an art with value in itself. Whatever his subject, an orator makes use of the richest, most florid, most elaborate language of which he is capable—often at the expense of clarity and meaning. The verbose style of oratory is carried over not only into literature but also into personal correspondence. Several elaborate styles may be used in addressing an envelope. A letter to a man named Mohammed al-Qudsi, for instance, might be addressed as follows: "To his noble honor Mr. Mohammed Effendi al-Qudsi, the respected, may God protect him and give him long life." Even the modernist who professes to disdain this ornateness would address the envelope with at least "The respected Mr. Mohammed al-Qudsi."

RELIGIONS

THE OVERWHELMING MAJORITY OF JORDANIANS ARE SUNNI MOS-lems. The only substantial religious minority are the 100,000 Arab Christians, about half of whom are Greek Orthodox; the remainder are divided among the Greek Catholic Church, the Roman Catholic Church, and a small but increasing number of Protestant denominations. The one sizable ethnic minority, approximately 12,000 Circassians, shares the Sunni Moslem faith. The 200 Samaritans of Nablus represent the remnant of a group which separated from the Jews in Old Testament times.

Islam (the Arab word means submission to God) is the monotheistic faith founded by Mohammed, who was born in Mecca in the year 570. According to tradition, Mohammed began to receive calls from God at about the age of forty while engaged in solitary contemplation upon the mountain of Hira. Mohammed's preaching in Mecca against prevailing practices and beliefs incurred the enmity of important personalities; in 622 the Prophet was forced to flee with his closest followers from Mecca to Medina. The flight (hegira) marks the first year of the Moslem calendar. Having put down the civil strife he found in Medina, Mohammed was able to repel the attacks of the Meccans and ultimately to bring all of Arabia under his control. Mecca became the holy city, and its principal shrine, the Kaaba, a large black stone in the wall of what had been a pagan shrine, became the focal point of an annual pilgrimage. In the theocratic order he established, Mohammed, the Prophet, became the judge, lawgiver, and social arbiter of his followers and laid down the principles incorporated later in the Koran, the Holy Book of Islam, and developed in the Sunnah, the supplementary body of the tradition of Islam.

After the death of Mohammed in 632 the countries of the Middle East succumbed in rapid succession to Islamic conquerors; by 636 the area which is now Jordan had been completely overrun. Its people, themselves Arabs, were Islamized within a few generations.

The Tenets of Islam

The fundamental article of faith of Islam is the testimony (*shahadah*): "There is no God but God (Allah), and Mohammed is His Prophet." The recital of this phrase, in full and unquestioning belief, is all that is required of one to become Moslem. Other Moslem dogmas require belief in the general resurrection and final judgment of all mankind, and the divine preordination of men's lives and destinies. Four sources of scriptural revelation are recognized: the Koran, the Pentateuch and the Psalms of the Old Testament, and the Christian Gospels.

The Koran, "the bountiful, the beneficial," sets forth all a Moslem needs to know to attain salvation. Acceptance of the four Gospels is qualified by the belief that the present texts are not as God revealed them. Other books interpreting the Koran but not regarded as divinely inspired are the Sunnah (a body of Islamic tradition) and the Hadith (the sayings of Mohammed). The Sunni Moslem majority, of which the Jordanians form a part, accept the Sunnah implicitly; the second largest Moslem group, the Shiahs, who live mainly in Iran and Iraq, reject the Sunnah as spurious and adhere to a tradition of their own. Sunnis and Shiahs both accept the Hadith.

Islam teaches that God has given mankind through his prophets a succession of revelations of divine truth, and that each time the human race falls into error God sends new prophets to lead it back into the way of truth. It is held that there have been altogether over 200,000 prophets since the creation of man; of these the great ones are Adam, Noah, Abraham, Moses, Jesus, and—the last and greatest —Mohammed.

The basic teachings of Islam closely parallel those of the Bible. The five guiding principles of Moslem conduct are embodied in what are generally known as the Five Pillars of Islam. These specify unquestioning belief in the oneness of God, frequent recourse to prayer (and praise), the responsibility before God to fast, the giving of alms, the spiritual value of pilgrimage to Mecca and other Moslem shrines. These are all in some form features of both Christianity and Judaism. Many of Islam's prohibitions—such as those against adultery, gambling, usury, and the consumption of carrion, blood, or alcohol —are similar to those of the Old or New Testaments.

Prayer

Every devout Moslem observes the Koranic injunction to pray five times a day in a prescribed manner. A series of obeisances are made, first from a standing position, then kneeling with the forehead touching the ground; the movements are accompanied by the intonation of set prayers, some of which are brief Koranic texts. Men should whenever possible say their prayers in a mosque, though they are free to pray by themselves; women usually pray in the seclusion of the home. The early morning prayer is said as the first light of dawn appears in the sky; then follow prayers at noon, in midafternoon, at sundown, and finally after dark. Ablutions are required before prayer, and the worshiper prays facing the holy city of Mecca. On Friday all males are expected to attend the mosque at noon to take part in communal prayer (the form of prayer advocated by the Prophet as being the most beneficial) and to hear the Friday sermon. Friday is not, however, the equivalent of the Sabbath, since the Koran enjoins the faithful to return to their business after hearing the sermon.

Fasting

The severest formal test of a Moslem's ability to practice his faith is met in Ramadan, the ninth month of the Moslem calendar. During this period all are required to fast from daybreak (reckoned from the moment a black thread may be distinguished from a white one) until the last rays of light have disappeared from the sky. The fast involves abstention from all food, drink, tobacco, and indulgence in worldly pleasure; exception is made for the sick, the weak, soldiers in front lines or on patrol, and travelers. Ramadan is widely and rigorously kept in Jordan. Backsliders—such as persons smoking in public or loitering in cafés—are frequently dealt with sharply by the police or by zealous civilians. A rather skeptical attitude toward full observance is to be found today among the westernized elements of the population. The bedouins, less devoted to ritual than the villagers or townsmen, largely ignore Ramadan.

Since the Moslem year consists of twelve lunar months and is shorter by eleven or twelve days than the astronomical year, Ramadan periodically falls during the midsummer heat and its observance then imposes real hardship. The psychological effect of the fast is very marked; as the month progresses tempers become shorter, personal violence and divorce statistics usually rise sharply, riots are frequent. The firing of a cannon at nightfall is the signal for all to repair home to break fast, and, as the days wear on, it is common for those who can afford it to rest all day and to banquet far into the night. Business generally comes almost to a standstill. Household servants may refuse to work. The tension is probably highest among the uneducated, who are likely to keep the fast rigidly and to dramatize their sufferings to find divine favor.

Children generally begin to observe the Ramadan fast when they are about eight years old. For the next few years they are obliged to abstain only until midday; the achievement of the first complete fast marks an important milestone in a child's life.

Almsgiving
The Koran assigns great importance to the giving of alms. In early times almsgiving was a moral obligation; it was customary to give a fortieth of one's annual income, either in money or in kind, to "the poor, the needy, those employed in the collection of alms, those who are to be conciliated, slaves and prisoners, debtors, and to mosques for the "Way of God." Almsgiving continues to be widely practiced in Jordan today. In addition to the voluntary contributions of the devout, a collection is also made and distributed by the government.

Pilgrimage
The pilgrimage to Mecca—the hadj—is regarded as the ideal culmination of every Moslem's religious experience. The Koran refers to Mecca as the "Station of Abraham"—according to tradition, the Kaaba was erected by Abraham. Adam is said to be buried in Mecca, and the tomb of Mohammed is claimed by some to be there. The Kaaba is regarded not only as the center of the earth but as the center of the universe; it is the place where heaven and earth join, where God is met face to face. The uncompromising insistence of the Koran on the true holiness of Mecca has from the beginning made the pilgrimage something to be achieved, at least once in a lifetime, if humanly possible. Those who are too poor to travel, however, are tacitly exempted, since authorities disapprove of a pilgrim's begging his way, as many do.

Jihad
In theory, jihad (literally, exertion) is a permanent struggle to make the word of God (the Koran) supreme among all men. In Moslem teaching it is presented as part of the collective duty of the faithful, and it is sometimes referred to as the sixth Pillar of Islam. Mohammed urged the feuding Arab tribes to compose their differences and divert their energies to the task of converting the world. The notion of many non-Moslems that jihad means "Holy War" is erroneous; with specific reference to Christians and Jews, the Koran makes it clear that as "People of the Book" these are not to be Islamized by force. The concept of jihad has, however, often been invoked by Moslem leaders to add a religious incentive to political motives in waging

war on non-Moslem states. A recent example was the preaching of jihad by the Sheikh al-Azhar in Egypt during the Suez Canal crisis of 1956.

The Institutions of Islam

The Moslem's relationship with God is a personal and direct one; there is no Islamic communion of saints to intercede for sinners; there are no holy orders or sacramental institutions. Mohammed, the founder, was born an ordinary man; the divine revelations did not change his nature. "Mohammed is dead," said the Prophet's successor, Abu Bakr.

Islam either lacked or consciously rejected those elements which elsewhere made for the ceremonial sequences of the ecclesiastical year. In addition to being devoid of the high days and holidays which characterize Roman and Orthodox Christianity and which are observed in varying degrees by Protestant sects, the religion of Mohammed has no priestly hierarchy nor is it strongly congregational. Mosques are not consecrated places; however ornate some mosques may be, they are all simply halls set aside for congregational prayer and the delivery of the weekly sermon. The only appointed mosque officials are the imam, whose duty it is to lead in prayer and preach the sermon, and the muezzin, who calls the faithful to prayer and is usually chosen more for his fine voice than for his learning. The muezzin is frequently employed as janitor of the mosque, sometimes living on the premises.

Stipends for the imam and the muezzin vary considerably according to the size, location, and type of congregation, and, particularly, on whether the mosque receives the income of a wakf. The imam of a large mosque, in Amman or Jerusalem, attended by considerable numbers of people will, for example, receive a much higher stipend than the imam of a smaller mosque in a city or in the countryside. He is, moreover, in all probability a distinguished graduate of the great Moslem University of al-Azhar in Cairo. The lesser imams, who live and work in unpretentious surroundings, are by comparison poorly educated—some are only semiliterate—and often receive such meager stipends that they are obliged to make ends meet by part-time employment, often manual labor.

The most important annual religious event other than Ramadan is Aid al-Kabir, the Great Feast. Lasting four days, it commemorates Abraham's readiness to obey God, even to the point of sacrificing his son, and is marked by the yearly pilgrimage to Mecca. Aid as-Saghir, the Lesser Feast, lasting three days, is also a time of high celebration marking the end of Ramadan. Mouled, the birthday of the Prophet, is a one-day commemoration, as is Ashura, the tenth day of the month of Muharram.

Islamic Law

Islamic law embraces the whole range of personal and social life. It tells the true believer how to live righteously and the community at large how to conduct its affairs, spiritual and temporal. Of the several schools of law, four have been preserved as equally orthodox. Named after their founders, and differing only in matters of detail, they have become identified with particular areas. The Hanafi school, dominant under Ottoman rule, is today prevalent in Turkey, Central Asia, Pakistan, and Jordan; the Shafiite point of view, once predominant in Jordan, is common among religious scholars in northern Egypt, Syria, Indonesia, and East Africa; the Maliki prevails in southern Egypt and North Africa; and the Hanbalite school is prevalent in Saudi Arabia, Yemen, Libya, and in isolated parts of North Africa.

Islamic law has always given wide latitude to local law and custom. It developed mainly as an ideal system, influencing concrete conditions through the wide dissemination of its basic doctrines and of learned writings and by the training of teachers and experts. In most Islamic countries today Islam is designated as the state religion, and, although versions of western legal codes have been adopted almost everywhere, questions of personal status (as to marriage, divorce, inheritance, orphans, endowments) are still adjudicated—except in Egypt, Turkey, and Tunisia—in sharia courts applying Islamic law. In Jordan civil jurisdiction is available and increasingly used.

In the days before western civil and criminal codes began to supplant Islamic law, the muftis, who interpreted the law, and the cadis (Moslem lower judges), who handed it down, were persons of considerable importance. The controversies between certain learned muftis are famous. Litigants were anxious to obtain the help of a mufti known for his compelling interpretations. Many much sought-after muftis became rich and influential. Western-based secular law has reduced their influence, but the specialists in traditional law still function in the limited jurisdiction of the sharia courts and are consulted, if frequently not heeded, in the adaptation of western laws to the Islamic tradition.

Islam in Jordan

Islam is being threatened by the relentless penetration of the secularism of the modern age. Though the secular impact in Jordan has been less strong than in Egypt and Turkey, it is increasingly felt among the educated urban minority and to some degree in the villages. It is significant, too, that in the West Bank regions the secularized element is much larger than in the still traditionally conservative eastern part of the country.

This situation is not yet reflected in any large-scale falling off of Jordanian mosque attendance or in failure to observe Ramadan. But such developments as the shrinking of the field covered by Islamic law and the adoption both of a constitution and an administrative structure based on western secular models have placed Jordanians in all walks of life in an environment where the Islamic tradition must compete with other values and ways of doing things. The emergence of Jordan as a political entity and the development of relations with secular powers abroad have also weakened the ideal of the Islamic theocratic state.

The result of Jordan's involvement in the modern world has been to accentuate the cleavage between the traditionalists and the modernists. High officials in the Jordanian Government continue to fulfill their religious observances, but for many the process appears to be a matter more of political convenience than of religious conviction. A law of January 1955, which made governmental authorization obligatory for speeches and sermons—in practice, those of a political nature —in the mosques, imposed a virtual censorship upon the free expression of political views in Moslem places of worship. A Bethlehem newspaper was closed down for criticizing the decree, and members of a Pan-Islamic group were detained on a charge of having violated it.

The forces working to bolster the beleaguered religious tradition are to be found among Jordan's ulemas (religious teachers), many of them educated at al-Azhar in Cairo, and among members or followers of the extremist politico-religious organization, the Moslem Brotherhood. The religious traditionalists are strengthened by the knowledge that the politicians are fearful of losing support and will therefore do nothing to undermine the position Islam still holds with the rank and file in the country. On the other hand, the power of the ulemas and the imams can be controlled by the government, which pays them. The combination of these factors has brought about an impasse. Meanwhile, the real strength of Islam is being tested under the pressure of external forces: those of the modern age in general, which challenge it to accommodate to new ideas and a new technology, and—most gravely—those of Soviet communism, which are directed at destroying Islam by subverting from within.

The Moslem Brotherhood, which was founded in 1928 by the Egyptian Hassan al-Banna, urged a return to Islam as preached by Mohammed. There were precedents for this organization in the long history of Moslem secret sects, and its glorification of the Moslem past appealed strongly to many who were ready to transmit discontent with the modern world into action. Whatever may have been the original purpose of its founder, the Brotherhood, fanatical and xenophobic in Jordan and Syria as in Egypt, plunged deeper and deeper into political intrigue. Its original religious goals, if not lost sight of, were de-emphasized in an extremist program of political action. In the 1956 elections in Jordan some indication of the strength of the Brotherhood was provided by the fact that it gained one tenth of the seats in the new chamber—four out of forty (see chap. 7).

The Religion of the Bedouins

Compared with the intense religious feeling of the devout among the settled population, the attitude of the bedouins to religion might seem casual, if not indifferent. Much of the ritual observance of the towns is never seen in the desert. The Five Pillars of Islam are neglected, and, although the bedouins are always willing to pronounce the shahadah—profession of faith—its meaning is vitiated by their strong belief in spirits, demons, and other supernatural beings. As for the other Pillars, there is little pretense of even formal compliance with them; the nomad does not pray five times a day, keep Ramadan, or perform the pilgrimage, and he substitutes hospitality for almsgiving.

The religion of the bedouins contains a resistant core of customary beliefs and practices which long antedate Islam. Transmitted orally from generation to generation, the indigenous tradition gives sanction to many aspects of the bedouin pattern of existence.

Folk Belief and Superstition

The use of magic to control nature and destiny is part of popular custom among uneducated townsmen and villagers as well as the nomads. The belief is prevalent that much that happens is the doing of spirits or demons (jinnis, afreets, ghouls) who are legion. Usually invisible, these supernatural beings can assume animal or human form. To counter their usually evil influence, one must repeat at the proper moment certain traditional sayings and key words or perform various rites. Protective amulets and talismans can be obtained from specialists, who, male or female, may remain within their own tribes or wander from group to group. When an evil spirit has entered the body of a person and caused him to sicken, a cure may be effected by exorcising the spirit in a public ceremony performed by a folk practitioner or a pious layman.

The "evil eye," a mysterious, harmful power which emanates from the glance of certain persons, is much feared among villagers and especially among the bedouins. Common countermeasures are amulets, disguises, invocations—such as *Ismallah,* "name of God"—and stipulated gestures. A sky-blue frame around the windows and doors of the home is also believed to possess the power of warding off the evil eye.

In or near practically every village there is a shrine, usually a small, rectangular, dome-capped building, beneath which is believed to be the grave of some man (or woman) locally esteemed as a saint. Cults that have grown up around these saints provide the villager with a sense of security (which the bedouin lacks) against the omnipresent evil spirits. A saint's popularity is compounded of the stories and legends about his life, miracles, asceticism, and reputation for granting supernatural help to his followers after his death. The shrines of the more renowned saints attract pilgrims throughout the year, especially on the saint's birthday. The supplicants, mostly women and not infrequently Christians, bring modest offerings to the hereditary keeper of the shrine and spend a night beside the tomb in prayer. Disease and childlessness are perhaps the two most frequent misfortunes against which the help of saints is invoked. The difficulty of finding a theological justification for saints in Islam has been traditionally overcome—not without opposition in orthodox circles—by declaring the saint to possess transcendental knowledge and to be closer to God than his fellow Moslems and able to perform miracles by the grace of Allah.

Religious Minorities

Arab Christian Communities

The largest Arab Christian community in Jordan comprises members of the Greek Orthodox Church. This Church is organized into several divisions, each of which is headed by a patriarch. The Patriarch of Jordan is also Patriarch of Jerusalem and of the Greek Orthodox community in Israel. The upper clergy of the patriarchates are Greek, the lower clergy, Arab; the liturgy is conducted in both Greek and Arabic. There is also in Jordan a small Syrian Orthodox community, which uses a Syriac rite.

The Greek Catholic, or Melkite, community is part of the Greek Catholic Church of the Middle East. Headed by the Patriarch of Antioch, Jerusalem, and Alexandria, the Church employs an Arabic liturgy and all its clergy are Arabs. Recognizing the supremacy of the Pope but retaining a certain local autonomy, the Melkite Church traces its origin to the reunion with Rome of part of the Greek Orthodox Church (hence the name "Uniate" which is often applied to it).

The Latin (Roman) Church originated in the area during the Crusades. It is under the jurisdiction of the Latin Patriarch of Jerusalem, who is appointed by Rome and is subordinate to the apostolic nuncio accredited to Jordan, Israel, Egypt, and Eritrea. There are some 15,000 Arab followers of the Latin rite in Jerusalem, Bethlehem, and Ramallah.

The Protestant Arab communities of Jordan all came into being in recent times as the result of European and American missionary activities. Practically all the members of these organizations were recruited from among the membership of the older Christian Churches, most of which existed in pre-Islamic times.

The conversion of Moslem Arabs to Christianity is very rare.

Non-Arab Christians
The few non-Arab Christians in Jordan include several hundred Armenians, who belong to the Armenian Orthodox (Gregorian) Church or (a small number) the Armenian Catholic Church. There are possibly as many as a thousand Nestorians (Assyrians), most of whom live in Jerusalem, who employ a Syriac rite. Most of the two or three thousand European Catholics are members of religious orders, and the few European and American Protestants are mission personnel stationed more or less permanently in the country.

Moslem-Christian Relations

The Jordanian Christians, more urbanized, better educated, and more prosperous than their Moslem neighbors, tend to look down upon the latter at the same time that their consciousness of being a small minority in an overwhelmingly Moslem country disposes them to seek tangible identification with the majority. This is evident in the fervor of their participation in Jordanian politics and in the disproportionately large number of positions they occupy in public life. Many of them see themselves as exponents of modern, western ideals and trends and as the natural connecting link between the Christian West, to which they are tied by religion, and the Moslem Middle East, of which they are a part in terms of language, culture, and history.

A similar ambivalence characterizes the attitude of many Jordanian Moslems toward their Christian compatriots. The tradition which regarded the Christians and Jews living in Moslem countries as protected minorities (zimmis) but second-class citizens still survives, although it is gradually dying out. At the same time, the relative educational and material advantages of the Christians have inevitably stimulated some resentment.

There have been reports of a growth of anti-Christian feelings in army circles since the dismissal of Glubb Pasha in March 1956. Many Christian officers have been relieved of their posts or transferred to the less esteemed National Guard. Actual clashes between Christians and Moslems, however, have been rare. The disorder—involving members of certain Christian communities on one hand, Moslems on the other—during the celebration of King Hussein's accession in 1953 was political rather than religious.

SOCIAL ORGANIZATION

THE THREE FUNDAMENTAL DIVISIONS OF JORDANIAN SOCIETY, and of Middle Eastern society in general, are the bedouin tribe, the village, and the town. These represent distinctly different ways of life within the society and they have often functioned with apparent independence. But the town in particular and the bedouin tribe to a lesser extent have been dependent on the food production of the village; and although each of these units may be for its members an essentially "closed" society, in varying degrees physical proximity, economic drives, and political motives have caused them to interact.

For the villager, interaction frequently has meant exploitation at the hands of both townsmen and nomads. The town, in addition to being the source of supply of items which the subsistence economy of the village cannot produce—sugar, salt, metal tools and utensils, and cloth—is also the seat of governmental authority, of the hard-dealing merchant and money lender, the tax collector, and the absentee landlord. The nomad, for his part, may have come to the village to trade, but he also came to plunder and to levy tribute.

Sharing a contempt for the villager, townsman and nomad have been no less contemptuous of each other. Historically, urban power has confronted bedouin mobile striking force. In times of urban strength, the nomads have been restrained from molesting the village agricultural production on which the towns depended; in times of urban weakness, the edges of the sown area reverted to nomadic pasture.

New sources of wealth and new political patterns are altering the traditional order in Jordan, but town, village, and nomadic tribe still constitute the three main sectors of life. Numerically, the village population is dominant, but the activity of the towns is strongly influencing the country as a whole; the nomadic minority, however, still retains considerable political power, and it displays most markedly the characteristic form of kinship organization less elaborately present in town and village. On the way in which these three sectors change and interact rests the outcome of the effort of the new Arab states like Jordan to remold the old Arab culture into national form.

The Bedouins

The greater part of Jordan is desert, where man can maintain himself only if he bases his livelihood on a kind of animal able to survive there for at least part of the year. The camel is such an animal, and the arid portions of eastern Jordan are the traditional range of the great camel-breeding nomadic tribes. Westward, the desert merges into a steppe belt of greater rainfall, which, though not sufficient to support cultivation, produces richer seasonal pasture. In this zone, which on its northwestern extension abuts the area of settled cultivation, the camel gradually gives way to sheep and goats. Closest to the cultivated area, some of the bedouins supplement the breeding of sheep and goats with cultivation; in a progressive process of sedentarization some have turned to village life and full-time farming.

The Jordanian nomads classify themselves and the people known to them in several ways. A broad distinction is made between the sedentary population—villagers and townsmen alike, who are called *hadar*—and the nomads, *ruhhal*. In the opinion of the nomads, only they themselves have the right to be called Arabs, a name denoting people of noble blood and to be applied only to tent-dwellers. They further distinguish, among themselves, between those groups whose main herds consist of camels and those whose flocks are predominantly made up of other animals. The term bedouin (literally, "inhabitant of the desert") is applied to the camel nomads; the others are *shwayah* (sheepherders), *maazah* (goatherders), and *baqqarah* (cattle nomads —found in insignificant numbers).

In the traditional social ranking of these groups the great camel-breeding tribes, independent in the sense that they were strong enough to resist the demands of others for protection money, *khuwwah*, have been at the pinnacle of the pastoral aristocracy. Until recently they could and did reduce many of the weaker sheep- and goat-breeding tribes to the status of tribute-paying vassals; the practice has been largely eliminated under government pressure.

Transitional between the nomads and the settled cultivators are the *raiyyah*, partially sedentarized groups, who during the spring and summer live in villages and cultivate crops and during the moister winter season move out with their flocks onto the steppe as tent-dwellers. The *raiyyah*, regarded by the pure nomads as of lower status than themselves, formerly were also required to pay tribute to the stronger camel-breeding or sheep-breeding tribes.

Still lower on the bedouin social scale than the vassal *raiyyah* tribes are the base-born tinker, smith, and artisan groups called *solubah* (a term, originally the name of an individual tribe, that has come to denote despised status). The *solubah* wander the desert and steppe, temporarily attaching themselves to noble tribes for whom, in addition to plying their handicraft skills, they provide entertainment as dancers, singers, and prostitutes. Nonfighters, completely dependent on their protectors, monogamous, and marrying only within their own group, the *solubah* claim descent from the Crusaders; there is the occasional occurrence among them of blond and red hair and blue eyes.

Every major nomadic encampment has its own blacksmith, or *sani.* The blacksmiths are set off from the herdsmen by their despised but important skill, and, although the same family of smiths may be attached to a particular tribe for generations, they do not intermarry with the tribe. The blacksmith does not take part in raids, and his noncombatant status is respected by enemy raiding parties. Like the merchants who visit the nomadic camps from time to time, every smith has a bedouin "brother" (*akh*) whose duty it is to protect him and to recover any property taken from him by a tribesman. For their work of shoeing horses and repairing and making weapons, the smiths are paid in food and equipment.

A final broad social classification employed by the nomads—and by the settled population as well—is based on the notion of northern or southern ancestry. The entire Arab population claims descent either from the north Arabian, Qaysi, tribes or from the south Arabian, Yamani, tribes. Both have equal claim to nobility in contrast with the ignoble tinkers, smiths, artisans, and other "riffraff who have no ancestry." The Qaysi-Yamani dichotomy, originating in pre-Islamic times, has today lost much of its meaning, particularly for educated urban groups, but traces persist of the rivalry and feuding which once hinged on it.

Tribal Distribution

Geographically, the East Bank of Jordan can be roughly divided into two unequal parts. The smaller part comprises a strip just east of the Jordan River and the Dead Sea. This is the domain of the sheep and goat nomads who wander through a narrow range. To the east and south of this region the more arid remainder of the East Bank is the territory of the wider-ranging camel nomads. On the uncultivated portions of the West Bank only sheep and goat nomads are found.

There are only a few major camel-breeding tribes in Jordan, and the largest of these, the Rwala, is not indigenous to the country but passes through it on its seasonal movement from its winter grazing grounds in Saudi Arabia to its summer pastures in Syria. The other principal camel tribes are the Beni Sakhr, the Huwaytat, and the Sirhan. These are the only nomads in Jordan with extensive wandering territories involving distances on the order of 100 miles or more between summer and winter pastures. Basing their economic activity on the camel, all of them have at least a few horses—prestige animals in the desert—and some have acquired sizable flocks of sheep and goats.

THE RWALA. The Rwala, reported to number between 4,000 and 5,000 tents and some years ago possessing 120,000 camels, 30,000 sheep, and 1,000 goats, belong to the Aneze tribal confederation originally centered in Arabia. Rwala territory cuts deeply into the pasturing area of the Jordanian Beni Sakhr, and this has produced a long-standing enmity between the two groups. Lately, however, contact of the Rwala with Jordan has been relatively slight, since in its seasonal passage between Syria and Saudi Arabia most of the tribe has followed a route which takes it through Iraq rather than the one that verges into Jordan.

The Rwala are divided into five subtribes, all of which recognize the chief of the al-Mered subtribe as their paramount sheikh, giving him the honorific title of emir. The ibn Shalan family of the al-Mered has headed the Rwala for several generations, demonstrating a quality of leadership which has given the tribe greater cohesion than any other in the Syrian Desert. The Rwala, who in World War I received large funds from the Allies, were once extremely well armed, averaging one rifle per tent in the 1920's. In 1919 they took the Oasis of Jawf in Saudi Arabia from the Shammar, but lost it six years later to King ibn Saud.

THE BENI SAKHR. The Beni Sakhr is the largest camel-breeding tribe with home territories entirely in Jordan; it reportedly numbers about 6,500 tents and some years ago owned 12,000 to 15,000 camels and some 500 horses. Its wandering territory extends from its summer pastures around Zuwayza, southeast of Amman, to Wadi Sirhan and Ard As Sawwan in eastern Jordan, where the tribe spends the winter. The two subtribes (each composed of several subdivisions) of the Beni Sakhr are the al-Huwaqah and the Kabinah. The larger of these, the al-Huwaqah, is said to have 4,000 to 5,000 tents and to own about 100,000 acres of good grainland. One 25,000-acre tract is operated with modern equipment and migrant laborers (mostly recruited from small tribes of the Jordan Valley) under the efficient direction of al-Huwaqah overseers (see chap. 14). The subtribe also owns some city property in Amman and has a permanent headquarters with large buildings.

The Kabinah (also known as al-Kharshan, the name of the most important subdivision) have acquired several thousand acres of dry-farm land, which is, however, situated on the submarginal side of the sown area. Plowing is done with camels, most cultivation by hand. In spring, when winter water and forage have been exhausted in the desert, the subtribe moves westward onto its farm lands, where it remains until after the harvest and the new planting in November or December. A few years ago the Kabinah were unique among the nomads in having a school, attended by some twenty boys, which was housed in a tent and moved with the tribe.

THE HUWAYTAT. Two of the several tribal groups which make up the Huwaytat, the Huwaytat ibn Jazi, and the Huwaytat ibn Nejad, have wandering areas in Jordan; other Huwaytat tribes live in Saudi Arabia, to the east and the south of Aqaba, and in Egypt north of the Galalah mountains. The Huwaytat claim to be descended from an Egyptian ancestor.

The Huwaytat ibn Jazi, reportedly with about 2,500 tents, range from their summer forage northeast of Aqaba to their winter pastures in the southeastern corner of Jordan. With the exception of one sedentarized subtribe, the nine subtribes and two attached groups constituting the ibn Jazi are camel-breeders. All of them recognize a paramount sheikh, who is also chief of one of the subtribes.

The smaller ibn Nejad, with some 500 tents, comprises 12 subtribes under the authority of a principal sheikh. Seminomads, who mix agriculture with herding, they use the numerous Roman ruins in the area as storehouses for their grain. Their wandering territory extends northward from Aqaba along the Jordan-Israel frontier.

THE SIRHAN. The only other Jordanian tribe which still does any large-scale wandering is the Sirhan. Numbering probably less than 400 tents, the tribe is divided into four subtribes, which recognize one paramount sheikh. The Sirhan before World War I had established themselves in several villages between Dara on the Syrian border and Al Mafraq. In 1925 they lost most of their camels in a large-scale raid by other tribesmen. They have not given up their pastoral life, however, still spending about three months in the winter in the Ard Ash Shamah, the mountain range which forms the northeastern boundary of the upper Wadi Sirhan, with Ayn Al Bayda as its main watering place.

THE SHEPHERD TRIBES. The great majority of Jordanian nomads are sheepherders and goatherders, scattered along the line of the Jordan River, the Dead Sea, and the Wadi Al Arabah. Closer to the cultivated areas and with much smaller wandering ranges than the camel-breeders, they are in various stages of the sedentarizing process which in differing degrees is affecting the whole nomadic population. Sheep, and to a lesser extent goats, are the mainstay of all these shepherd groups, but some also own sizable herds of camels as well as some horses, donkeys, and occasionally cattle. The Beni Atiyah, for example, who winter in the lowlands south of the Dead Sea and move eastward no more than 60 miles in the summer to the uplands and to the environs of Kerak, are said to pasture 10,000 sheep and 2,000 camels. The proportion of sheep to camels, where the latter are present at all, is usually much higher. Thus, another large tribe, the Beni Hasan, reportedly has 100,000 sheep and 2,000 camels, and in the limited area of its range in northwestern Jordan it also engages in agriculture.

JORDAN VALLEY TRIBES. The nomadic tribes of the Jordan Valley are generally small, sometimes consisting of no more than a few families. Many of their members are the descendants of slaves escaped from larger tribes to the east or from Egypt or Nejd in Saudi Arabia and show Sudanese or Ethiopian physical characteristics. Most are tent-dwellers, but some are semisettled, living in mud huts. An economically depressed group in a country where the general living standard is low, their circumstances are often worse than those of the refugees in the nearby camps. Those fortunate enough to own livestock follow the seasonal pastoral round, moving into the hills in summer and back to the valley in winter. Others have migrated to the Transjordanian plateau or to the towns; some are charcoal burners, lime burners, and woodcutters and the remainder constitute a cheap labor supply for the villages, public works projects, and commercial enterprises of the valley.

The Wandering Cycle

The term "wandering," as applied to the movements of the nomads, is misleading insofar as it suggests an aimless drifting in the desert and steppe. The various tribal groups have a very clear knowledge of the boundaries of their pasture lands, and each tribe moves its herds on a fixed itinerary which finds it more or less at the same

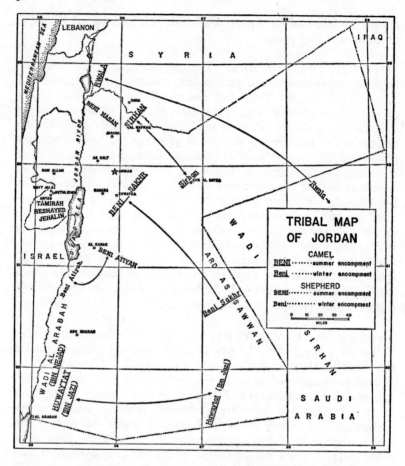

TRIBAL MAP OF JORDAN

CAMEL
BENI ········ summer encampment
Beni ········ winter encampment
SHEPHERD
BENI ········ summer encampment
Beni ········ winter encampment

0 10 20 30 40
MILES

spot at the same time year after year. Water and forage and freedom of movement over the traditional routes by which these are reached are for the nomad life-and-death matters about which he cannot be haphazard. (See Tribal Map.)

Well-defined landmarks, such as waterholes or wells, boulders, dry water courses, mountain ranges and hills, and other natural features, usually delimit the wandering territories of neighboring tribes. Tribes who count themselves related by blood, such as the Rwala and the Weld Ali of the Aneze confederation, may share pasturage during certain seasons of the year. A tribe also may conclude a treaty with an unrelated one, permitting it to use its pastures and watering places for a specified period. Again, powerful tribes have invaded the territories of weaker groups, as when the Huwaytat displaced the Beni

Atiyah from the Ash Sharah area. In other cases, tribal territories may overlap, so that the wandering route of one tribe crosses that of another. In a year of subnormal rainfall a tribe may have no choice but to encroach upon the more favored lands of a neighboring group, a necessity which has often precipitated clashes.

The political boundaries which were drawn across the desert after World War I imposed fewer restrictions on the movements of the Jordanian tribes than on those of the wider-ranging Syrian tribes to the north. The wandering territories of practically all of Transjordan's shepherd tribes and most of its camel nomads were encompassed within the borders of the new state. One of the few exceptions, other than the Rwala already noted, was the Beni Sakhr tribe, which formerly penetrated into Syria and occasionally into Saudi Arabia, and which is now largely confined to Jordanian territory.

Jordanian wandering territory, whether it is that of a large camel tribe or of a small shepherd tribe, whether it measures a hundred or only a few miles in length, has one common characteristic: it extends from the cultivated zone toward the desert. In the dry summer months the more abundant rainfall and ground water of the cultivated area draws camel-breeders and sheepherders alike. Summer is thus the season when the two types of nomads are brought into contact with each other, when—in the old days, but no longer—protection money (*khuwwah*) was paid by the weaker tribes to the stronger and when the nomads visit the towns and villages to buy and sell or simply to exchange conversation (see chap. 16).

The summer camping grounds are occupied by the tribes for three to five months every year. As soon as the first autumn rains have fallen on the desert, camp is broken and the tribe, now divided into its constituent wandering units, begins its movement eastward. The journey is longer for the camel nomad than for the sheepherder, but even the sheepherder winters at some distance from the settled area. These weeks of respite from the summer heat, when conditions of pasturage make it possible to camp in one place for relatively long periods, are the most pleasant time of year for the bedouin. Removed from the complexities of interaction with the settled population and secure in the compact wandering units into which the tribes have divided, the nomad can turn to those social activities which do not satisfy the primary needs of livelihood but which make his life worth living.

Tribal Structure

In Jordan and elsewhere in the Arab world both the structure of the nomadic tribe and the terms applied to the tribe and its subdivisions vary greatly. In size, the tribe may consist of only a few families, as do some in the Jordan Valley, or it may number 3,000 tents, as in the case of the Beni Hasan. As to tribal origins, a complex process of amalgamation, division, reamalgamation, and redivision has been going on for a long time. Thus, the generalizations that follow will certainly not apply to all Jordanian tribes but do reflect basic principles which are apparent in the structure of most.

The tribe (*qabilah*) is usually subdivided into two or more subtribes (*ashirah*). Each subtribe, in turn, is commonly divided into two or more subdivisions (*firqah*). Each *firqah* may again be subdivided into two or more parts (*fakhdh*); the *fakhdh* into two or more subdivisions (*hamulah*); and finally the *hamulah* into two or more related extended families. Throughout this structure kinship is reckoned through the male line; as a rule each tribe propounds the tradition that it is composed of the descendants of a single ancestor, whose name it often bears. The ancestor may be a more or less remote historical figure, whose progeny developed into the tribe, or he may be a fictitious figure whose existence is affirmed to explain and give luster to the tribal name. An example of the latter seems to be Annaz, the supposed ancestor of all the Aneze tribes, to which the Rwala belong.

The six levels of this ideal tribal scheme can be found in some of the large and complex Syrian tribes, but it is doubtful that all of them are present in any group in Jordan. The Jordanian tribes, smaller and more simply organized, most often show above the extended family no more than three levels—lineage (*hamulah*), subtribe, and tribe. Moreover, two or more subdivisions of the same level in any particular tribe are rarely symmetrical; of several related subtribes, for example, one may be built on two levels, while the others will contain three or four.

Lineage and Family

Whatever the number of layers in the nomadic tribal organization, two—the lineage and the extended family—are always present, and they represent the basic social units with which the larger social aggregates are constructed. The *hamulah,* or lineage, consists of several related extended families, who as a rule trace their descent to a common ancestor. Next to the extended family, the *hamulah* is the group with which the individual identifies himself most closely and which functions as a unit in wandering and camping and for protecting its members.

The extended family, the nucleus of all Arab tribal organization, typically consists of three generations of parents and children who reckon descent in the male line. Such a family is commonly composed of paternal grandparents, the married sons and their wives, their married and unmarried sons, and unmarried daughters. The group may also include widowed or orphaned female relatives of the senior males (see chap. 18). Formally, authority in the family is vested in the senior male, a pattern which, however, may be altered by circumstances and the accidents of personality. Marriage, by preference but by no means exclusively, is within the lineage; occasionally a prosperous man may take more than one wife, as sanctioned by the Koran. The number of tents occupied by an extended family varies with its size and economic status. A small and poor family may be sheltered by a single tent, while the head of a large and well-to-do group may have a tent for himself and separate ones for each of his wives and his married sons. The cohesiveness of the family is visibly expressed in the close clustering of the family tents, that of the *hamulah* in the grouping of the tent clusters of the constituent family groups.

Khamsah

An important social unit among the nomads, and to a lesser extent in the settled population, is the *khamsah,* the "group of five." A man's *khamsah* embraces all his patrilineal kin who are within five degrees of relationship. The method of counting the five steps of relationship varies from tribe to tribe, but the actual extension of the *khamsah* would ordinarily include relatives as remote as a grandfather's brother's son's son. The *khamsah* functions largely in cases of conflict, particularly in the blood feud. The intervention of the police power of the government is altering the pattern but traditionally, if a tribesman had been murdered the circle of his relatives within the *khamsah* were expected to seek vengeance, and all the members of the offender's *khamsah* were regarded as sharing responsibility and could legitimately be killed in revenge.

The Wandering Unit

The pastoral wandering units—the actual groups into which the nomads divide when they are on the move—vary considerably in size, depending on such factors as quality of grazing lands, abundance and distribution of water supply, and type of livestock. Sometimes the wandering unit may be an entire tribe; in the case of the larger tribes, it is almost invariably a subtribe or some further subdivision, which under adverse natural conditions may be as small as the lineage or extended family. The security of the group against enemies increases in direct proportion to its size, and the wandering unit tends to be as large as ecological factors permit; these factors vary from season to season and from one part of the tribal territories to another, and the size of the wandering unit changes accordingly.

The plasticity characteristic of the wandering unit is evident throughout the organization of the bedouin tribes. Far from being rigid and static structures, they are subject to a constant process of change in composition and in the relative position of the subtribal groups. A tribe may attach itself to a group of tribes and, although of alien origin, may in the course of a few generations come to regard itself as a kindred group. In another instance, a tribe or subtribe may detach itself from the larger group, move into another area, and in time appear as an independent tribe. The Huwaytat, for example, who claim descent from an Egyptian named Huwayt, were actually recruited chiefly from among the Beni Atiyah. Developing into an independent group about three hundred years ago, they became strong enough to drive numbers of the Beni Atiyah back into Saudi Arabia.

Leadership

Leadership in nomadic tribal society is vested in the heads of successively larger kinship aggregates. Every competent male can count on becoming in due course the head (sheikh) of his own extended family. When a father dies, each of his sons becomes the head of a family consisting of his own sons and grandsons and their womenfolk. Generally, among the extended families making up a lineage, one family has the hereditary right to the headship of the lineage, and one of that family's senior males—usually but not always the most senior, depending upon such factors as wealth and reputation for ability—heads the lineage. Again, one of the lineage-head families inherits the right to the headship of the next higher group in the tribe, and so on up to the leadership of the tribe itself. In this succession of interlocking authority each leader exercises authority in his own extended family and on those additional levels to which family position and personal ability may have brought him. The traditional title of all these chieftains is "sheikh"; such designations as "emir," taken by the sheikhs of a large and powerful tribe such as the Rwala, represent a relatively recent development.

It is by no means always easy to distinguish between a bedouin group which ought to be called a tribe and one which is properly a subtribe. The leadership role, however, provides a general criterion—which is simply that the tribe is headed by a sheikh who is subordinate to no one, while the sheikh of any subdivision is subordinate to a tribal sheikh.

Although the position of sheikh is usually filled from particular families who enjoy that hereditary prerogative, no strict rule of inheritance governs the actual selection within the family. It is not felt, for example, that the first-born son of a sheikh should always succeed him. If the sheikh is ill or old and weak, the tribe will be intensely preoccupied with the question of succession, and out of the deliberations of the elder men a consensus emerges as to which of the sheikh's sons (or nephews or other close relatives) is most suitable to fill his place. A sheikh who has a definite preference for one of his sons or relatives may entrust him with the handling of tribal affairs to give him a chance to prove his mettle, while the sheikh, now in emeritus status, supports him with his prestige and advice. With the death of the sheikh, however, there is usually no doubt about which of his surviving male relatives has the support of the tribal elders, and, through them, of general tribal opinion, and it is to this one that leadership usually falls. Should two members of a sheikhly family aspire to leadership and both have a considerable following, the tribe may split into two separate, independent units.

The sheikh is assisted by the *majlis,* the tribal council. Composed of the heads of the various subdivisions of the tribe, the majlis meets daily in the guest tent of the sheikh when the tribe is encamped. At its sessions, which last from midmorning to about noontime, there is informal discussion of such questions as when to break camp, where to find grass, news of other tribes, and cases of litigation. No vote is taken, and the sheikh in his capacity as chairman is able to influence the deliberations only through the force of his personality, wisdom, and understanding. The autocratic sheikh is not unknown, but traditionally the position carries no power to compel the members of the council against their wishes. Traditionally, the sheikh's position depended upon the good will of the elders, and his tenure was ultimately in their hands. Foreign indirect rule under the British and the present central authorities have interfered with this pattern and prevented the deposition of sheikhs upon whose political reliability the government can depend.

It is the sheikh's duty to represent his tribe, to rule on water rights, to act as arbiter and judge in litigation (in this he may be assisted by tribal judges, hakim), to give consent to marriages and divorces, to protect the feeble, to receive guests, to make the first move in breaking camp, to protect the honor of the tribe, and to work for its welfare. Formerly, before governmental intervention halted these practices, it fell to the sheikh to make the final decision as to raids and welfare and to receive the protection money paid by tribes and villages or by passing caravans.

The impact on the tribal chiefs of the recent growth of governmental power has been not only proscriptive but also has replaced old duties with new ones. Among the latter is the responsibility of the sheikh to collect taxes in the tribe or to assist the visiting tax collector. This unpalatable task—among a people whose tradition has acquainted them with tribute exacted from the weak by the strong but not with taxes—has been only partly mitigated by the payment of subventions by the government to the more powerful sheikhs. Today, confronted with increasing contacts with the government and the settled world, a few sheikhs of the larger tribes have secretaries or business managers who are not tribesmen (most tribesmen are still illiterate) but are brought in from outside.

The Decline of Nomadism

The influences of the twentieth century are bearing hard on the nomad and are hastening a major process of social change which has been affecting him for many centuries. That process is sedentarization. In the past the transformation of a nomadic camel-breeding tribe into settled agriculturalists might have taken as long as three hundred years; today, under the pulls and imperatives generated in the new urban centers and the larger world beyond, a generation or two may suffice.

In contrast to such countries as Syria, Saudi Arabia, and Iraq, where governmental authority has sometimes operated to compel the nomads to adopt a settled life, in Jordan this change has been almost always voluntary, however reluctant. Behind the motives for sedentarization lie certain economic pressures that are undercutting the traditional foundations of bedouin life and that make the alternatives of the village or the town seem inevitable if not attractive. Where motorized transportation reduces the need for camels, with a consequent drop in the price of camels, where raiding and the extortion of protection money is made impossible by the increasing control of the government over the desert routes and the steppe fringes, and where the extension of cultivation takes away the best grazing lands, the nomad is driven by sheer economic necessity to supplement his livelihood by cultivating the arable parts of his wandering territory on the borderland between the steppe and the sown areas. Once this first step is taken, complete sedentarization follows gradually but almost inevitably.

Another motivation for spontaneous sedentarization is created by the enticements of modern life to which some of the nomads are exposed in their contacts with the towns and through the development of governmental and industrial enterprises in the desert and steppe areas. Unable to satisfy their desire for the amenities of settled life in the desert, the wealthier nomads are drawn to the urban centers. Thus, the sedentarizing process, at work at both ends of the economic scale, first affects the very poor and the very well-to-do.

Once through the transitional stages of sedentarization, situated in villages in permanent houses, and completely dependent, or nearly so, on agriculture for its livelihood, the settled group finds itself in a new relationship with its peasant neighbors whom it formerly regarded as beneath notice. Economic cooperation and social interaction sooner or later result in intermarriage with the older peasantry, and the nomadic past remains only as a nostalgic tradition, the values and ideals of which have but limited practical relevance to the earth-bound existence of the agricultural village.

The replacement of the camel caravans by motor vehicles and railways has greatly diminished the role of the nomads in the economic life of Jordan. Bedouin political power, however, today focusing on the Jordanian royal authority, primarily through the army, is a force to be reckoned with, and the economic and social problems of the bedouin population loom large in the life of the country. Moreover, the historic values of nomadic society continue to influence the popular ethos in Jordan and in the rest of the Arab world. The effort to translate these ideals and values into meaningful terms in the context of modern life is in Arab states like Jordan, not merely a romantic exercise, but a part of the struggle in this part of the world to articulate a renewed Arab identity in national terms.

The Village

In Jordan the peasant majority comprises at least two thirds of the total population, but the importance of these village cultivators—the fellahin—is not merely a function of their numerical preponderance— their labor feeds both the towns and the nomads. Village life, reaching back into prehistoric times, may well be older in the area than the more spectacular bedouin nomadism; its resistant patterns are pressed upon the nomad when he becomes sedentarized and they are injected into the urban setting with the increasing flow of villagers to the towns.

The Jordanian village shares its basic characteristics with thousands of others dotting the arc of cultivable land extending through Lebanon, Syria, and Iraq. Beyond the broadest generalizations, however, the details of the village pattern vary, and in Jordan certain specific factors further complicate the picture of village life. Among these factors are the strong influence of nomads and seminomads even in the most agricultural parts of the country; the establishment of new villages by the influx of peasants from other areas; the marked decrease in recent decades of collective land ownership; the traditional Qaysi-Yamani division of the population; and religious and ethnic diversity which, though not so marked as in some other Arab countries, is nevertheless noticeable.

Nomadic influence is brought to bear on the villages both through the continuous interaction of nomads and villagers and through the absorption into village society of sedentarized nomads. Nomadic influence has been more pronounced on the East Bank than in recently annexed West Jordan, where most of the villages are very old, stable settlements, and this circumstance is another aspect of the Jordanian East Bank–West Bank division.

Throughout the Fertile Crescent, the cultivated area has been expanding and contracting since early times with the rise and fall of the governmental authority needed to protect the settled population from the nomads. During the Roman period, present-day East Jordan was the site of elaborate and extensive settlements. Some climatic change and, more importantly, the political insecurity resulting from the decline of Roman power forced the gradual withdrawal of this settled population, and their fields became nomad pastures. On the other hand, whereas in the middle of the nineteenth century there were almost no villages east of the town of Salt, the area of cultivation has pushed eastward ever since, expanding over about 1,500 square miles of territory. The new settled population has been recruited not only from migrant villagers—Christians, Circassians, and Moslem Arabs from adjacent areas—but from nomads turned farmers. The result has been a complex array of villages, ranging from those with a purely agricultural economy to those which combine agriculture and pastoralism.

Communal ownership—the mushaa tenure system—engendered difficulties from which Jordanian agriculture has not yet recovered. This system might have been expected to equalize landholdings and to stimulate cooperation among village cultivators, but in practice certain individuals were able to acquire and retain a disproportionate number of shares of the communally held land, and there was some growth of absentee landlordism. Government action has greatly reduced mushaa holdings, which are giving way to individual ownership, but the problems of absentee landlordism, sharecropping, and land fragmentation remain (see chap. 14).

The Qaysi-Yamani division is apparent in the social structure of many Jordanian villages and in the way in which people tend to align themselves in conflict situations into Qaysi and Yamani factions.

There is also a sizable contingent of Christian Arabs, mostly

Greek Orthodox, among the villagers and among the seminomads as well (see chap. 5). The Circassians, although they do not appear to have kept aloof, until recently preserved their own distinctive ways. These and a few other groups give Jordan no significant minorities problem, but they add to the diversity of the village scene.

The Village Setting

Under the conditions of Jordan's physical and social environment, three considerations enter into the choice of a village site: access to water, soil fertility, and defensibility. It is not always possible to meet all three conditions. In some districts there is no ground water; the soil varies in fertility from place to place; and villages in the flat lands lack natural defensibility—the fortified village, in fact, being extremely rare in the area.

The typical Jordanian village is composed of a tightly clustered group of houses and other buildings, surrounded by the fields which are worked—but may or may not be owned—by the inhabitants. There are few, if any, isolated farmhouses. The entire village, houses and fields, may be designated by the Arabic word *kharaj*, while the house cluster alone is commonly distinguished by the term *dayah*.

The dayah is usually divided into a number of sections or quarters (*harah*), and each of these tends to be occupied by people belonging to the same lineage. Ordinarily, there are no visible demarcations between the several sections of the village, which is typically a jumble of houses connected by narrow paths. The whole gives no appearance of plan beyond the tendency for the houses to be similarly oriented with relation to the dominant topographical features of the site.

Most villages have an open space (*sahah*) where biweekly or monthly markets are held and which serves as a gathering place on social occasions generally. The village mosque is apt to be situated at or near the sahah, as are whatever stores or coffeehouses the village may possess. In larger villages, or in those in which more than one religious sect is well represented, there may be more than one sahah, each with its own mosque or church.

The stone architecture of the typical Jordanian village varies from region to region, and dwellings may be large or small. Almost universally, however, the houses consist of one room for each family of parents and unmarried children and another room for equipment and livestock.

The cultivated area commonly extends outward from the village in several zones of specialized use. Small garden plots for vegetables and fruit trees lie nearest the village and sometimes reach into it. Next may come a belt of orchards, then the zone of cereal crops, finally, on the periphery, pasturage and wasteland. This scheme, however, is not universal, for some villages specialize in only one or two crops and there is also a general practice of letting at least a third of the cultivated land lie fallow each year and an increasing tendency to rotate crops on the same parcel of land. Physically, the fields are much fragmented, being constructed on terraces in the mountains and divided in the plains by hedges, ditches, and stone walls.

The land is the main pillar of village life, and the overwhelming majority of the inhabitants of most villages are farmers. Every village, however, has a number of occupational specialists to serve its needs— carpenters, smiths, shopkeepers, and a few others. There are also some villages whose inhabitants have turned to a particular craft, masonry for example, and many of the men of such places may be absent from their villages for extended periods while plying their trade in the surrounding area. Increasing numbers of villagers are also finding seasonal and permanent employment in the towns.

Class and Status

Jordan's rural population, complexly fragmented in other ways, shows little economic class stratification. The notion of a hereditary aristocracy, by which the bedouins distinguish noble tribes from base-born groups, finds little expression in the actual social organization of the village, although families and individuals frequently claim to be of noble descent. For the mass of Jordanian villagers, the harsh and arid land has yielded too little bounty to permit the growth of any wide difference in economic situation. The few who have acquired real wealth have by that fact been impelled and able to move to the towns; the rest—from the landless tenant, through the peasant who works his own few parcels of land, to the small landlord sea-sonally employing a few laborers—live on an economic scale which does not set them very far apart from each other. Socially, of course, these differences are reflected in differences in prestige and influence in the village community, and the limited opportunities available to the villager for accumulating wealth do provide a narrow range of social mobility.

Other factors than wealth contribute to social differentiation within the village. The mere fact of owning land carries prestige, and traditionally the farmer has ranked above the handicraftsman; in the villages of recently sedentarized and partly sedentarized nomads, at least, the bedouin contempt for such occupations as blacksmithing and tinkering remains, while the attitude toward the newly adopted agricultural way of life is no doubt still ambivalent. The shopkeeper and the merchant of the larger villages—often outsiders—probably stand apart from the village social scheme, as do any resident military or civil representatives of the central government.

Certain lineages, through wealth, numbers, or the capacities of their leaders, acquire high prestige, which in one degree or another is reflected on all their members. Such a lineage generally contains poor families as well as prosperous ones, and, if the bond of lineage membership does not level these economic differences, it does tend to soften or obscure them. The principal families of the more important lineages constitute the village elite, and their senior men stand high in village affairs.

Among the village leaders, the main status markers of Jordanian rural society—relative wealth in land, advantageous family connections, age seniority, and reputation for personal capacity—only approximately coincide. Not all of these qualifications are always present, for the propertied man may be influential but not a leader; the most powerful lineage in the community may put into the office of village headman, not its actual leader, but a lesser kinsman through whom the lineage chiefs choose to work; or a man from a relatively unimportant family may by energy and the force of his personality acquire a personal following which makes him a power in the community.

The Kinship System

The basic principles of kinship organization which obtain among the nomads are also found in the villages: male descent, paternal residence and authority, the extended family, and the lineage are all present. Save for recently settled nomads, however, the village, as a local entity, replaces the kinship-based tribe as the largest immediate social unit with which the individual identifies himself.

Jordan's 900-odd villages range in size from those made up of only a few families to settlements of several thousand persons. A small village may have but one lineage, all of its members tracing their descent through the male line back to a common ancestor, but two or more lineages are common in the larger places. Marriages are preferably with lineage-mates—ideally first cousins—but intermarriage between lineages is common.

The individual villager is bound to the other members of his lineage by a network of mutual obligations, which is strongest within the circle of the extended family but which can also draw the whole lineage together in the face of any external threat. Whether it is the lineage or the village as a whole that operates as a unit and defines the individual's identity depends upon the circumstances of the particular situation. Obviously, in the village with a single lineage, the two operating principles coincide, but where there are multiple lineages, rivalry within the village is common, and in relation to each other the inhabitants of such a village view themselves as members of this or that lineage. In dealings with the outside world, however, the village is capable of acting as a unit, and the particularity of kin group is then transcended by the cohesiveness of the village as a local entity.

As among the nomads the extended family, uniting a group of closely related males and their wives and children, has long been the important unit in the Jordanian village. In the traditional pattern the bonds between husband, wife, and children were strong, but they existed within the framework of the extended group, the interests of which were expected to come first. The authority of the senior male, shared residence, common property, and daily economic co-operation all combined to make the extended family the center of the individual's existence. Western influence and the changes of the modern period are eroding the unity of the extended family, and this process, most active in the towns, but present in the villages as well, is reducing more and more Jordanian families to their simpler dimensions of husband, wife, and children.

Intervillage Relations

Despite the kinship and religious affiliations which tend to divide Jordan's larger villages internally, village cohesiveness and the sense of attachment to the local community as a whole are not lacking. Beyond the preference for marrying within one's own lineage, there is the feeling that one ought at least to marry within one's own village. The relations between neighboring villages are often colored by traditional enmities or friendships. Kin ties, religion, Qaysi-Yamani partisanship, and economic exchanges have worked both to divide and to unite neighboring villages. In all of this, however, the villager is conscious of his local origins and retains a special loyalty to his home place.

Intervillage marriages are far more common than the popular ideal suggests. Open feuds between lineages were once frequent, and embattled groups sometimes sought to strengthen themselves by marital alliances with lineage mates in other villages. Another pattern is illustrated in a village study completed some years ago. The people of the West Bank village of Artas are all Moslem and Qaysi, but Artas has close economic relations with predominantly Christian and Yamani Bethlehem, the trading center of the area. Despite the Qaysi-Yamani division, there were some marriages between Moslems of the two places. In these marriages the companions of the bride and groom conspicuously displayed their respective Qaysi or Yamani colors, although the bride was encouraged to change hers to that of the groom. Another village in the vicinity, Bayt Jala, although Qaysi like Artas, is Christian, and no marriages took place between the two. The Qaysi tie, however, made it a convention that Artas and Bayt Jala exchange wedding invitations.

The Changing Village

Four primary themes have traditionally characterized village life in Jordan and throughout the Middle East: devotion to the land, immersion of the individual in the kinship group, adherence to religious sect, and community cohesiveness. Though these characteristics are still dominant in the area, they are being weakened and altered by the forces of the present.

The strongest influences are those emanating from the towns, which, in addition to generating an urban dynamic of their own, are serving as channels for the influx of western ideas and techniques. The subsistence standards and the unvarying agricultural toil of the village seem less rewarding than formerly to the peasant who has been to town and encountered more amply compensated ways of work. The cohesion of the extended kin-group tends to break down as more individuals, through choice or the force of economic circumstance, strike out on their own, and the old forms of paternalistic authority become less compelling and command less respect as the wage-earning husband finds himself more dependent on his own efforts than on the cooperative economic activity of a circle of relatives. The force of religion remains strong, but the secular influences of the town are bringing into question the traditional meaning which religion has had for the countryman, and with the spread of education he is beginning to find the religious tie alone insufficient to bind him to his former place in the village scheme. The accelerating movement of the rural population to the urban centers in itself would affect the cohesiveness of the village community, but the contemporary political currents are also pushing outward the boundaries of village exclusiveness. The nationalist ferment in the Arab world, the competition of political ideologies, and the efforts of the Jordanian Government are presenting the villager with new and vastly more inclusive definitions of personal and group loyalty than those traditionally marked by the perimeter of his village.

The impact of the modern world has only begun to be felt in Jordan's villages, particularly in those on the long-isolated East Bank.

Change, however, is taking place, and its probable directions can be gauged from the experience of other and now more urbanized Arab areas.

The Town

The contrast between life in the Jordanian village and in the nomadic tribe is marked; the contrast between either of these patterns and the life of the town is far greater. The elaboration of Islamic culture was the work of the towns, and the secular patterns that were developed in this way remained essentially urban. The city looked to the rural districts only for tax revenues, food, and some raw materials. Concerned only to maintain the minimum controls needed to insure the continued flow of these things from the countryside, the city through the Islamic Middle Ages stood as an island in a sea. During this time the townsman in Damascus in his daily pursuits and outlook, in the complex ordering of his community life might have more in common with the inhabitants of Cairo or some other distant city than with nearby villagers. The gap between city and country was preserved until well into the modern period, and it still marks a major cleavage in Middle Eastern society.

The immediate outcome of the impact of the West on the Arab world was to widen the gap between the city, which showed a comparative readiness to absorb western influences, and the village, which was relatively remote from the new forces. This stage is now being left behind in Jordan, as it was earlier in more developed Arab countries. For some time the rural population has been economically self-sufficient only in that it could satisfy its barest dietary needs from its fields and was able to produce simple utensils, apparel, and housing by handicraft methods. Today, with the introduction of commercial agriculture and a cash economy, even this capability has largely disappeared. Through or from the towns come food and all kinds of consumer goods which the peasant—and increasingly the nomad—desires and on which all but the most isolated depend.

The new economic role of the town is matched by its heightened importance as a center of administrative, political, judicial, religious, and educational activity at a time when these functions are affecting the country as a whole. In the towns are concentrated the minority of the population engaged in these and other professional fields and the still smaller minority of well-to-do landed proprietors and modern businessmen.

The traditional urban monopoly of wealth, power, and cultural pursuits made of the town, for all those who were conscious of its existence, the seat of everything desirable. That attraction has not waned, and it has combined with the pressure of contemporary economic and social conditions to accelerate rural migration to the urban centers. Spectacular as has been the growth of Jordan's towns in the past two decades, none are of really metropolitan proportions. The capital city of Amman, the largest, is remarkable, not for size, but for the expansion of its population from a few thousand in the 1920's to nearly 200,000 today. Other smaller Jordanian towns have grown almost as rapidly.

The Urban Setting

Aside from Amman, Jordan's 18 principal towns vary in size from Jerash's few thousands to the nearly 80,000 in the Jordanian sector of Jerusalem. Generally, a town has a hospital or at least a government clinic, one or more public and/or private schools, a number of mosques and churches, shops, business houses, and government offices, and in some instances a newspaper. Most of the principal towns have electricity and piped water, but these utilities are by no means within the reach of the whole population, and the well, the communal privy, and the kerosene lamp are common. Architecture varies, but stone construction predominates; housing ranges from the mud huts of the poor and the tent encampments of the bedouins to the western-style accommodations of resident foreigners and the well-to-do Jordanians.

One or more men's literary or other clubs—generally political in their objectives—are to be found in most centers. Public entertainment is restricted to coffeehouses, which are exclusively for men, and to movie houses, which are attended by men and women—either at separate showings or segregated as to seating—and in the largest centers to the small number of legitimate theater productions (see chap. 20). Some hotels in Amman, Jerusalem, and Ramallah that cater to western tourists have dance bands, but hotels of any kind are lacking in many East Bank towns.

Like the villages, Jordanian towns are internally divided into quarters (*harahs*), each of which tends to be occupied by a particular lineage or lineages. The population of Irbid (about 25,000 in 1952), for example, is divided into a number of large lineages, each occupying its own quarter. On the other hand, the several quarters of Amman are not organized on the traditional lineage lines but are inhabited by both Moslem and Christian families. The old Shabsugh quarter of Amman, however, is predominantly Circassian; such residential segregation of ethnic or religious communities is often characteristic of the towns, where the country's few minority groups have tended to gather. And some towns are inhabited only, or predominantly, by Christians, as in the case of Ramallah (until 1948), Bethlehem, and Madaba.

Class Structure

Until the end of Turkish rule over the territory of the present state of Jordan, the towns in the area were characterized by what in broadest terms was a two-class system. At the top were a small number of landlords, merchants, civil, military, and religious officials, whose status was defined by wealth or family connections and occupation; below were the mass of artisans, small shopkeepers, workmen, and in the smaller towns agricultural laborers. While the upper levels of the latter group approached the status of a middle class, a wide economic gap separated the wealthy minority from the rest. This gap was in part bridged by the kin ties which might connect a poor family with a wealthy one, giving the latter at least a sense of protective patronage. Various families tended to be identified with particular occupations, and the hereditary character of many skills made it natural for the individual to accept his allotted place in the economic scheme. The sanctions of religion, too, asserted that man's fate was predestined by God and that it was man's duty to submit to God's will. In this traditional order, the forms of relationship between superior and inferior, master and man, were patterned on those of the family institution. The equation of the role of superiors and inferiors with those of father and son, respectively, made it easier for people to accept lowly position.

Economically, this society, though heterogeneous by contrast with the homogeneity of the village and the nomadic tribe, was relatively static. The ultimate source of wealth was the land, which the urban upper class exploited directly or indirectly through rents and taxes, and it was the produce of the villages which fed the towns and made possible the commercial and cultural activities which were concentrated there. The urban owners of landed estates had no motivation to put their capital into other than agricultural and related commercial pursuits. Possibilities for economic, and hence for social, advancement existed, but there was little room at the top of the ladder and the system did not provide for its enlargement.

A new middle class has begun to appear in the towns. Still insignificant in numbers, it is nevertheless exerting an appreciable influence on the political, economic, and cultural life of the country. A direct outcome of western contact, this new group is the carrier of the new ideas, values, and techniques which today are presenting the Arab world with so many problems and possible solutions.

Occupationally, Jordan's young middle class consists mostly of a very small number of doctors, lawyers, teachers, social workers, writers, journalists, and a few other professionals. It is revealing of the persistence of the traditional disdain for manual work of any kind that Jordanians are reluctant to assign professional status to the mechanical skills which the country lacks. Nor do old-style merchants, owners of real estate and of workshops, and lower government officials count as members of the middle class; these are identified rather with the fringes of the old upper class into the ranks of which they aspire to rise.

The members of the middle class seem to be recruited from three main sources: from well-to-do families in the rural areas who can afford to educate their sons, some of whom continue on to professional training; from the families of the higher-paid urban workingmen, whose sons are sometimes able to acquire an education; and from the urban upper class, most of whose sons receive a high school education which leads some of them into the professions. Professional persons who belong to the "great" families are regarded as members of the upper class.

Kinship

A distinction must be made between old and new towns, between those with long-established populations and those like Amman and Ramallah, which have mushroomed with the influx of refugees and other settlers. Little is known about the details of the changes which the settlers have undergone in their new environment. Obviously, they bring with them the social patterns of their home localities, but it is not clear how resistant these patterns are to the confused and generally poverty-stricken conditions of contemporary Jordanian urban life or what detailed changes are taking place.

The social organization of the older towns shows a general resemblance to that of the nomadic tribe and the village. Extended families are grouped into lineages. Paternal descent and authority, family loyalty, and intra-lineage cooperation are components of the pattern, although the actual integrity of the extended kin-group may vary from the strong cohesiveness of the conservative lineage to the attenuated unity of the family scattered by misfortune or influenced toward a more individualistic pattern by western education or residence abroad.

One result of the traditional urban residence pattern of particular lineages, ethnic, and religious groups congregating in special quarters has been that these quarters have functioned almost as though they were so many independent villages. The inhabitants of a quarter of any size might range on the economic scale from poor to wealthy, but they tended to focus on a number of particular occupations, and the ties of kinship, residence, and common occupation set them off from, and sometimes against, the other sections of the town population. Jealousies, hatreds, and blood feuds between different lineages have been a feature of town life as well as of the villages and the tribes.

The Town in Transition

The mold of the old order in Jordan is cracked but not broken. Western influences, the problems which came with the tripling of the population as a result of the annexation of the West Bank and the refugee influx, the nationalist ferment in the Arab world, and the tensions which all of these have engendered focus with particular intensity on the towns. New ways of work and new social forms compete with traditional ways and forms which still half-serve the needs of a crowded, impoverished, and confused population. The indigent man in a refugee camp cannot look for support from kinsmen as helpless as himself, and in the absence of large-scale and expensive resettlement measures his status as refugee is tolerable only if he retains hope that he will some day be restored to his home. Workman and employer alike in one of Jordan's few modern industrial plants find it difficult to deal with each other in the old paternalistic and personal way. The upper-class landlord, once secure in his wealth and status of family, is confronted with novel demands, not only from the villages but from a government which must be concerned with the plight of the farmer. The member of the new middle class, equipped with ideas and skills developed in the West but not yet adjusted to the conditions of Jordanian life, finds it hard to employ his knowledge effectively or to place himself in the tradition-bound but changing social scene.

Whatever the course of events, the Jordanian town is influencing the rest of the society as it has never done in the past. The continued development of new economic forms and the efforts of the government to substitute a pattern of unified political administration for the local and family controls of the past seem certain to move the town, and with it eventually the other main sectors of Jordanian life, closer to patterns familiar in the modern world.

DYNAMICS OF POLITICAL BEHAVIOR

JORDANIAN POLITICS IN RECENT YEARS HAVE BEEN COMPLICATED by the annexation in 1950 of the interior of central Palestine on the West Bank of the Jordan River. The relatively urbanized West Bank population brought with it new allegiances, new divisions, and new sources of discontent with which the predominantly rural and tribal order of the East Bank was ill equipped to cope. The internal complications of the Jordanian political scene were aggravated by regional and international politics.

Political activity in Jordan, as elsewhere in the Middle East, is at once more superficial and more intense than that in the West. Violence of feeling, street demonstrations, mob action, choleric oratory, all are characteristic political phenomena in the Arab world. But the consequences of such activity—even including the overthrow of a government—almost always have a slighter effect on the society as a whole than would comparable events in western Europe or the United States. In Jordan, as in other Arab states, the formal apparatus of government is only beginning to acquire the importance it holds in the West, and many of the essential social controls and services are maintained by the traditional institutions of kin-group and village.

Jordanians interested in politics tend to range themselves at any given moment for or against many more purposes and personalities than ordinarily hold the stage in western politics. As a consequence, the community may appear to be gravely divided, but the seriousness of such division is greatly modified by the impermanence of political allegiances and loyalties and by the relative ease with which persons may move from one end of the political spectrum to the other.

New political types and personalities are emerging in Jordan as elsewhere in the Middle East. Notable among them are leaders, and aspirants, who are acutely aware of the nature of local politics. They have learned to manipulate for their political ends the complex of the traditional and the new in the area; and their ends more often than in the past find political expression in ideologies which reach outside the region. The masses, preoccupied with local interests and until recently politically accessible only to the strong personal leader, are now not only being manipulated by the new type of leader but also moving toward an awareness of larger issues. A manifestation of this is the way in which mob violence is today employed for political ends. What appears to be the popular spontaneous outburst of public indignation is most often a rigidly controlled demonstration; moreover, the participants are motivated not only by the old desire for loot and excitement but by newly developing political attitudes.

Two main sources of political subversion exist in Jordan. Organized elements of both have at various times been outlawed, at other times tolerated. Politically, one is on the extreme left, with the Communists as its most important element; the other, on the extreme right, is made up of religious extremists of the kind found in the Moslem Brotherhood, which until Nasser's coming to power had its major strength in Egypt.

More generally, in early 1957 two thirds of Jordan's population was actually or potentially opposed to the royal authority and to the maintenance of government under the terms of the existing constitution, or even to the preservation of the state itself.

Nature of Jordanian Politics

Prior to 1948

The East Bank population—settled, seminomadic, and nomadic alike —was before 1948 left much to its own devices and gave the government little trouble. Whatever opposition there had been under the emirate was suppressed by Abdullah (1921–1951) during the first dozen years of his rule as Emir of Transjordan. Such opposition was largely centered in the few towns; professional circles particularly resented Abdullah's policy of collaboration with Britain. Doctors and lawyers who had been trained in Germany often brought back a pro-German point of view which complemented their anti-British bias. Although few in number, they became increasingly important as the Palestine question developed. After Abdullah's successful repression of opposition, most of their activity was confined to places of enforced or voluntary exile in surrounding countries, such as Lebanon and Syria. The rest of the population almost completely acquiesced in the existing form of government—parliamentary in name only.

Abdullah built up a bureaucracy because his rule, first as Emir and then as King required executive machinery. The country's politics became largely that of a bureaucratic oligarchy conditioned by the traditional family and tribal patterns of the area. After the King's murder in 1951 the state organism remained in the hands of the oligarchy. The men forming it had originally come from widely different backgrounds: Syrians opposed to the French Mandate and Palestinians opposed to British rule; local landowning magnates; Circassians transplanted in the early years of Turkish Sultan Abdul Hamid's reign (1876–1909); Moslem jurists sympathetic to Abdullah. If the bureaucracy had remained intact and unswerving in its loyalty to the throne, the internal politics of Jordan would not be so much in doubt today.

The tribal and local character of loyalties and the low educational level of the primarily rural and nomadic East Bank population prevented any large-scale concern with issues on the national level and discouraged grassroots involvement in politics. The rule of Abdullah was maintained under British guidance and supported by the dominant tribal chiefs as well as the conservative merchants, property owners, and religious leaders in the towns. Under British influence, Abdullah's role was largely that of a superior sheikh given a modern quality by the trappings of a constitutional monarchy. While the British Mandate continued (1921–1946) the pattern was not challenged, and it is unlikely that any serious opposition to royal prerogatives has appeared among the rural and nomadic peoples up to the present time.

The West Bank, on the other hand, has had quite a different political history. Direct British administration evoked more widespread political activity than in Transjordan. Educational facilities were superior, and western influence reached farther. The ruling families constituted an aristocracy whose prestige was based on historical grants of position and honor by Mameluke and Ottoman Turkish rulers between the thirteenth and eighteenth centuries. A relatively large professional and white-collar group formed the nucleus of a growing middle class; many of its members had been educated in Britain or continental Europe. The political consciousness of this population was heightened by such large issues as increased Jewish immigration into Palestine, the political future of the Mandate, and the choice of spokesmen to deal with British mandatory authorities. The growth of Israeli nationalism was an irritant which intensified the factionalism of the Palestinian Arab leadership. The differences were increased by the recriminations which developed after the failure of Arab arms in the Arab-Israeli hostilities in 1948. Petty intrigue and endless attempts at self-justification became the hallmarks of West Bank politics. A general disillusionment with the old leaders opened the way for a new, often more leftist, leadership, which understood how to make use of confusion and chaos. The new West Bank leaders are on the whole relatively young men who have little use for the traditional bases for authority. Demagogic and intransigent, some of them have emerged as heroes of present-day West Bank politics.

Since 1948

The new elements brought into Jordan by the annexation of the West Bank produced trouble immediately. Feeling at a disadvantage in relation to the established East Bank group, the Palestinians began by demanding more representative government. The political friction which followed was but one expression of the difficulty of incorporating into the country a largely uprooted and embittered population which outnumbered the original inhabitants by two to one.

The demand of the West Bankers for representative government appears to have come less from any devotion to democratic institutions than from the urge to develop means of ending the alliance with Britain and of renewing the war with Israel. Whatever the motives, the Palestinian demand for a larger voice in government exaggerated the differences between the East and West Banks.

The satisfaction which might have been felt in Jordan upon the end of the Mandate in 1946 was more than offset by new tensions and frustrations. Not the least of these stemmed from the presence of the refugee camps, which by 1954 still held over 100,000 refugees. Many of the inmates of the camps, caught in an unproductive and substandard existence, became in a sense professional refugees. Disillusioned and despairing, their principal active emotion was anger, and they became one of the main sources of anti-British as well as anti-Israeli sentiment. They concentrated their wrath on the Arab Legion—especially on Glubb Pasha and his British colleagues, who symbolized for them the British imperialism to which they had come to attribute their woes. As for Israel, they felt that there could be but one solution—a war which would destroy the interloping new nation utterly and restore the displaced Palestinians to their lands and homes. They also took for granted that the anti-Israeli objective required the elimination of all British influence from Jordan. This extreme point of view was fostered chiefly by the anti-Hashemite supporters of Hajj Amin al-Husseini, the former Mufti of Jerusalem. It also became a convenient and effective weapon of all other anti-royalists at home, including the crypto-Communists, and of the anti-Hashemite and anti-British Arab governments abroad, notably Egypt and Saudi Arabia (see chap. 10).

Economic insecurity, and often actual hardship, rendered the whole Palestinian group susceptible to the refugee mentality, but they were not uniformly opposed to the monarchy, and there were pro-Hashemite and anti-Husseini elements among the Palestinian Arab leaders. Some of these entered the government bureaucracy, but the core of the ruling oligarchy remained small and largely composed of East Bank leaders: in the first decade of independence, 31 politicians occupied at least 155 posts, 15 held 96 posts of cabinet rank. The hold of the bureaucracy on the government apparatus—behind the façade of the Constitution, which it had largely drafted—might have continued intact if the bureaucracy itself had been cohesive. But competing ambition and differences of policy—between ins and outs, conservatives and liberals, those favoring cooperation with Britain and the West and those opposed, pan-Arabs and those favoring the development of a Jordanian nationalism, and others—splintered the ruling elite and introduced a new and more chaotic era of Jordanian politics.

Jordanian political activity since 1948 has been conducted in an atmosphere of prolonged crisis involving war, civil disturbance, constitutional change, problems concerning the royal succession, and constant alarms in the unstable armistice with Israel. Political issues and political action began to more generally affect the population and to take on a more personal meaning: the permanent loss or the reacquisition of a villager's ancestral lands might hinge on one political decision, an opportunity for employment which would take a refugee out of a camp, on another. Heightened feeling in the political sphere was exacerbated by the East Bank–West Bank division, and the differences in the situation and experience of the two populations made satisfactory decisions extremely difficult to reach. Under the circumstances, it was remarkable that the government was able to act effectively as often as it did.

The old elite around the King continues to be confronted by a group of younger men, eager for power and convinced that it can best be grasped and held in terms of this or that version of an Arab left-wing authoritarianism. The increased tempo of Jordanian political life has been accompanied by the growth of techniques of mass communication, and ideological appeal is being added to the traditional reliance on the attraction of the personality of the individual political leader. New organizational lines have not, however, clearly emerged.

Political Alignments

Parties in the western sense, with platforms and defined positions on particular issues, developed organizations, and large popular national followings, have not until recently existed in Jordan. The Communist

Party is perhaps an exception but it does not have a large following. The average Jordanian tribesman or villager comes into contact with the government only through the village chief (*rais al-baladiyah*)— or the headman (*mukhtar*) if the village is very small—and the local police. He probably knows of, and may even have seen, the provincial governor (*mutasarrif*). He is conscious of the king as the most exalted figure of all, but, save in its limited local manifestations, government remains for him a distant and shadowy entity. Until recently he has been almost entirely unaware of national issues. Family, tribe, village constitute the significant units within which social life is lived; within these circles relationships are characteristically personal. In this pattern, politics becomes less a matter of principles and issues than of allegiance given or withdrawn on the basis of attitudes toward the personality of the individual leader. Men turn to the figure most able to help them and their families personally—to lend money, provide food when it is scarce, give employment, and act as advocate before higher authority.

The patron-follower relationship remains a basic factor in Jordanian life, even among urban dwellers. In the villages the patron is usually a man whose family has long exercised neighborhood authority. Such local leaders themselves tend to repeat the pattern by clustering—however temporarily—around other, still more influential individuals, and it is in the shifting, unreliable web of these personal allegiances that the larger pattern of Jordanian politics is formed. The emphasis on the personal factor in leadership and organizational life has tended to make of political parties rather loose groupings around a leader whose success is worked for because it is shared in various ways with his followers.

Given the key role of family loyalties and alignments, it is not surprising that family feuds and rivalries are characteristic features of political life in Jordan. Many of these conflicts are centuries old and have left a deep and lasting imprint in the history of the region. For example, the Husseini family, claiming descent from Mohammed and a high place in the early Islamic aristocracy, bitterly rejects the counterclaims of the Hashemite family, traditional defenders of Mecca. In Jordan today such rivalries often divide even political moderates who might be expected on other grounds to cooperate with one another.

Legal Parties—1956

In conformity with the Constitution, a law pertaining to political parties was adopted in 1953. It laid down the principle that party aims must not be harmful to "Arab unity" nor calculated to create dissension among the different communities in the country. The Ministry of the Interior is required to reply within six months to an application for party organization. Emergency regulations issued in 1954 further stipulated that the Cabinet might refuse to grant a permit to any group or might dissolve any existing party, "if deemed in the public interest." The construction placed by successive cabinets on the constitutional and legislative clauses about party formation has been extremely narrow, and most of the approved parties have been not real political groupings but private instruments of individual and family interests. Such parties as have existed tended in their early stages to be formal groupings and to be of only regional or local importance. Most candidates have usually run as independents and have made a bid for office mainly on the strength of their personal reputations. The East Bank–West Bank division, the Israeli question, and the new crisis precipitated by the problems of Suez and of Middle Eastern relations with the Soviet Union, all were stimulating the growth of political parties in Jordan. By the time of the national election of October 1956, which witnessed the victory of leftist, anti-West, pro-Nasser candidates, seven parties were contesting for seats in the legislature, although only three of them were legally recognized. The three legally recognized parties were the National Socialist Party, the Arab Resurrection Party, and the Arab Constitutional Party. The other four which, although illegal, participated in the elections unmolested were the Moslem Brotherhood, the Islamic Liberation Movement, the Arab Nationalist Party, and the National Front, a front organization of the Communist Party.

With the ousting of Prime Minister Nabulsi and the appointment to the premiership of Ibrahim Hashim Pasha during the political crisis of April and May 1957, political parties were legally abolished. Their return presumably awaits a government decision that they no longer constitute a subversive threat. Precedent suggests, however, that some of them continue to function.

The National Socialist Party (al-Hizb al-Watani al-Ishtiraki) emerged from the 1956 elections as the strongest party in Jordan. It secured eleven seats in the new legislative chamber, and Suleiman an-Nabulsi, its leader, although failing in his bid for election in Amman, was called on by King Hussein to form the new Cabinet. Nabulsi, a former Jordanian envoy to London, was the center of opposition to the Baghdad Pact. He and his party favored close cooperation with Egypt and Syria, modification if not abrogation of the treaty with Britain, and neutralism in the East-West struggle. President Nasser of Egypt has called the party "the symbol of Arab awakening." Although it calls itself "socialist," the National Socialist Party includes many moderate elements. Its socialism refers to mild social reforms rather than to a Marxist program. It draws most of its strength from western Jordan.

The Arab Resurrection Party (Hizb al-Bath al-Arabi) is one of the better organized parties in Jordan. It is to the left of the National Socialist Party and to the right of the (Communist) National Front; it has in the past been treated as subversive by the government. Vague in its ideology, the Arab Resurrection Party was once broadly anti-foreign. Recently, it has modified its xenophobia to a pro-Soviet, anti-western position, as exemplified in the actions and pronouncements of the Minister of State for Foreign Affairs in the Nabulsi Cabinet, Abdullah ar-Rimawi. The Party, linked with the Syrian party of the same name, also pro-Soviet, was not permitted to enter the national elections in 1954, but did so in 1956, when it elected two of its candidates to the Chamber of Representatives. It had evidently suffered a loss of support among its main sources of strength, the intelligentsia and students, who were being attracted by the more moderate National Socialists, on the one hand, and the National Front, on the other.

The Arab Constitutional Party (al-Hizb ad-Dusturi al-Arabi) is more a collection of notables than a party with popular roots. Its strength depends on the strength of its leaders, most of whom are feudal landlords. Although it had enjoyed a majority in the previous legislature, its representation after the 1956 elections was reduced to eight deputies, most of whom are from the East Bank. It is the least anti-West of the Jordanian parties, but, like all of them, it is Cairo-oriented.

Illegal Parties—1956

Despite their small numerical strength in Jordan, the Communists (most of whom were acquired in the annexation of the West Bank) now constitute the most serious subversive threat to the country. Prior to the annexation of the West Bank, they were of little consequence. In Palestine, during the period of the Mandate (1921–48), however, they were able not only to infiltrate workers' organizations but also to attract significant numbers of intellectuals and professionals. Moreover, the Communist Party in Palestine found favor among Arabs for its opposition to "bourgeois Zionism." And before the implementation of the Palestine partition in 1948–49, the Communists found it advantageous to collaborate with the former Mufti of Jerusalem against the interests of King Abdullah.

Following the annexation, the Palestinian Communists, who then became Jordanians, had to carry the burden of an unpopular program which favored partition and tacitly, therefore, the maintenance of Israel. Moreover, there was confusion in the Party organization, for although prior to partition a large proportion of the rank-and-file had been Arabs, most of the leadership had been Jewish. There was also a clannish distinction between labor and white-collar members.

By 1950 the Party had reorganized and was engaging in considerable activity. In 1951 it abandoned support of partition and the policy of peace with Israel and changed its name to the "Arab Communist Party of Jordan." Meanwhile, the Communists had opposed the establishment of the National Guard, had worked to boycott the national elections in 1950, and had identified themselves with elements opposing King Abdullah and his policy of cooperation with the western powers. Premier Said al-Mufti obtained special legislation to deal with Communist activity. Heightened antisubversive efforts by the government, however, did not impede the increasing activity of the Party under Fuad Nasir. Nasir, an Arab of Christian background from Nazareth, the most important Communist center in Israel (where the Party is legal), seems to have been able to move back and forth across the border at will, thereby escaping detection. This involved collaboration with the Communist Party in Israel, but the collaboration did not prevent changes in the Communist line in 1951 which ranged the Jordan Party with other Arab Communist parties behind the slogans of anti-Israeli Pan-Arabism.

King Abdullah was assassinated in July 1951 by adherents of the former Mufti of Jerusalem. The government reacted at first with a relaxed security policy, apparently to appease the various opposition forces. The Communists took advantage of the opportunity by running candidates in the August elections of that year from behind the façade of a "People's Bloc." None of its candidates were elected. The government, which in October had freed all those in prison or in custody on charges of subversion, in December struck at the Communists by arresting Fuad Nasir and sentencing him to a ten-year prison term. This action appears to have been made possible by the presence within the Communist movement of planted government agents. The Party, which then numbered about 700, had been further weakened by the appearance of a "Titoist" faction. Nasir's successor as head of the Party is believed to have been Radwan al-Hilu, a Palestinian labor leader. The government's anti-Communist measures continued during 1952 with the arrest of other Party members and the tightening of legal measures providing severe penalties for making money contributions to Communist organizations or distributing their propaganda, while the legal definitions of conspiracy and incitation were broadened.

Despite efforts to suppress it, the Communist Party in 1953–54 extended its activities and influence. In this it was assisted by the "experiment with democracy," under Premier Fawzi al-Mulqi, which involved abandoning earlier repressive measures. Throughout, the Palestinian Arab refugees constituted an important political target of the Communists. The miserable conditions in the camps and the hopeless prospects of the refugees made them highly vulnerable to Communist appeals. The younger refugees, reacting against the defeatism of the older generation, are particularly vulnerable.

The Communist threat, however, was not immediate as long as the British stayed and the Arab Legion remained loyal to royal authority. On the other hand, the Party's capabilities were considerably greater than its small membership might indicate.

The ten cells said to be operating in Jerusalem in the early 1950's were made up mostly of professional men, the best known of whom was Dr. Yakub Zayidin, who had been head of the Augusta Victoria Hospital, Jordan's largest. Additional advantage accrued to the movement through its close cooperation with the Israeli party. Nevertheless, in late 1953 the head of the Criminal Investigation Division, a British official, revealed that the country had been divided into nine surveillance districts, and declared that he could round up 80 percent of the leadership in the course of one day.

The Communists, recognizing their most important antagonist, in 1953 directed their main propaganda offensive against Glubb Pasha, exploiting the charge that he was responsible for the Qibya tragedy (involving an Israeli raid on a Jordan village) in failing to use the Arab Legion effectively to protect the villagers. The Party was very active in the 1954 election campaign, working through a new front group known as the National Socialist Front (al-Jabhah al-Ishtirakiy-yah al-Wataniyyah) or as the National Democratic Front (al-Jabhah ad-Dimuqratiyyah al-Wataniyyah). The group did not acquire legality, but eight of its candidates—all Communists—ran as independents. Five eventually withdrew; none were elected.

Most observers agreed with the official Jordanian investigating commission that the Party was the most important influence in the election-day riots, which in the capital amounted almost to full-scale rebellion. Again in 1957 the demonstrations protesting King Hussein's dismissal of Premier Nabulsi began in Nablus, the center of Communist activity and of a population known for political explosiveness.

The years following the Arab-Israeli war saw the growth of Communist influence and of the Party's capacity to provoke violence as a technique for weakening the government. The government, however, vacillated between stern and weak measures. Clearly, the refugees and the inhabitants of the West Bank, who after 1950 made up two thirds of the country's population, posed almost unsolvable problems, but inconsistency and weakness in meeting Communist exploitation of these problems only worsened the government's position.

Since 1954 the international situation has increasingly complicated Jordan's internal politics. British pressure upon Jordan in late 1955 to join the "northern tier" states associated in the Baghdad Pact precipitated a crisis in which successive ministries were overthrown and anti-western, pro-Soviet, pro-Egyptian feeling reached new heights (see chap. 10). Russian diplomatic, trade, and propaganda activity in the area were being intensified, and Saudi Arabia by 1954 had injected itself into Jordanian politics, working against the Baghdad Pact through payments of money to the Jordanian press and the corruption of local politicians. Egypt was similarly engaged and was making its influence even more strongly felt through the aggressive and targeted propaganda broadcasts of Radio Cairo. By the time of the crises of April and May 1957, in which King Hussein halted Jordan's leftward drift, the situation had been somewhat changed. Saudi Arabia had become alarmed over the penetration of Communist ideological as well as Soviet influence into the Middle East and even into its own territory. Moreover, it had begun to recognize Egyptian President Nasser's pro-Soviet neutralism as dangerous to its own interests.

The external pressures on Jordanian politics are further suggested by the fact that the most influential figure among local Communists is almost certainly Khalid Bakdash, secretary of the Syrian Communist Party. The Jordanian Party has found fertile ground in which to cultivate the Soviet propaganda line which equates the West with colonialism, imperialism, and interference. It also promotes the pro-Soviet, anti-western "neutralism" of which President Nasser of Egypt is an important protagonist. The Communists have found special opportunities in the frictions between Jordan's East Bank and West Bank, and in the events of 1956 and 1957 when Egypt seized the Suez Canal and Britain, France, and Israel took military action against Egypt.

In 1956 the Communists entered the election through a party called the National Front (al-Jabhah al-Wataniyyah), composed of Communist and pro-Communist elements. The government did not greatly interfere with the party, and three of its candidates were elected. Although the election represented a major gain for the Communists in Jordan, it did not necessarily indicate a substantial increase in Communist Party membership. The National Front appears to have gained much of its support in the last election as a result of Arab bitterness over what is regarded as the pro-Israeli policy of the western nations.

The subversive threat of Jordan's Communist Party should not be judged in terms of its small hard-core membership, but rather in terms of its capacity to organize the activity of a considerable number of active sympathizers and to influence strongly the political activity of perhaps 25 percent or more of the Palestinian refugees in Jordan. Some sympathizers come from the best-educated sectors of the population. Frustrated and embittered, they are among those most apt to identify their own aspirations and the demands of the Pan-Arabic nationalism vigorously promoted by Egypt with what they are ready to believe are the friendly policies of the Soviet Union. The alternative appears to them to be acceptance of a permanent Israel and capitulation to the superior strength of the "western imperialists." In seeking to spread this outlook, the Communists have had particular success among Jordan's small and relatively isolated professional and middle classes.

The Jordanian sector of the Moslem Brotherhood, which was founded and has its main strength in Egypt, must be called subversive, both in its fanatic insistence on a return to the social and political order of early Islam and in its readiness to resort to terrorism in furthering its aims. It has, however, shown no particular regard for consistency in its short-range policies. One of its proposals directed at the problem of unemployment involved the use of foreign capital, notwithstanding its basic, extreme xenophobia. During the period when the Brotherhood in Egypt favored the Nasser regime, the Jordan branch organized demonstrations in Amman supporting Egyptian demands for British evacuation; later, when the Cairo government executed six members of its Brotherhood, a demonstration of a thousand persons took place before the Egyptian Embassy in Amman and the local organization called for a general strike in the city. It currently supports the throne and regards Jordan as a haven from the repressions of both the Egyptian and Syrian regimes.

Although for a time in 1954 the Permanent Bureau of the Islamic Conference (an organ of the Mufti and related to the Brotherhood) was established in Jerusalem, the Jordan government in August of that year refused to permit the Egyptian Said Ramadan, the Conference secretary and son-in-law of the assassinated Supreme Guide of the Brotherhood, Hasan al-Banna, to return to Jordan. In October of that same year, members of the Brotherhood were involved with the Communists in election riots. The Director of its Permanent Conference was requested to leave Jordan. An order issued early in 1955 for the arrest of the controller general, Mohammed Abd ar-Rahman al-

Khalifah, was rescinded in May and he returned to Jordan. In 1954 the Brotherhood's candidates were presented in the Jordanian election and four were elected. On the other hand, the crisis precipitated by the dismissal of the Nabulsi Cabinet in April 1957 brought Brotherhood members into the streets in clashes with the Communists. There was no indication, however, that the Brotherhood, despite its attacks on the Communist opponents of the King, was any the less subversive.

Before 1956 the Moslem Brotherhood took part in politics not directly but through a subsidiary called the Islamic Liberation Movement, which was not legal in the 1954 election, although six independent candidates were said to support it. In 1956 the Liberation Movement entered the elections independently, electing only one member.

The Arab Nationalist Party (al-Hizb al-Watani al-Arabi) is an old Palestinian party sponsored by the former Mufti of Jerusalem, Hajj Amin al-Husseini. Two of its prominent members were elected to the new legislature, one of whom, Dr. Dawud al-Husseini, is a cousin of the ex-Mufti. The ex-Mufti of Jerusalem still exerts a certain amount of influence among the Palestinian Arabs. He is widely suspected of bearing the ultimate responsibility for the murder of King Abdullah in 1951. The Mufti's hatred of the King goes back to the period of the Mandate, when Abdullah supported the Husseinis' political opponents in domestic Palestine Arab politics. The Mufti's cousin and close political associate since the mid 1920's, Jamal al-Husseini, was retained in the mid 1950's by King Saud of Saudi Arabia as a confidential adviser. Jamal is believed by some to have been the organizer of the Saudi program in Jordan against the Baghdad Pact; certainly, many pro-Mufti West Bankers were among the angry mobs who in December 1955 caused the downfall of two cabinets within a single week.

Another subversive group is the Syrian People's Party (al-Hizb al-Qawmi as-Suri), which employs terrorist methods and is organized on totalitarian lines. Its main goal is the incorporation of all the northern Arab countries into a greater Syria. Its concept of amalgamation is "Syrian" rather than "Arab," a fact which sets it off from other subversive groups in the region—and no doubt modifies its popular appeal.

Political Role of Religious and Ethnic Minorities

The small Circassian community and the Christians are the only two minority groups that have any significance in Jordanian politics. King Abdullah, in drawing on the Circassians for his bodyguard, gave them an importance out of proportion to their numbers. At present each of the two groups is represented in the Jordanian Cabinet by two members, one from the East Bank and one from the West Bank. Politically the Circassians have generally appeared to be cautious and stable in their political activities; they have supported the government in power. On the whole the Christians, whether supporting or opposing the government, are more violent and intransigent, and are usually found taking extreme positions.

Jordanian Elections and Representation

Jordanian elections operate under an extremely liberal nationality law, which provides that any Palestinian Arab may choose Jordanian citizenship, thereby receiving the franchise; it is scarcely more difficult for any other non-Jordanian to acquire the same rights. An electoral law, several times amended, enfranchises every male Jordanian eighteen years of age and above who has not lost his civil rights because of a court conviction, is not mentally defective, or is not a relative of the king within certain degrees. Elections are direct, with the successful candidate required to receive a majority of votes—except in the case of the two bedouin members of the Council of Representatives, who are chosen by a council of 10 from among the chiefs of the tribes to be represented. A fixed number of seats in the Council of Representatives is also reserved for the principal ethnic and religious minorities: 2 seats for the Circassians and 7 for the Christians on both banks of the Jordan. In the latter case there is overrepresentation, since there are only 40 members of the chamber altogether (20 from each Bank) and the Christian population of Jordan is not more than one tenth of the total.

Although there is an active feminist movement in Jordan—called the Arab Women's Union—which has worked for women's political rights, women are not permitted to vote. The Council of Representatives in January 1955 recommended to the government that the latter study "with sympathy" the request of the Union for such rights.

Elections are conducted under the Ministry of the Interior, which draws up an electoral list. This list must be posted for popular challenge in public places well before the election. Popular exercise of the ballot varies considerably from election to election. The refugee population is often particularly active in elections, despite appeals of some sections of its leadership to abstain as a protest against government policy.

Most elections have been conducted without overt interference, although those of 1954 witnessed government use of the army to meet the challenge of demonstrations, riots, and increased political activity by leftists and by the Moslem Brotherhood. Charges were made that the government had been guilty of fraud in the elections and that it had employed a reign of terror to gain its ends. It was alleged, also, that Glubb Pasha had interfered in the elections in favor of certain candidates. Many of these charges emanated from sources outside Jordan, including Egypt, Lebanon, and Syria. On its side, the government clearly was confronted with a serious threat from extremist elements, and in suppressing the violence of the extremists and seeking to win at the polls it no doubt went beyond the bounds of the Constitution.

The elections of October 1956 witnessed a victory for those elements, largely West Bank and often leftist and oriented to the Pan-Arabism of Cairo and Damascus, who continue to demonstrate their ability to exploit the dissatisfactions and emotions of a confused and politically disorganized people.

Forces for Change

Three events—the annexation by Jordan of the West Bank on April 24, 1950; the assassination of King Abdullah on July 20, 1951; and the dismissal of Lieutenant General John Bagot Glubb Pasha, the British commander of the Arab Legion on March 2, 1956—have involved the progressive weakening of the royal control over the government.

Whereas to the end of his life Abdullah remained an embodiment of effective patriarchal authority and stoutly resisted significant constitutional limitations upon this authority for three decades, by early 1957 his grandson, King Hussein, was in fundamental conflict with the ministries and with the legislature over domestic and foreign policy. Abdullah possessed a sharp political intelligence that made him one of the most important forces in the Arab world (see chap. 10). His removal from the scene left power in the hands of persons either less astute than he or without his powerful personal prestige. Hussein, the present King, has shown some capacity to resist the forces of division and to defend his royal prerogatives, constitutional or traditional, but it is a question whether the values he strives to speak for can become identified with the popular forces at work in Jordan.

The annexation of the West Bank raised a real question as to whether the kingdom could long remain intact in view of the many internal and external forces pulling upon the fabric of the state.

The dismissal of Glubb Pasha in the spring of 1956 was a blow to British prestige in the Middle East, but its significance to Jordan went much deeper—revealing the increased influence of the anti-British Palestinian Arabs in the Arab Legion and in the political life of Jordan in general. The presence in the Arab Legion of officers who carried their opposition to the British to the point of insubordination made it clear that the Legion had ceased to be a completely loyal instrument of the royal authority.

The increasing insecurity of the monarchy involved a broadening of the contest for power. This did not necessarily mean more popular participation in politics, although the mob was increasingly active in the towns in manipulated demonstrations. By early 1957 it had become almost certain that, in the intensifying contest, the army would emerge as the formal central political force, as had happened in Syria and Egypt a few years earlier. It was also clear that the army, in asserting its power in the political arena, would come to speak in part also for certain new forces. Notable among these were the numerically superior and dissatisfied Palestinian Arabs of the West Bank. Politically, the accents in which some army elements spoke were Pan-Arab and leftist, a circumstance no less pleasing to Syria and Egypt than to the proponents of communism within and without the country. During the political crisis of April and May 1957 the army elements supporting the royal authority were victorious.

The rise of the power of the military was accompanied and partly countered by the increasingly active role of the legislature. This tendency was first manifested in the legislative rejection of the government's budget in May 1951, an event which presaged difficulties for the orderly development of constitutional government in Jordan. The pressures of the mob, of the Palestinian Arabs, of anti-western nationalists, and of leftists were more and more finding expression in the legislature. In this situation, the effort of the King to assert the traditional and constitutional royal prerogatives became only one among a number of competing forces. Meanwhile, the system of constitutional law could impose only weak restraints upon the exercise of power by a government which at any given moment was little more than the instrumentality of this or that special interest group. The Constitution in Jordan remained important, however, for political forces and parties in their struggles for power appealed to it and in some degree conformed to its principles.

THEORY AND STRUCTURE OF GOVERNMENT

THE CONSTITUTION OF JORDAN DATES FROM ITS PUBLICATION IN the government's *Official Gazette* in January 1952; it succeeded a constitutional instrument of December 1946, which in turn supplanted that of 1928 as amended in 1939. These constitutional developments have moved haltingly toward executive responsibility. Aside from what the Constitution owes to an Islamic background its inspiration was drawn from western sources by way of Syria. Beyond this, the decisive elements have been the precedents of the British mandatory system, the influence of British administrators, and the personality and intelligence of both King Abdullah and the collaborators who aided him in building the formal constitutional order of Jordan from its inception. In general, the progressive phraseology of the Constitution pertaining to civil rights and social welfare was borrowed substantially from the Syrian Constitution of 1950; the conservative features were rewritten from the Transjordan Constitution of 1946, which in turn leaned heavily on the original Transjordanian Organic Law of 1928.

Actually, the formal organic laws and constitutions which Jordan has known during its brief existence as a political entity have been relatively unimportant in determining the real locus of political power in the country. Even at the royal court in Amman, as among the nomadic bedouins, there is little notion of a formal higher law beyond tribal custom and convention (see chap. 22). If Jordan is able to continue its independent existence, however, it may move away from the politics of clan and tribe toward those of the nation-state.

The structure of Jordan's government became more complex in the years immediately after the termination of the British Mandate. During this time, new ministries were established, the bureaucracy increased in size, and with the elaboration of governmental functions intragovernmental relationships became more complicated. Independence brought increased contacts with other countries, particularly with those outside the Middle East. The existing machinery of government was not equipped to cope with the new problems presented by this entry into the international arena. On the other hand, Jordan still depended on Great Britain; the financing and ultimate control of the country's armed forces resided in London. Formal independence notwithstanding, Jordanian leaders found it desirable to accept British guidance on major domestic and foreign decisions. The union with Arab Palestine compounded the difficulties of conducting the government. With the attempted absorption of a larger and more sophisticated population, the demands upon the government accumulated at a pace faster than that at which the requisite agencies could be created.

Formally, the structure of government in Jordan conforms with the Constitution of January 1952. In fact, however, the real patterns of power in the government structure are in a process of flux, a state of becoming rather than that of being. They have undergone—and continue to undergo—the influence of a series of major political events which began before the promulgation of the constitution: the annexation of the West Bank region; the assassination of King Abdullah; the dismissal of Glubb Pasha. Superficially, the effect of these events seemed to be a weakening of the crown's authority and a commensurate development of greater popular control over the structure and process of government; in reality, they put the further evolution of governmental forms at the mercy of a struggle for power in which the supporters of the King were pitted against the leaders of the Palestinian Arabs and their Egyptian and Saudi supporters.

Central Government

The King

The 1952 Constitution declares (Article 1) that the "government is a hereditary monarchy, and its form representative."

The succession to the throne in Jordan is governed by the principle of inheritance through the male line, eldest living son succeeding eldest son, eldest brother succeeding upon termination of the original line, and eldest paternal uncle, if there is no brother or he dies without male issue, and their heirs. Should a king die without an heir as specified, the National Assembly chooses a king from the family of the late King Hussein son of Ali. During the king's minority his functions are exercised by a regency council chosen by the previous king or, failing that, the Council of Ministers.

The monarch has been vested with wide powers over the executive branch, the legislature, and the judiciary. He appoints (Article 35) the prime minister and may dismiss individual ministers or the entire Cabinet. He also appoints (Article 36) the members of the upper chamber (Council of Notables) of the legislature and designates its president. No member may be expelled from that body without the king's approval (Article 75). The king may dissolve the elective Council of Representatives, the lower chamber (Article 34). But if that action is taken, "general elections shall be held so that the new Council will meet in extraordinary session within a period not exceeding four months from the date of the dissolution" (Article 73). The king must confirm all laws and enjoys the right of legislative veto which may, however, be overridden by a two thirds vote of both chambers (Article 93). Judges are appointed and dismissed by royal decree (Article 98). No amendment of the Constitution may come into effect without his approval (Article 126). He is commander in chief of the armed forces (Article 32). He has the power to declare war (Article 33). The decisions of the Council of Ministers (Cabinet), the judgments of courts, and the currency are issued in his name. He is immune from all manner of liability for his acts (Article 30).

Despite the monarchical form and the specified royal powers, the "people" are declared "the source of all powers" and are enjoined to exercise them in accordance with the Constitution (Article 24). Certain theoretical difficulties exist in the application of this principle, because the Jordanian precedent had been that the organic law emanated from the royal will—in keeping with Abdullah's view of his patriarchal authority. The difficulties occasioned debate in the Constituent Assembly. The ambiguous resolution of the problem was to allow the popular principle to stand alongside a concept of royal authority as emanating from its own will.

The king exercises his ceremonial functions as head of the state through a royal diwan (council); he makes executive and administrative decisions, and maintains liaison with the legislature and the judiciary, through the Cabinet or Council of Ministers. While King Abdullah lived, the Cabinet remained his personal instrument. During the brief reign of his son Talal, and by the terms of the Constitution, the Cabinet became technically responsible to the Council of Representatives (*majlis an-nuwwab*), the lower house of the National Assembly (*majlis al-ummah*). Talal, because of the mental illness which led to his early deposition, could hardly be said to have exercised his royal prerogatives. In consequence, the Council of Ministers tended to acquire much greater executive authority, a development not seriously challenged by the legislature.

The Cabinet continued to manage the affairs of state without legislative hindrance and, until early 1957, without any serious challenge from the young and inexperienced King Hussein, who did not reach his majority until May 2, 1953. Hussein tended to rely heavily on the elder statesmen, trained in his grandfather's service, for the principal posts in the Cabinet. It was they, rather than he, who were to keep the West Bankers under control. The King, however, was by no means a nonentity: he still had the support of a well-disciplined, loyal army.

Glubb Pasha had built the Arab Legion into a force remarkable not only for its ability in combat but for its maintenance of civic discipline and political order; on his departure it changed. The assumption of command by Arab officers might have strengthened its morale, but the entry of more and more Palestinians into its ranks complicated and diluted the erstwhile single-minded allegiance to the crown. It was no longer certain that Hussein, without Glubb Pasha and without the loyalty to the royal authority he had instilled in the Legion, could continue to impose his will and authority in future crises. In the crises of April and May 1957, however, the young King by his vigorous actions against disloyal army factions and the leftist Nabulsi Cabinet dispelled for the time being fears for the safety of the monarchy and the country's unity.

The Cabinet

There is no statutory table of organization of the Council of Ministers or Cabinet. The respective powers of the prime ministers, the ministers, and the Council of Ministers are determined by the Council and confirmed by the king. The most important changes in the structure of Jordan's government, particularly in the implied or real arrangement of power relations within it, took place after the annexation of the West Bank in 1950 rather than after the promulgation of the present Constitution two years later. Before the annexation the average council of ministers might have comprised six or seven members; by 1955–56, the number had grown to ten or twelve. Important ministries such as those of foreign affairs, justice, education, and communications have acquired much larger staffs and a broader range of functions in order to cope with the needs created by the merger with the West Bank and the tripling of the population.

The Ministries of Interior and Defense have been of central importance from the beginning, especially because of their control over local government and public order and safety. The Ministry of Foreign Affairs was reorganized in 1950. At the head of its permanent hierarchy, which directed the Ministry below the cabinet level, stood a permanent under-secretary and a secretary-general who supervised the various departments—divided into two classes, specialist and functional. Among the specialist departments were those to do with political affairs, the United Nations, treaties and conferences, Arab, Islamic, and oriental affairs, press and publicity, protocol, and consular affairs. Geographic departments were added after 1950. Functional departments included those of economic and legal affairs, external liaison, clerical matters, accountancy, translation, and personnel affairs.

The Legislature

The Council of Representatives, the lower chamber in the National Assembly, comprises 40 deputies, who are required to be above the age of 30 and are elected by universal male suffrage. The upper chamber or Council of Notables (*majlis al-aayan*) is appointive. It is made up of 20 members, who serve for 8 years and are chosen from among former premiers, high judges, religious dignitaries, retired general officers, and others above the age of 40 "who have gained the confidence and trust of the public . . . in their work and service to the people and the fatherland." The Council of Notables has amounted, in fact, to a gathering place of "the king's friends," an oligarchical force more resistant to change than the Council of Representatives.

The membership of the lower house has been extraordinarily disparate. It has included well-educated West Bankers with western-derived notions of social and political responsibility; Pan-Arab nationalists devoted to a cause that would do away altogether with Jordan as a separate national state; leftists of varying shades, including crypto-Communists; other West Bankers for whom the reversal of the verdict of the Arab-Israeli war seemed to provide an exclusive political purpose; bedouin sheikhs speaking for their tribes; scions of wealthy landowning families defending their private interests; Christian and Circassian deputies representing their communities.

The Judiciary

The judiciary is declared independent and subject to no authority except the law and the monarchical power of dismissal (Articles 97 and 98)—power that was not exercised until the political crisis of early 1957.

The organization of the judiciary follows the lines laid down in the court establishment law of 1951 and the Constitution.

Magistrate's courts, sitting in each large town, handle all civil cases where the matter in contention does not exceed JD 150 ($420). Courts of first instance (each comprising three judges), established in every *qada* (district), deal with all cases not referred to the magistrates' courts or reserved to the sharia courts or to the High Court of Justice.

Two courts of appeal (each consisting of three or more judges), one on the West Bank and the other on the East, hear appeals from the lower courts. The Court of Cassation (last resort), located in Amman, listens to appeals from the two courts of appeal in all civil cases in which the matter in contention exceeds JD 500 ($1,400), as well as appeals of major criminal offenses and any judgment involving an important legal point of general interest. There is also an *ad hoc* High Court of Justice (an innovation imported from the West Bank) "to hear habeas corpus and mandamus petitions and issue injunctions or restraining orders against wrongful acts of public servants in respect of illegal orders issued in the course of the performance of their official duties."

The Court has reversed acts of the Council of Ministers on at least two occasions. In 1953 it overrode an order of the Prime Minister dismissing the mayor of Amman on grounds of corruption. It also upset a ruling of the Interior Ministry that all journalists must belong to the press syndicate (established in accordance with the press law) and abide by that body's decisions; the High Court held the ruling prejudicial to the constitutional freedom of the press. The Ministry accepted the verdict without appeal.

The sharia courts (Moslem religious courts) are vested with exclusive jurisdiction (Articles 105 and 106) over questions of the personal status of Moslems (marriage, divorce, succession, guardianship, inheritance, and the like); in matters concerning Moslem religious trusts (wakfs); and in purely religious cases. Cases involving "blood money" (*diyaah*—compensation paid by one who has committed homicide or has wounded another) are the province of Tribal Courts (arbitral boards).

The sharia is an inclusive body of traditional Islamic law which once regulated social and political as well as religious affairs. From the early days of Islamic power, Christians and Jews, as *ahl al-kitab* ("People of the Book"—see chap. 5), were endowed by Moslem rulers with a wide measure of autonomy in cultural matters and in the conduct of their own legal and even political affairs. This tradition was preserved in Jordan under the British Mandate, and it was confirmed by the 1952 Constitution, which authorized (Articles 108–109) the established non-Moslem communities to employ their own religious councils to handle questions of personal status and matters affecting community endowments. These communities were also assured protection (Article 14) in "the free exercise of religious ceremonies and beliefs in accordance with the customs observed in the kingdom, unless detrimental to public order or contrary to morals," and the right (Article 19) to operate their own schools, subject to governmental supervision of curricula and educational policy.

The sharia establishments operate at two levels, as courts of first instance and of appeal. Appeals from the second level are made to the High Court of Justice. Membership in the sharia courts is drawn from among the ulemas, doctors of the religious law. Religious councils for matters of personal status function in the Greek Orthodox, Roman Catholic (Latin), Armenian Catholic, and Greek Catholic communities. A civil court of first instance serves the members of the small Protestant community.

The Constitution provides for two special courts, the Supreme Council and the Diwan Khass. The Supreme Council consists of nine members: the president of the highest civil court, four of his colleagues, and four members of the Council of Notables selected by that body. In the event of vacancies it was laid down (Article 57) that the presidents of the lesser courts in order of seniority should become members. The Diwan Khass, originally created in March 1930, comprised under the 1952 Constitution (Article 123) the president of the highest civil court, two of his colleagues, and one member named by the responsible minister from among the senior officials of the ministry charged with the execution of the law under review.

The Constitution further requires that all trials should be open except "in the interest of public order or . . . morality" (Article 101), that civil courts should have jurisdiction over all persons, except those cases reserved to the religious or special courts (Article 102), and that all civil and criminal jurisdiction should conform with the law in force, except in certain cases involving personal status of foreigners or commercial and civil suits, "in which it is customary by international usage to apply the law of another country" (Article 103).

Government Responsibility

The Constitution establishes (Articles 6 and 23) the concept of a welfare state. The right of the citizen to employment and the duty of the state to provide, by governmental direction of the national economy, opportunities for work are expressly phrased. The state's obligation to protect labor is to be executed by legislation that would provide for the following: wages proportional to the amount and kind of work accomplished; maximum hours; a weekly day of rest and annual leave with pay; workmen's family compensation for unemployment, illness, old age, and accidents resulting from their work; regulation of health conditions in industry; and the free functioning—within legal limits—of trade unions. This last provision was given concrete, if limited, expression in July 1954 with the approval of a Federation of Workers' Trade Unions by the Ministry of Social Affairs (see chap. 12).

Elementary education is compulsory and is free in government schools (Article 20). The first provision of this Article has never been enforced since demand far outruns facilities, and although the second provision was put in force by Cabinet decree on February 15, 1954, those who can afford to pay are charged a small fee (see chap. 19).

The economic and social provisions stirred protracted debate in the Constituent Assembly—the deputies insisting on the state's duties, the government demanding, and obtaining, language that confines the state's actions in certain respects "within the possibilities" (Article 6), owing to Jordan's scanty resources. The Constitution (Article 111) asserts that the principle of progressive taxation must guide the financial policy of the state so that social justice and equality may be safeguarded.

Public Administration

King Hussein has actively intervened in military and foreign affairs but has seemed to avoid exercising his powers in the economic sphere —where, because of the great and ever-growing demands of the refugee problem, change and experimentation have been most notable. A new ministry, variously styled "reconstruction and rehabilitation" or "rehabilitation and development" has been assigned in successive Cabinets to the members holding the portfolios for commerce, economy, or agriculture. The idea of rehabilitation is politically repugnant because West Bank leaders deliberately cultivate the demand for repatriation and oppose any appearance of permanently accepting the *status quo.* The shifting of the new ministry to the control of the heads of three other economic ministries is one expression of the futility of all efforts so far to integrate the refugees into Jordan's economy. The Ministry of Social Affairs and the Ministry of Education have also assumed responsibilities for refugee care. A number of interdepartmental committees, mostly concerned with issues inherited from the Arab-Israeli war, have been created, among them the Supreme Council of Defense, the Civil Defense Committee, and the Higher Council of Education. Similarly, semiautonomous bodies such as the Bank for Reconstruction and the Aqaba Port Trust have been formed, bringing the government into partnership with international agencies and with private groups.

The United States, the United Nations, and the United Kingdom have furnished technical aid missions which, by creating services previously unknown in the country, have helped give Jordan the appearance of a modern state. Among the services are maternity and child welfare centers (UNICEF); a research clinic (American) in the

Ministry of Social Affairs; an economic planning section (British) in the Ministry of Economy; many secondary and technical schools (UNESCO jointly with the United Nations Relief and Works Agency for Palestine Refugees) under the Ministry of Education. The Arab Legion—which became the Jordan Arab Army on July 4, 1956 —had also provided a species of technical assistance, in the sense that until March 1956 the armed forces were trained and commanded by British officers and its maintenance wholly covered by a British grant to Jordan—reflected in the 1955–56 Jordanian budget as about 50 percent of the budget. The states of the Arab League provided a much more modest subsidy to finance the National Guard or voluntary reserve units formed for local defenses along the Israel border (see chap. 10).

The constitutional promise of a regularly constituted civil service posed a thorny issue for successive cabinets. The habit of most Middle Eastern governments, including Jordan's, is to hire civil servants, not to fire them. The 1954–55 budget set aside funds for a bureau of personnel to create a real civil service. Under a "purge law" semijudicial machinery exists to investigate standards of official conduct and to punish malefactors. An audit department vested with extraordinary powers and immunities was organized in 1952 to control the disbursement of public funds. Since Prime Minister Said al-Mufti on taking office in May 1955 promised to establish "justice, capability and honesty" in public life, however, it appears that, although some progress may have been made in certain departments, Jordanian governmental machinery had then not yet been retooled to create anything like a modern civil service.

Rights and Limitations

Part II of the Constitution sets forth in abundant detail the civil and religious rights of citizens. Jordanian citizenship is declared subject to definition by law (Article 5), and the citizen's rights are guaranteed "within the limits of the law," a stipulation which in conjunction with the special emergency powers reserved to the government gives the authorities considerable latitude in restricting or suspending the actual enjoyment of rights.

Personal freedom is declared to be safeguarded. There may be no discrimination among citizens on grounds of race, religion, or language. No person may be detained or imprisoned except according to law. No Jordanian may be exiled or put under restraint except under provision of the law. The government may not levy compulsory loans, nor may it confiscate or expropriate property for any but public use and under provision of the law duly enacted. The inviolability of dwellings, except under writ of law, is also established. Forced labor may not be exacted except in a national emergency or under the provisions of a criminal conviction by a court.

Freedom of opinion expressed orally, in writing, or by other means is guaranteed "within the limits of the law," as is freedom of the press and publication. In a period of martial law or in a state of emergency "the law may impose on newspapers, pamphlets, publications, and on broadcasting, a limited censorship in respect of matters pertaining to public security and national defense" (Article 15). Operation of the press law enacted under these clauses has given rise to frequent charges that the government was violating the spirit of the Constitution. A number of newspapers have been suspended for attacking in language considered inflammatory. In another effort to control the press the government was defeated in the courts, and the two most influential dailies, *Falastin* and *ad-Difa,* which between 1952 and 1956 at times expressed sharp criticism of the government, continued to appear without interruption.

The right of peaceful assembly is guaranteed within the law (Article 16). The right to form political parties and associations is assured, on condition that their purposes are lawful and that the means they employ are peaceful (Article 16); questions of party organization and finances were deferred for separate legislation (Article 16). In abolishing political parties in 1957, the King was evidently taking the position that their purposes and methods had become unlawful.

The right of petition is guaranteed (Article 17), subject to such conditions as may be imposed by law. This right, particularly dear to the Arab, is exercised in Jordan with liberty and frequency.

Every Jordanian is declared eligible (Article 22) for appointment to public posts. It is stipulated that such appointments must be made on the basis of merit and qualification. Almost every incoming cabinet since the adoption of the Constitution has promised an end to corruption and favoritism. The frequent promises suggest a wide discrepancy between constitutional theory and practice in these matters.

Extradition of persons because of political principles or actions in "defense of freedom" is forbidden, while extradition of ordinary criminals must be regulated by law and international agreement (Article 21). In other words, the Constitution forbids treaties with such intent as well as executive action.

The operation of the so-called "National Defense Law" has in practice sharply curtailed the constitutional rights of citizens and has correspondingly enlarged the effective powers of the government. In view of the significance of the law, its constitutional basis (Article 124) is cited here in full:

If in emergency anything occurs which might make necessary the defense of the country, a law shall be passed which will be known as the [National] Defense Law, which shall empower a person to be specified therein with full authority and jurisdiction to take all necessary steps, ways and means, including the power to order the suspension of the ordinary laws of the realm, for securing the defense of the country. This National Defense Law shall only come into force by declaration issued by Royal Decree made upon the decision of the Council of Ministers.

If the emergency should exceed the capacity of the National Defense Law to safeguard the realm, the king is authorized (Article 125) to declare martial law and rule by decree, irrespective of any law in force.

The enactment of the National Defense Law actually preceded the adoption of the Constitution, and successive governments have invoked this law on the ground that the continuing danger of aggression from Israel makes it imperative. Particularly vocal in their resentment, West Bank deputies have accused the several cabinets of concealing tyranny behind the mask of the emergency legislation.

Amendment and Interpretation

The Constitution may be amended by a two thirds vote of both chambers of the National Assembly, but such decisions must be confirmed by the king. Constitutional interpretation may be initiated at the request of the prime minister or by decision of an absolute majority in either house; a special Supreme Council comes into being for this purpose. Decisions of the Supreme Council in constitutional affairs become operative as law on publication in the *Official Gazette* (Article 122).

The interpretation of any law not previously tested by a regular court may be made at the prime minister's request by an extraordinary court called the Special Board (Diwan Khass). Decisions of the Special Board have the effect of law upon publication in the *Official Gazette* (Article 123).

DIFFUSION AND CONTROL OF INFORMATION

THE SMALL BUT GROWING LITERATE AND SOCIALLY CONSCIOUS Jordanian elite is today able to keep closely in touch with national and world events through all the usual communications media. But interchange of information among the uneducated sectors of the public and between the public in general and the outside world presents all the problems common to technologically underdeveloped and largely illiterate communities. Although the standard of radio information services is improving and a network of newspapers and information sheets covers the country, the illiterate majority's awareness is still dependent largely on hearsay. The average townsman, more likely to be able to read than the villager, is still not literate to a degree that would permit him a full appreciation of the content of newspapers; radio news and commentaries, delivered in classical or modified-classical Arabic, are equally difficult for him to comprehend fully (see chap. 4).

Interpretation of newspapers and broadcasts comes often to be left to those members of the coffeehouse coteries who profess an ability to explain the news content, and these persons, overestimating their skill, more often than not prove to be as unreliable as the gossips—a fact which does not go unnoticed by their hearers. The same problems are intensified in the villages; indeed, many village communities are completely illiterate and have no member capable of producing an accurate colloquial version of a radio broadcast. As a result the impact of modern media is felt only lightly by the majority of Jordanians. By and large, travelers, peddlers, merchants, middlemen, and soldiers on leave are still the chief purveyors of information and misinformation. The coffeehouse whisper, the gossip and rumors of the market place and the courtyards of the mosques are still invested with more credibility than the communications of a mechanical device, though it is probable that the rumors themselves are originally radio-inspired.

The bedouin, removed for long periods from sources of news, obtains his information during his infrequent visits to markets and other centers of population, and from wayfarers and merchants who come to trade in bedouin encampments, and travelers to whom he extends hospitality. Most of what he hears means little to him since he is dominantly interested in family and tribal matters. Tribal chiefs, many of whom are educated, attach greater importance to news and many own radio sets.

From the modern western point of view it would also seem that Jordan lacks most of the elements which combine to permit a government to initiate and sustain an effective and sophisticated system of political indoctrination and propaganda. Such a system usually requires adequate funds, the possession of adequate tools, and special skills that come only from training and experience. Jordan is very poor, even by the low Middle Eastern standards; it has only two radio stations, four daily newspapers, four weekly papers, twenty-four movie houses. Except for a very few men who had some experience of Nazi methods during World War II or of those, more recently, of the Egyptians, Jordan has no trained personnel in a field which, given the country's state of political flux, has assumed an importance comparable to that of diplomacy.

Nevertheless, propaganda has played a not inconsequential role in public affairs and the evolution of policy in Jordan. The royal court has sought to mold and to influence—if not always to direct—the currents of opinion. Courtiers and politicians have manipulated the rumors in the coffeehouses, the market, and the street; they have exploited the loyalties of the family, village, tribe and, above all, those of the displaced Palestinian refugees.

Press and radio output in Jordan bears the imprint of the hearsay background of Middle Eastern methods of communication. Exciting and intriguing presentation tends to take precedence over accuracy of content. Public withdrawals of inaccurate items are rarely printed; a study of newspapers over any given period will reveal inconsistencies which are never cleared up and hurried switches of editorial position which are not explained.

Radio

Jordan's major modern mass communications instrument is the radio. As elsewhere in the Middle East, the importance of this medium is not to be reckoned purely on the basis of the number of receiving sets per capita. Loudspeakers in the shops and coffeehouses of the towns and villages bring the message of the radio to almost everyone in the settled area, and word-of-mouth "retransmission" carries it to the remotest reaches of the kingdom. The high rate of illiteracy (estimated to be as much as 80 to 85 percent) and the small number of newspapers, periodicals, and printed books make the radio a far more effective instrument for molding public opinion than the printed word. Moreover, the spoken word, particularly in the context of the flowery rhetoric and extreme statement which are so much a part of talk and argument in the Arab world, has a more direct emotional appeal. The speaker on the radio in his imagery of all-black or all-white political issues or in his far-fetched analogies can go farther and be more forceful than the editorial writer whose direct appeal must be made to a more limited and somewhat more discriminating audience.

The radio broadcasting facilities in Jordan are owned and operated by the government. The Hashemite Jordan Broadcasting Service has its headquarters in Ramallah, about nine miles from the Old City of Jerusalem; its senior officials in 1956 were Thabet N. Khalidi, controller, and Abdel Qader Taowry, assistant controller. The Jerusalem (Ramallah) station was the only one in Jordan until January 1956, when a second, called the Arab Radio Station, was put into operation at Amman. The first station, with a 20-kilowatt medium-wave and a 550-watt short-wave transmitter, operated six and a half hours a day in Arabic and one and a half hours a day in English. This transmitter has been a "palace station" in the sense that the daily newspaper *al-Jihad* of Amman has been considered a "palace newspaper." But it has been more than merely a vehicle for the court's views and those of the King; over a three-year period during which Jordan has had a series of governments, at times with contrasting policies, the Ramallah station has most often been used by the authorities to project government measures and to furnish the appearance—if not the reality —of a sense of direction and continuity to national life.

The difference between the planned purpose of the Arab Radio Station at Amman and the reality of its activities is a reflection of the fluidity, in the recent past, of Jordanian policies, and hence of propaganda aims. The older Jerusalem station was designed primarily for domestic consumption; the Amman station was to do defensive counterpropaganda against the Voice of the Arabs station at Cairo. When Glubb Pasha and his fellow British officers not only led the Arab Legion but had great influence at the palace, the Jordanian Government found it desirable to go on the air to try to counteract Cairo's incitement of the Jordanian population against the British. After 1954, Cairo attacked the Baghdad Pact, which includes Great Britain, and Amman, while not defending the theory or the fact of the "northern tier," tried to hold a balance between the two sides and above all to maintain a degree of independence. But gradually Jordan's new West Bank population—violently hostile to Britain, whom it blamed for the creation of Israel—whittled away at the Jordanian version of neutralism. In 1955 the Palestinians found excellent fuel for the fire they were fanning: London invited Jordan to join the Baghdad Pact, an offer which turned out to be a disaster for the neutralist position and a boon for the former Palestinians. Three governments rose and fell in Amman, and soon afterward, in March 1956, Glubb Pasha was dismissed. The Voice of Amman, as heard over the station during the year between that event and the final abrogation of the Anglo-Jordanian alliance, was directed by Yunis al-Bahri, who had gained experience in modern techniques of political propaganda in Nazi-occupied Europe during World War II; it may not have spoken entirely in harmony with Cairo's Voice of the Arabs, but it was moving steadily closer in themes and treatment to the Egyptian output that originally it had been set up to counter. In 1957 there was another and complete reversal at the order of the King. These changes are in a sense a measure of the importance of this medium.

Licensed radio receiving sets total 14,000, not counting village loudspeakers. Of the 14,000 receiving sets, only about 2,000 are in the East Bank region—about 1 for each 200 inhabitants. In the whole country, there is about 1 radio for each 100 inhabitants. There is no television service.

Broadcasts in Arabic are received from other Arab countries and from the United States (Voice of America), Great Britain, France, other western European countries, the Soviet Union, and Israel.

The Press

The press in Jordan, as in all countries of the Middle East, is more a vehicle of opinion than of information, and often more of political propaganda than of opinion. The men who own and run the newspapers and periodicals have, therefore, been directly affected by laws and decrees regarding political parties, such as the law of December 30, 1953, and the emergency regulation of August 21, 1954. They also have been affected by the fortunes of the Arab Legion, which once controlled the police and whose antisubversive Criminal Investigation Division was headed by a British officer until March 1956. The fact that the Jordanian Government since 1956 has been dependent financially on other powers than Britain has been reflected in the changing preferences of the press in the international sphere.

In 1952 there were five daily newspapers—three in Amman, two in Jerusalem. By 1955 two of these had been discontinued, and a new daily had been created. In 1957 there were four dailies, two in Amman (*al-Jihad* and *al-Urdunn*) and two in Jerusalem (*ad-Difa* and *Falastin*). The largest of these, *ad-Difa,* had a circulation of only 7,000; none of the others exceeded 2,500 copies a day. They average four pages of the size of a standard American newspaper; since they carry little advertising, the amount of text per page would roughly equal that of an American paper's front page.

The four weeklies constitute a source of supplementary and background information. They have more pages than the dailies, and carry many pictures. Total circulation is estimated at between 7,000 and 8,000 copies. *As-Sarih,* published in Nablus, has a circulation of about 2,000 copies. The government weekly *Official Gazette,* which has a circulation of about 8,000 copies, is the only nonprivate publication; it usually contains laws, government regulations, and official news.

The Press Bureau of the Ministry of Foreign Affairs does not put out regular news bulletins but constitutes an important source of information because it distributes all government news and some domestic news. The Controller of Press, Radio, and Publicity has an office in Amman, with additional staff in Jerusalem. In general, arrangements for the transmission of news to foreign countries are better than the facilities for the supply of world news to the local press.

Distribution of the dailies and weeklies is solely on a local or regional basis; no one publication may be said to circulate throughout the entire nation. Generally speaking, the press is principally concerned with publishing domestic news. Individual newspapers obtain their information from correspondents in the major cities. World news is supplied principally by the Arab News Agency (ANA), which maintains an office in Amman and to which all the dailies subscribe. The news service originates at the central ANA office in Cairo, which also distributes news furnished by the British Reuters agency. The dailies also obtain world news from the Agence France-Press (French), the United Press (American), and from foreign broadcasts, especially Arabic news broadcasts from Cairo.

Government control over the press in Jordan is manifested in many different ways. An application to license a newspaper can be arbitrarily rejected by the government; the suspension of the license of an existing newspaper is frequent procedure and may be carried out either under the press law or the criminal code. Until 1953 censorship was exercised by the court and was capricious but not particularly severe; since then, however, it has been put on a rather more formal basis without greatly increasing its efficiency. Internal censorship is haphazard but substantial. On the whole the Jordanian press has less freedom than that of the Arab countries to the north.

The principal means used by the government to control the press —when other, less obvious means failed—has been to ban or suspend the offending publication. Under the emergency regulations of 1954, as well as under previous laws, suspensions could be carried out at the will of the Cabinet. The reasons given, although perhaps not the complete reasons, often seemed unreasonable or trivial to those accustomed to western attitudes toward discussion of public issues. For example, *al-Hawadith* was suspended in September 1954 because it was said to be "apt to agitate and deceive." What was seen as agitation and deception in 1954 may be praiseworthy "national guidance" in 1957. One of the political parties not allowed to participate in the 1954 elections, for example, was later a power in the press—the Arab Resurrection Party (Hizb al-Bath al-Arabi), popularly known as the "Bathists."

The Jordanian press, like that of other countries of the Middle East, is not financially independent; linked to personalities, it has been "for sale" almost without limits. Since 1953 the official tendency has been to try to make all forms of journalism difficult; the demand that editors and journalists accept responsibility seems to mean that they are called upon to accept obedience to the official will, bordering on subservience. In September 1953 the Cabinet stipulated that the publisher of a periodical must have a secondary education and that the editor-in-chief must be above the age of twenty-three, have a college education, be neither an official nor a member of parliament, and work for one newspaper alone. In 1954 several suspensions were decreed and the Cabinet's broad rights of supervision asserted. In 1955 new registration was prescribed. Today an editor-in-chief has to show a record of five years of experience in journalism. Physicians, lawyers, pharmacists, and engineers may not engage in journalism while active in their professions. Foreigners may not appear as publishers. Above all, the Cabinet is to have the right and power to grant or refuse permits for the publication of newspapers.

Jordanians of the upper classes read, in addition to local publications, Egyptian and to a lesser extent Syrian newspapers and magazines. Those preferred specialize in political polemic; whether imported secretly or openly, they are more widely read than Jordanian material. The Egyptian weekly *Rose al-Yusuf,* a journal with communist tendencies, was until banned, so widely read it was called the "school of politics." The Egyptian Embassy has been a rich source of books, periodicals, and pamphlets, all with a strong propagandistic bias. It is estimated, moreover, that as much as half the literate population reads clandestine Communist literature printed or mimeographed by the Arab Communist Party of Jordan, which though illegal is still openly active.

Films

All films are imported. The annual total for feature films is about 700, of which 45 percent come from the United States, 30 percent from Egypt, 15 percent from the United Kingdom; 10 percent from France, Italy, and Turkey. There are 24 movie houses, including 2 new ones in Amman; the total seating capacity is about 12,000 and the annual attendance is estimated at two million. Six of the cinemas are open-air and function only during the summer. Until the decisive changes in Jordan's political relations with Great Britain in 1956, the British Council gave educational shows in cooperation with the Jordanian Ministry of Information.

Role of the King

Not only on the radio but in the street and in public appearances and state ceremonies, Jordan's youthful King is the protagonist par excellence of propaganda. All of his appearances have been staged with the greatest and most colorful panoply. During the period of the Arab Legion's ascendancy—and, to a lesser extent, after Glubb's departure—armed men in dress uniforms provided the setting. Such spectacles have usually been staged in Amman, but the Jordanian sector of Jerusalem has not been neglected as a center which plays a role in forming public opinion at least as significant as that of the capital. The combination of such armed might as Jordan could display and the unassuming and modest demeanor of the King was clearly found to be effectively persuasive.

The King's speeches on such occasions are full of colorfully dramatic imagery and often strike a highly hortatory tone. In April 1954 on the occasion of the anniversary of the Arab revolt (see chap. 2) he opened his address with the name of his great-grandfather, the leader of the revolt against the Ottoman Empire. He called attention to "the supreme objectives of the blessed movement"—that the Arabs were one people and had one homeland—and appealed to Jordanians to continue the war on disunity and oppression. These objectives formed "a bright torch to illuminate the road of the future," and he saw signs that the spirit of revolt was reviving and would furnish "miraculous power to resume the march to glory." In this setting Israel was the enemy, a foreign people who, he said, had come into national existence in the heart of the Arab homeland, where there was room for no one but Arabs.

At the time of his enthronement Hussein addressed the Arab Legion in the same tones: "Jordan is nothing but a part of the Arab nation and the Arab Legion is but one of its armies." He pleaded for understanding of his own "personal misfortune"—his father's illness and deposition—as he assumed his "noble task." A year later he called the nation to its duty:

> Brethren, the cause we defend is the most just cause in history. . . . What has happened is that people from all over the world invaded the homeland and dispersed its inhabitants. Then they claimed they wanted peace. . . . They make light of international resolutions, attack peaceful villages, and threaten expansion. They boast of strength, but it is aggressive strength. As to us, we feel strength, but it is the strength of right—the right of the Arab nation and the Islamic nations, supported by fair minds throughout the world, the right we shall defend with all our might. . . . Let everyone carry out his duty with faithfulness and determination. The future is ours, and hope and confidence in God and in right is our slogan.

The position of the King has also been invoked at times of Cabinet crisis. In the serious election riots of 1954, the Premier published a message from the King, expressing "deep sorrow that certain subversive elements have exploited the circumstances of the elections to provoke disturbances which led to loss of life." The presence of such elements, the message said, was "prejudicial to the dear homeland and treason to the nation, which is facing enough catastrophes by resisting a treacherous enemy preparing to exterminate it."

In March 1957, however, the King referred to a different threat to the nation, one coming from a different quarter. A year after the dismissal of Glubb Pasha the Anglo-Jordanian alliance was ended, and on the eve of March 14, the date of the official termination of the treaty and declared to be permanently a Jordanian national holiday, Hussein made a broadcast, which was printed in full the next day by all the newspapers. During wild celebrations in Amman, in the hours before the King's broadcast, truckloads of young men drove through the streets, clapping their hands, chanting, shouting slogans that denounced Britain and the Eisenhower Doctrine and praised the Soviet Union and Arab solidarity. There also were processions of Bathists and members of the Moslem Brotherhood.

In his radio address the King said:

> We Arabized the army as an answer to a threat from a certain great power, which asked us to accept the policy she advised. The threat was that we may lose our throne and even that Jordan may lose her independent existence. . . . When I intended to Arabize the army I received many threats but I ignored all of them. I was alone at that time, but I was sure that you were all with me. . . . My life was threatened also, but I did not care because I knew I was doing good for Jordan.

Then he spoke favorably of Britain's "good will" in the treaty-termination negotiations and said that the British "proved their good intentions by dealing with us nobly and on an equal basis."

The language of the address was simpler, more forthright, less rhetorical than that of previous speeches. It was assumed that the help which the King had been given in preparing it might have come from advisers with experience outside the Middle East. The "great power" from which the "threats" had come was not identified. By a common device of a more sophisticated type of propaganda than had previously been used in Jordan, the identification was left to rumor-mongers—professional or amateur—so that spokesmen at the palace could make the ritualistic denials, while men in the street mobs, the coffeehouses, and the countryside could make their choice by "thinking" with their hearts, or with their blood.

In addition to relying very heavily on the personality, prestige, and influence of the King, the government has employed for propaganda purposes the traditional Islamic pieties, invoking the direct aid (and implying the direct responsibility) of the Deity. Official statements often begin with the phrase "Trusting in God" and end with the Koranic quotation "God is the renderer of success."

At the opposite end of the scale of motivations, the government has sought to exploit material dissatisfactions of one sort or another as a point of departure for propaganda. Improved economic and security conditions have been repeatedly promised to the "front line" villages on the Israel border. An unpopular Cabinet pledged to the politically sensitized students cheap school texts and easing of requirements for secondary school certificates.

Statements on current public issues by public officials are almost always an occasion for propaganda. Rarely is a relatively realistic note sounded on current issues, especially the touchy subject of refugees and their repatriation in Israel. A former Minister of Defense, himself a Palestinian, declared:

> We make a big mistake if we consider the Palestine catastrophe the end of the journey and not its starting point. . . . Refugees are a source of wealth—that of working hands. We are mistaken if we exploit their catastrophe to gain cheap sympathy—it is a generator which will push this country toward the regaining of its usurped rights.

FOREIGN RELATIONS

BEHIND JORDAN'S POSITION IN CONTEMPORARY INTERNATIONAL affairs lie two central facts. (1) Jordan, since its inception as a political entity, has been decisively dependent on foreign economic assistance. (2) It has been impossible for Jordan to have a foreign policy supported by a general consensus of the politically articulate sections of its population. It is appropriate to speak, not of a Jordanian foreign policy, but of alternative Jordanian foreign policies, each a product of diverse and conflicting interests and groups within the arbitrarily established Jordanian political order.

By late 1957 Jordan was caught in the play of international politics, regional and general, too weak really to go it alone but chary of accepting the clear-cut protection of any major power. The situation was dangerous for a country which has no well-defined natural boundaries, lies in a strategic area, and is too young to have developed any widespread sense of national identity and loyalty among its people.

In the decade after World War II opposition to Israel and resentment of the West might have seemed sufficient bases on which general Arab unity could be constructed and maintained. The Jordanian crisis of 1957 made it clear that this was not so. Threatened by dissident elements encouraged from Egypt and Syria and from the Soviet Union, King Hussein of Jordan took strong measures to secure his control of the country. In this he found support not only in Iraq, which as a member of the Baghdad Pact had been ranged against Egypt and Syria, but in Saudi Arabia, which, with Egypt and Syria and Jordan itself, had recently been ranged against Iraq. The division among the Arab states might not necessarily lead to an open break, and old slogans calling for unity against "western imperialism" and against Israel continued to be compelling, but evidently the Pan-Arabic ideal had not transcended local and national ambitions in the area. If this situation posed dangers for Jordan from and through certain of its Arab neighbors, it also implied the presence of Arab allies concerned to preserve the independence of the strategically placed state and to keep it out of the hands of rivals or from becoming an advance post of Soviet power in the area.

The establishment in 1952 of a new military regime in Egypt has become an external factor of major importance to Jordan and the rest of the Arab world. In that year, coinciding with the proclamation of the new Constitution in Jordan, the Egyptian monarchy was replaced by a group which in the course of time showed itself determined not only to turn its back on a century of political and cultural ties with western Europe but to remake the Egyptian and general Arab social order with the help of techniques and slogans resembling Soviet and Fascist models. This development, particularly the person of Colonel Nasser, provided a rallying point for several Jordanian political groups, most of them determinedly anti-British, some anti-regime, and some revolutionary (see chap. 7). The appearance of the new Egyptian regime produced another centrifugal pull in Jordanian politics, and added to the multiplicity of values and motives through which, and despite which, Jordanian foreign policy must be made. Establishment of the United Arab Republic increased that divisive force and required an answer.

Foreign Policy Problems

Jordan occupies a central position among the Arab lands in the eastern Mediterranean. This geographical circumstance and the absence of an organic unity within the new country have shaped many of Jordan's major foreign policy problems.

King Abdullah, looking back on Jordan's long history as a part of Syria, hoped to use it as a base for the creation of a Greater Syria. That ambition came to be in a sense reversed, in that many Jordanians would have approved absorption of the country by Syria.

Jordan's geographical position immediately north and east of the Sinai corridor makes the country an object of prime interest to Egypt. Domination of Jordan would provide the Egyptians with a central avenue of communication with the Fertile Crescent, where Egypt aspires to leadership.

Having the longest common frontier with Israel, Jordan feels the presence of that country more intimately than does any other Arab state. One third of Jordan's population consists of refugees from Israeli territory; to many of them Israel has become a blood enemy whose ultimate defeat takes precedence over all other public questions. Policy makers in other Arab states may stress or de-emphasize the Israeli problem; those in Jordan do not have that option, and the miles of barbed wire marking the common boundary, the endless series of provocations and counter-provocations, the stalemated issue of the utilization of the waters of the Jordan, and Jordan's severed access to the Mediterranean, all help maintain the destructive tension.

Jordan has always been vulnerable to the incursions of raiding bedouin tribes from Saudi Arabia, and the Hashemite dynasties of Jordan and Iraq in modern times have been in opposition to the Saud rulers of Saudi Arabia. The Hashemite bond has been both an advantage and a disability for Jordan. Iraqi support has at times bolstered Jordan against increasing pressure from Syria and Egypt; on the other hand, the Hashemite connection has rendered the Jordanian royal house vulnerable to the charge, pressed so hard by Cairo against Iraq, that it is pro-West. Hashemite-Saudi differences were transcended, however, in 1957 when King Saud chose to throw his weight behind King Hussein in the face of the imminent threat that Jordan might be brought under Egyptian or Syrian control. In late 1957 it appeared that there might be emerging a new alignment among the Arab states, with Iraq, Jordan, Saudi Arabia, and perhaps Lebanon countering the Egyptian drive to leadership in the region. The two mergers in early 1958 confirmed that alignment in its major aspects.

Relations with Other Arab States

The events in early 1957, which brought a halt to Jordan's drift into the orbit of Egyptian and Syrian control, revealed something of the complexity of the forces and motives at work in the contemporary Arab world and underscored the difficulty of any attempt to make long-range generalizations about intra-Arab relations. What in late 1956 might have appeared to be a relatively solid Arab front in the eastern Mediterranean—excluding perhaps Iraq—by March 1958 had realigned itself into two counterbalancing, if not conflicting, blocs.

Scarcely ten years earlier Abdullah, under whom Jordan (Transjordan) had achieved independence, was projecting a Hashemite kingdom of "Greater Syria." This was to include present-day Syria, Transjordan, and such parts of Palestine as might fall to the Arabs in the negotiation of the boundaries of the Jewish "National Home"—an idea the King had not opposed in the 1930's. Abdullah even went so far at one time as to propose a general "Syrian" constituent assembly to bring about the unity of the "country" as described above. These policies brought him into conflict with other Arab leaders, particularly in Syria. Abdullah's occupation in 1948 of the Palestinian territory remaining to the Arabs after the Arab-Israeli war and his subsequent annexation of this area—Jordan's present-day West Bank —appear as steps in the direction of his unification program.

The annexation of the West Bank was a defiance of the Arab League that might have brought about Jordan's expulsion had it not been for the intercession of Hashemite Iraq. Long charged with being an "imperialist tool" because of his acceptance of Jordan's tie with Britain, Abdullah was now condemned as a traitor to the cause of Arab unity, one who had exploited Arab difficulties for his own advantage. Much of this criticism emanated from Egypt, whose claim to Arab leadership Abdullah, with his orthodox conception of Arab political institutions and legitimacy and his belief that the center of gravity of Arab power was in the Fertile Crescent, could not accept.

It is said that Abdullah shortly before his death was working toward union between Jordan and Iraq as both a move toward the larger Arab unity for which he hoped and an approach to the solution of a refugee problem which was too great for Jordan's unaided resources. Possibly he recognized also that his unstable son Talal was unfit to succeed him. Upon Abdullah's death the Iraqis pursued the project with enthusiasm, and there was some favorable response in Jordan. The lower house of Jordan's National Assembly demanded, with many Palestinian representatives concurring, that it be called into special session to consider the project. The subsequent failure of that plan was attributed by Prime Minister Abu al-Huda to the purely political character of the arrangement as conceived by the Iraqis and to the absence of any economic benefits for Jordan.

The failure of the plan coincided with King Talal's (or Abu al-Huda's) policy of ingratiating himself with the Arab leaders his father had offended, in particular King Abd al-Aziz ibn Saud of Saudi Arabia (father of the present King), Abdullah's principal enemy. Under Talal, Jordan joined the Arab League's Collective Security Pact, which together with Iraq it had refused to do in 1950. After the incapacitated Talal was succeeded by his son, the present King Hussein, Jordan attempted to pursue a policy of avoiding too close association with the emergent blocs among the Arab states and of staying on good terms with all. An Iraqi proposal in 1954 for unification with Jordan was rejected as offensive to Jordan's allies in the Arab League. Jordan, on the other hand, found reason to complain of the only partial fulfillment by the other League members of their pledge to contribute to the financial support of the Jordanian National Guard in recognition that Jordan bore the burden of manning the longest common frontier with Israel.

Iraq's adherence in 1955, through a defense pact with Turkey, to western plans for defense against the Soviet bloc brought a sharp change of opinion in Jordan, particularly among the Palestinians who earlier had been the chief proponents of unity with Iraq. Under their influence, Jordan moved away from Iraq and toward the Egyptian "neutralism" which sees no threat from the Soviet Union but condemns the western powers as imperialist and pro-Israeli. Foreign Minister Salah stated that Jordan opposed Iraq's decision, taken without consultation with the other Arab states, and censured it as calculated to widen the cleavage in the Arab world. In May of 1955, however, King Hussein indicated his desire for a return to a less partisan policy by demanding the relief of Salah from the Foreign Affairs portfolio and then the resignation of the entire Cabinet; the new Prime Minister was charged to maintain a foreign policy based on general agreement and cooperation with all Arab states.

At the year's end in 1955 a major political crisis was precipitated by the efforts of Sir Gerald Templer, on behalf of Great Britain, to draw Jordan into the Baghdad Pact (the other signatories are Great Britain, Turkey, Pakistan, Iran, and Iraq). The public demonstrations which immediately broke out in the country were on such a scale that the Cabinet fell and was finally replaced by a new one pledged to keep Jordan out of the Baghdad Pact. The Suez crisis in mid-1956, the Israeli-British-French attack upon Egypt in October, and the elections, in the same month, that brought to power the leftist government of Prime Minister Suleiman an-Nabulsi (see chap. 7) all served to strengthen the increasingly pro-Egyptian, pro-Syrian orientation of the government. It appeared that the Jordanian left wing was only waiting for an occasion on which to call the street mobs of Amman, Jerusalem, and Nablus into action in a coup which would subordinate, if not oust, the monarchy and bring the country under the domination of Egypt and Syria. An important factor in the success of the countermeasures taken by King Hussein in April and May 1957 was the support from Iraq and Saudi Arabia. Iraq's position represented nothing new, since the Hashemite Kingdom had long been in opposition to Egypt over the latter's claims to Arab leadership and the issue of the Baghdad Pact. Saudi Arabia, however, associated with Egypt and Syria in the Arab League, registered a change in point of view, apparently reflecting, in part at least, King Saud's concern over the effect of Egyptian Suez Canal policy on his oil revenues and his fear of the long-range consequences for his own government and the Middle East generally of the nationalist and anti-monarchic, if not pro-Soviet, maneuverings in both Egypt and Syria.

The collective security pact which binds the members of the Arab League, including Jordan, and their agreement for a unified military high command (entered into in 1956) have not been implemented.

Slogans of Arab unity have always concealed deep cleavages in the Arab world and the events of 1957 revealed the strength of the centrifugal forces at work among the Arab states and which for the time being centered on Jordan. Jordan, itself torn by the division between its East and West Banks, had seemed to be bound to a combination of Egypt, Syria, and Saudi Arabia, who were jointly pledged to make up to Jordan the discontinued British subsidies on which the country was dependent—even to pay its troops. Only Saudi Arabia made any contribution to Jordan under this commitment. The reported offer of loans to Jordan from Iraq and Saudi Arabia in 1957 reflected the breakdown of the unity of the Arab League and a realignment in which two previously opposed powers concerted to aid a third against Egypt and Syria. The form of the earlier unity, however, continued to be preserved, and Jordan, in accepting a ten million dollar loan from the United States in the midst of the crisis, found it necessary to assert its nonacceptance of the Eisenhower Doctrine and its rejection of any terms which might reflect on the royal government's loyalty to the Pan-Arab ideal.

Despite the fluctuations which internal weakness and external pressure have produced in Jordanian policy, Jordan has been notably persistent in seeking concrete means of cooperation among the Arab states. It was among the first to sign the Arab League Nationality Agreement designed to create uniform Arab nationality laws. It was one of the first to agree to the establishment of an Arab High Court of Justice for the settlement of disputes among Arab states. It has actively helped to reconstruct the Hejaz railway, and it has come to agreement with Saudi Arabia on the mutual demarcation of frontiers. The Arab Federation undoubtedly embodies a desire to wrest Pan-Arabism away from Egypt's Nasser.

Relations with Israel

The General Armistice Agreement reached under United Nations auspices in April 1949 still formally governs Jordan's relations with Israel. The agreement terminated hostilities which broke out between Israel and the Arab states in 1948; it provided principally that neither side would commit acts of war against the other or violate the armistice line established in the agreement, and it stipulated that the agreement was without prejudice to a future political settlement. A Mixed Armistice Commission was set up under a chairman representing the United Nations Truce Supervision Organization. A local Commanders' Agreement was signed on March 14, 1955, to facilitate an exchange of information on border violations.

Although it is evident from the language of the agreement that it was expected that the work of the Armistice Commission would be finished in a short time, the Commission is approaching the end of a decade of service in which it has had to deal with one incident after another. Each side claims that it acts only in self-defense or in reprisal for the aggression of the other, and the close proximity of thousands of Arab refugees along the armistice line to their former homes greatly exacerbates the situation. The self-perpetuating seesaw of violence continues and the prospect of any real settlement remains remote.

The days when an Abdullah could entertain the possibility of establishing peaceful relations with Israel seem distant indeed. Peace negotiations with Israeli officials were undertaken but came to nothing, and Abdullah's successors proved even less able than he to run counter to popular feeling against Israel. When Tawfiq Abu al-Huda, long associated with Abdullah, was appointed Prime Minister in June 1954 —his eleventh occupancy of that office—he had to allay popular suspicions that he intended to negotiate with Israel by declaring that peace or negotiation was impossible. In the 1957 crisis the King felt it necessary to be more anti-Israeli in his public statements than Suleiman an-Nabulsi, the ousted Prime Minister. In any event, even if it were disposed to do so, Jordan, could hardly act on a peace settlement with Israel without the concurrence of the other Arab states. There have been few signs pointing to such a development. The Israeli attack upon Egypt reinforced the popular conviction in Amman no less than in Cairo—notwithstanding the tension between the two —that no accommodation to Israel is possible. There are some Arabs who believe that the fact of Israel's existence must eventually be accepted, but such views are not stated publicly nor do they carry any weight in the formulation of public policy.

Relations with the United States and the USSR

Jordan is caught up in the global struggle which, focusing on the United States and the USSR, has affected would-be "neutrals" hardly less than the committed allies of the protagonists. Located as it is in the eastern Mediterranean sector of the Middle East, the country is influenced by this conflict of forces where their meeting is particularly violent. The weakness of Jordan and the other Arab states constitutes an invitation to the Soviet Union to extend its influence into this area, which Russian power has never before penetrated; and by that token the United States and its allies must face the consequences of allowing it to succeed.

Among the Jordanian Palestinians, about half of whom are refugees, there is a widely held conviction that America has been the main champion of Israel and is therefore a major cause of their miseries. Neither the earlier favorable impression of the United States as a source of philanthropic, educational, and technical assistance, nor the general approval with which Arabs greeted the opposition of the United States to Israel's attack on Egypt in 1956 has sufficed to overcome popular suspicion of American motives. Jordanian critics resentfully compare United States aid to Jordan with the larger grants to Israel. King Hussein, as he did in May 1957, may contrast United States assistance, given without conditions, with the threat to the country of Soviet imperialism; at the same time, however, Foreign Minister Samir ar-Rifai is at pains to distinguish between communism as an ideological menace and the Soviet Union as a national state, and to indicate Jordan's appreciation of Soviet aid to the Arab world at the time of the Israeli attack. The pattern is the classic "neutralist" one of other governments elsewhere in the Middle East and Asia whose recognition of the Soviet danger is still qualified by the historically rooted suspicion of the West, which remains so strong an accompaniment of nationalism.

One of the issues in the Jordanian political crisis in 1957 was whether Jordan should establish formal diplomatic relations with the USSR. An announced decision to do so was reversed by the King. Meanwhile, Soviet propaganda continued to attack the King's policy as "pro-West," "reactionary," and "submissive to imperialism."

Relations with Great Britain

The state of Jordan had its origins in a British policy decision at the end of World War I (see chap. 2). A Transjordanian government was established over which the British retained controls with respect to foreign policy, defense, and finance. Over the years the relationship was gradually modified in the direction of greater Jordanian independence, and in March 1948 a treaty of preferential alliance was signed by Britain and Transjordan which regulated their relations until its mutual abrogation in early 1957. Britain is now receiving no preferential treatment in its relations with Jordan.

The 1948 treaty did not remove British influence in spite of the disappearance of such obvious restrictions on sovereignty as the mandatory authority and resident advisers; until 1957 the influence remained as an object of resentment and a critical issue of Jordanian politics. Although the treaty contained assurances of mutual aid in time of war or threat of war, Jordanian critics attacked its provisions for the stationing of Royal Air Force units at Amman and Al Mafraq, for standardizing Jordanian army equipment with that of Britain and coordinating plans and training through a joint defense board, for giving British forces access to lines of communication in Jordan, and for permitting the stationing of other British forces in Jordan by mutual agreement. The treaty required Britain to reimburse Jordan for these privileges and to provide the country with the military equipment needed to meet its mutual defense obligations, but even this reciprocity did not suffice to soften Jordanian resentment of what was considered an onerous subordination to British interests. With the influx of the Palestinian refugees, Jordan's dependence increased and from 1949 onward Britain found it necessary to go beyond the terms of the treaty and grant considerable sums in interest-free loans and other forms of aid.

Jordanian opposition to the relationship with Britain continued to mount, and in early 1957, on the heels of the military action against Egypt by Britain, France, and Israel, negotiations were precipitated which brought about the termination of the 1948 treaty within a few weeks. Jordan agreed to provide necessary facilities and assistance for the evacuation of British forces, which was to take place within six months; other understandings pertained to the disposition of property and equipment.

Other International Activities

Jordan became a member of the United Nations in December 1955, after several vetoes of its application—beginning in 1947—by the Soviet Union. Before its admission to membership Jordan had participated in the activities of numerous special agencies of the United Nations, including the International Monetary Fund, International Bank for Reconstruction and Development, Food and Agriculture Organization, World Health Organization, UNESCO, United Nations Children's Fund, International Telecommunication Union. It is also a member of the advisory council of the United Nations Relief and Works Agency for Palestine Refugees (UNRWA).

Jordan sent a delegation to the Bandung Conference of Asian and African nations and was successful in obtaining from the Conference a statement of support for the repatriation of the Arab refugees. It also sent a delegation to the Convention for Peaceful Uses of Atomic Energy held in Geneva in the summer of 1955. It has signed five Geneva Conventions of the Red Cross on the treatment of war victims and prisoners.

Popular Attitudes

It is clear that in the conduct of the country's foreign affairs the Jordanian Government must contend with strong and divergent attitudes among its people toward other peoples and states. One factor especially—the tradition of close association with Syria and Syrians—has worked against efforts of the government to pursue an independent policy. For those Jordanians who have been disposed to describe themselves as Syrian rather than Jordanian, Pan-Arabism has meant throwing into question the desirability of Jordan's existence as a sovereign entity. To these persons, no foreign policy was acceptable which did not lead to the political realization of a "Greater Syria" or some other larger Arab unity. In their eyes the alternative was an artificial Jordanian state created originally by a foreign power in pursuit of its own interests and to satisfy the ambitions of an Arabian princely family. Their ultimate reaction to federation will in large part be determined by whether or not Iraq pulls out of the Baghdad Pact.

The fragmentation of social life in Jordan and elsewhere in the Middle East into local groups and kin-groups has as one of its corollaries a degree of xenophobia. Even the material and technical contributions of foreigners, if they are not opposed as running counter to Moslem tradition, are often interpreted as having some hidden ulterior motive. Western-supported activity in particular is likely to be viewed as a continuation of the foreign domination of the recent past. During the riots of 1955–56 protesting Britain's efforts to draw Jordan into the Baghdad Pact, mobs attacked the American hospital in Ajlun, the installations of a small Quaker-sponsored community project in the village of Dibbin, and several United States technical assistance (Point Four) projects. The depredations were committed by rioters shouting anti-imperialist slogans. Communist influence was evident in this, but such influence was and continues to be the kind which falls on the fertile ground of long-established anti-western feeling.

Israel, an alien, culturally western enclave in the Arab world, stands as the chief international villain in Arab eyes. The United States, thought by Arabs to be the main support of Israel and Zionism and identified as an ally of British and French colonialism, has been viewed with growing dislike, but when the United States opposed Britain, France, and Israel in their military action against Egypt in the autumn of 1956, American stock in the Arab world, including Jordan, rose. It was evident, however, that this changed climate of opinion might change again, and the proffer of United States aid to King Hussein in the Jordanian crisis in the spring of 1957 saw the revival of anti-American feeling among those Jordanians and other Arabs whose opinions were taking direction from Cairo, Damascus, or Moscow.

The attitude of the Jordan Government toward the Soviet Union since the dismissal of Prime Minister Nabulsi, whose policies had pointed toward closer relations with the USSR, has been openly accusatory. The USSR, nevertheless, enjoys an advantage in the fact that many Arabs have experienced and bitterly resent western European political domination while few have ever seen a Russian. Communism aside, on the principle of "the enemy of my enemy is my friend" there is a tendency among the politically articulate in the area to approve of the USSR. The anti-Israeli, anti-Zionist position with which the USSR has been at pains to identify itself in the area has been a strong factor in creating Arab good will, especially in the face of the widespread conviction among Arabs that Israel is not merely supported by the major western powers but is nothing less than a consciously conceived instrument of "western imperialism."

Foreign Assistance

Popular attitudes toward Israel and the West go far toward explaining Jordan's foreign economic relations. The Arabs remain categorically unwilling to resume normal economic relations with Israel. The politically articulate segments of the population, convinced that Israel is a creation of the West and a sign of continuing western imperialism, oppose western economic and military assistance. This antiwestern sentiment is being fully exploited by the USSR, as a part of its larger drive to eliminate western economic and military influence from the whole Middle East, and by Egypt, which sees in the West an obstacle to its aspirations to leadership in the Fertile Crescent.

The importance of both the Arab-Israeli impasse and the antiwestern sentiment to the economic relations of Jordan was underscored when King Hussein, critically in need of economic aid and confronted by a major political crisis in which he was threatened by a vociferous pro-Communist, pro-Egyptian, pro-Syrian opposition, declared in April 1957 that American economic aid totaling ten million dollars would be accepted only if not tied to the Eisenhower Doctrine and that he would not depart from the principles of the conference of the preceding February in which four Arab nations—Egypt, Syria, Saudi Arabia, and Jordan—pledged not to join pacts with non-Arab powers.

British Assistance

The most important single source of foreign currency for meeting Jordan's deficit in the past were grants and loans from the United Kingdom (some $35 million in 1956). Until the termination of the British-Jordanian alliance, Britain subsidized almost all the expenditures of the Arab Legion and contributed also to other military expenditures. British assistance in the military budget increased from approximately 50 percent in 1955–56 to 70 percent in 1956–57; Britain also provided loans without interest for economic development projects.

Development loans were apportioned by the Jordan Development Board in accordance with annual bilateral negotiations. These funds were designed primarily to assist in absorbing nearly half a million refugees into the economy and were allocated principally for agriculture and transportation, with major emphasis on village loans, rural cooperatives, the Aqaba deep water port, airports, and roads.

In March 1957 an exchange of letters terminated the British-Jordanian alliance of 1948 and with it the British military subsidy. Under the terms of the negotiations ending the treaty, Jordan retains buildings, land, and permanent installations of the British forces as well as military equipment and is to reimburse the United Kingdom $11.9 million over a period of six years. British assistance in the form of interest-free loans, now totaling $16.8 million, can continue outside of the treaty. The Jordanian Ministry of Economy approached the British Government early in April 1957 to settle the remaining commitments to the Joint Development Board for 1956–57, amounting to $3.8 million; meanwhile Jordan failed in March 1957 to meet a payment due on its present loan commitments.

Arab Grants and Loans

Under a treaty signed in January 1957, Egypt, Syria, and Saudi Arabia promised to replace the British military subsidy to Jordan. Of the three nations, however, only Saudi Arabia has made a contribution. Estimates of assistance from Saudi Arabia in April 1957 vary all the way from $1.5 million to $14 million. The latter figure has been cited in the press but has not been officially confirmed.

United Nations Aid

United Nations Relief and Works Agency (UNRWA) projects for Palestine refugees are financed by a rehabilitation fund established in 1952, of which $51 million was set aside for Jordan. To assist refugees to become self-supporting, one tenth of this amount was programed from 1952 to 1955. In addition to supporting the balance of payments ($13 million in 1955), UNRWA is the largest employer, supplier, and distributor in the country and somewhat relieves the serious unemployment problem through its small development schemes.

A special fund of $40 million was expended by UNRWA in 1955 for an engineering survey of the Jordan Valley.

United States Aid

United States technical and economic assistance contributed 37.5 percent (a total of $34.1 million) of the total public expenditure for economic and social developments in Jordan for the period from 1950 to 1956. United States contributions until April 1957 were divided between technical cooperation—with major emphasis upon agriculture and water resources—and the Economic Development fund for roads and irrigation. The Economic Development Fund gave a stimulus to the Jordanian economy by providing $400,000 for the development of small industry and $700,000 for community development in 1956. United States aid reached a peak of $18.9 million in the fiscal year 1956 and dwindled to $1.8 in the fiscal year 1957; in April 1957, King Hussein accepted an additional grant-in-aid of $10 million from the United States, outside the formal provisions of the Eisenhower Doctrine. The grant was given to alleviate the country's urgent economic need and as a means of contributing to its political stability in a time of crisis.

BASIC FEATURES OF THE ECONOMY

THE OUTSTANDING ECONOMIC FACT ABOUT JORDAN IS THAT IT IS dependent on outside aid for its very survival. What economic benefits will accrue from membership in the Federation are still a matter for speculation.

Dependence on foreign assistance was increased by various consequences of the Arab-Israeli war. The population was tripled. Normal trade routes to the Mediterranean were severed. Trade with Israel ceased. The West Bank, which had been dependent on income from the rest of Palestine—now Israeli territory—was cut off from that source while the East Bank continued to produce barely enough livestock and farm products to maintain its original population at a low consumption level. Jordan had to absorb a large refugee population, reorient at great expense its entire transportation network toward Beirut and Damascus in the north and Aqaba in the south, and begin building an industry despite high costs and lack of capital.

Foreign assistance has accounted for a considerable part of the rise in employment and the increase in the national product since 1952 and it has made possible an expansion in the transportation network, of cardinal importance to the exploitation of phosphates, one of Jordan's few mineral resources. It has also paid for a major portion of Jordan's imports.

The single most important supplier, distributor, and employer in Jordan is an international organ—the United Nations Relief and Works Agency for Palestine Refugees (UNRWA); it also plays a key role in stabilizing agricultural income through the purchase of wheat, the major cash crop of the nation.

Considerable improvements may be realized in the next decade in mining, transportation, small-scale irrigation, agricultural marketing and production, but the general outlook for the development of a self-sustaining economy seems unpromising. The extremely limited industrial base will continue to reflect the shortage of raw materials and power; broadening that base will require basic improvements in transportation, access to industrial skills, and a considerable increase in the purchasing power of the population—all very long-range goals. Improvement of agriculture continues to be impeded by, among other things, the chronic Arab-Israeli tension which prevents the development of the Jordan Valley.

Agriculture

Jordan's agriculture cannot at present meet the food needs of the country's expanded population; the principal agricultural products—wheat and livestock—must be supplemented by imports. Given Jordan's poverty in natural resources, and the natural increase of its population, dependence on outside help in the foreseeable future is likely to become greater, even if such long-term development schemes as that planned for the utilization of the waters of the Jordan River can be carried out in cooperation with neighboring states.

Government-sponsored improvements in agricultural techniques have increased the production of certain crops, notably through the intensive irrigation of fruits and vegetables, but the basic reforms needed to transform agriculture from a subsistence to a commercial pattern have not yet been made. Such changes as have been introduced have affected only a small sector of the rural economy and have not yet come seriously to grips with basic problems.

The problems are numerous: excessive fragmentation of the land, a land tenure system which discourages improvements, inadequate seasonal credit, high transportation costs, poor marketing facilities, low quality and lack of standardization, primitive methods of cultivation. Moreover, the country's two most important crops, wheat and olives—which can be raised on nonirrigated land—are subject to extreme fluctuations in price and production. Scanty and unreliable yields, low produce prices, and high interest rates on agricultural loans mean that the average cultivator cannot set aside a surplus to maintain himself and his family in the bad years or to invest in improvements in the good years. Adequate credit and marketing facilities and protection from speculative prices would help give the Jordanian farmer the incentive he now lacks to make maximum use of his land.

The greatest potential for agricultural development seems to be offered by the nonirrigated crops, particularly olives and fruits. Before these crops can compete on the world market, however, they will have to meet higher standards of quality, grading and packing, and be distributed more efficiently.

Industry

Industrial potential is ultimately limited by a scarcity of fuel resources and of raw materials other than the abundant salts of the Dead Sea, agricultural products such as olives and fruits, and the substantial reserves of phosphates, which could provide the basis for a sizable fertilizer industry. Other limitations, such as the small size of the domestic market, the lack of skilled labor and trained managerial personnel, and the high cost of transportation could perhaps be ameliorated or overcome. Despite these handicaps, industry in Jordan has made greater relative progress since the Arab-Israeli conflict than has agriculture.

Since 1950 a few relatively large-scale modern enterprises have been established in urban areas. The most notable examples are cement and phosphate plants, where modern technology and standards of quality require skills not previously known in the area. These industrial beginnings are too recent and too restricted to have had important effects for more than a small part of the population, but there are signs that changes are taking place: an increase in the amount and variety of domestic consumer demand; the appearance of a small but active group of investors willing, with government cooperation, to put money into relatively large-scale as well as small-scale enterprises; and the founding of vocational schools. These developments owe much to the initiative of Jordan's Palestinian population, many of whose members acquired, under the British Mandate, skills, capital, and receptivity to modern techniques.

Most Jordanian industry is still organized on a family basis, and the corporate form remains in its infancy. The pattern of investment focuses on speculation for immediate gain, and profits tend to be distributed rather than reinvested.

Transition

The transition from a traditional to a modern economy is far more rapid in the towns, of course, than among the villagers and tribesmen. But trading and financial transactions in the towns retain many important traditional characteristics, particularly those which emphasize personal relations (see chap. 21). There is, for example, a widespread preference for collecting gold, jewelry, and property rather than saving currency, even among Jordanians who have access to banks. Nevertheless, the impact of westernization is beginning to appear in the class structure of the country—the waning of the great families and the emergence of a small but influential middle class and of an urban proletariat—as well as in various specifically economic phenomena.

The Jordanian wholesale and retail systems remain underdeveloped. Trade in goods is primarily on a basic personal level, and the exchange of goods between town and village is limited to a few commodities the rural economy cannot produce. The exchange of goods between the nomad and the villager continues to be mainly on a barter basis.

The traditional self-sufficiency of the villages, particularly those distant from major towns, still persists. Since 1950 many villages, however, present a picture of conflict between traditional ways and the forces of change. Large villages near major centers are transitional in culture between the more self-sufficient isolated village and the city. This fact is reflected in the number of delegations coming from such larger villages to request schools, clinics, health centers, and other improvements.

In a different way the nomad also feels the impact of modernization. His traditional role is being seriously altered (see chap. 6). To adjust to new circumstances he is becoming increasingly sedentarized. Some of the more powerful tribes employ peasants and sometimes even settle their own members on agricultural land. Exposed to modern influences, they are adjusting to new methods of production and organization (see chap. 14). The organization of the larger tribes, and the extensive tracts of land they possess both favor the use of modern production techniques.

Within the tribe the extended family controls the available capital, including the livestock. Tribal leadership, both economic and political, is based on a consensus of leading families. Within the village the family owns and works the land and runs the local industry.

In the city the family as a self-sufficient economic unit is gradually declining in significance. But most urban enterprises still operate on a family basis and have as their primary objective the satisfaction of family needs rather than the maximization of profit.

Role of Government

The government is actively promoting industrial and agricultural development and domestic and international trade. Businessmen, some of whom accumulated considerable fortunes during World War II, are beginning to show a disposition, when they can get government backing, to reinvest in industrial undertakings. Banking is developing, and the government, in addition to being itself a subscriber of capital to the Development Bank of Jordan, guarantees a dividend of 5 percent to private investors. The Development Bank is designed to grant medium- and long-term loans to industry and agriculture, to take up equity participation in enterprises, and to provide technical assistance to potential borrowers. The Agricultural Bank, the Jordan Development Board (which makes loans to the inhabitants of border villages), and the Rural Credit and Thrift Cooperatives (which depend heavily on loans from the government) have all shown increasing business activity in recent years (see chap. 13).

Jordan's incipient industry also depends to some extent on official support, and the government is a large investor in the phosphate, manganese, and Dead Sea minerals projects. The government also owns 49.5 percent of the shares in the country's only and highly efficient cement plant and is a major shareholder in an olive oil refinery, valued at about $280,000.

The most important projects planned by the government for the next few years are a petroleum refinery, a sugar refinery, and a textile mill. A road, rail, and port building program is already under way. The accomplishment of these schemes, in giving further impetus to the development of modern patterns of domestic trade, not only would constitute a move toward self-sufficiency in areas in which Jordan is at present almost completely dependent on imports but would enlarge local markets for domestic products by increasing the purchasing power of the general population.

ORGANIZATION AND USE
OF MANPOWER

INFORMATION CONCERNING THE COMPOSITION OF THE JORDAN-
ian labor force and the conditions under which it works is scanty and
unreliable. The general picture is of a predominantly rural, young, and
rapidly growing population, with a surplus of cheap labor reserves.
The presence of large numbers of refugees, the shortage of natural
resources, and the slow rate of economic development have combined
to create serious problems of both unemployment and underemploy-
ment. Modern industry, established only recently, has not had time to
bring into being a significantly large body of workers trained in mechanical skills, however, and there is a consequent shortage of skilled
and professional persons.

It may be said that until quite recently labor problems as understood in western countries did not exist in Jordan. The bulk of the
population consisted of nomads, seminomads, and small cultivators.
There was no modern industry, and the few small towns that existed
were market centers in which commerce was the province of small
shopkeepers hiring few or no assistants. The picture changed somewhat
after the Arab-Israeli war—the Palestinian Arab workers who became
Jordanians had some experience in union organization—but not
enough to make any real difference soon.

Labor Force

Of an estimated total population of 1,440,000, some 200,000 are
nomadic or seminomadic bedouins, some 400,000 are townsmen, of
whom approximately 175,000 live in Amman and 80,000 in Jerusalem, and the remainder are settled villagers engaged in the country's
basic economic activity, agriculture. The total labor force was estimated in 1955 to be just under 400,000 (see Table 2).

The population is probably about evenly divided between the sexes, as in neighboring Arab countries for which figures are available, and, in the absence of official statistics, it may be assumed that the breakdown by age groups is about the same as that of the Palestinian Arabs during the Mandate: 42 percent under 15 years of age; 52 percent between 15 and 59; and 6 percent over 60.

Composition

The bulk of the labor is supplied by the male population, though women and children play an important part in agriculture, helping during the harvest and doing most of the dairying and poultry raising. Most domestic help is female and a few women are employed in the lighter industries. An assessment of the role played by women in the labor force is complicated by the fact that while most women work within their families relatively few of them are in the paid labor force. Since unpaid family labor plays a large role in Jordanian agriculture the concept of a clearly distinguishable agricultual labor force is difficult to apply.

The number of women between the ages of 15 and 65 who are free to seek and can obtain paid employment—negligible in the villages, higher in the towns—represents perhaps 5 percent of the total. With education for girls increasingly available, it is likely that opportunities for women in industry, commerce, and government will increase and the percentage of female employees will rise.

The natural increase in population—between 2 and 3 percent per annum during the last few years—is estimated to be sufficient to add between 5,000 and 7,000 annually to the total labor force. Age statistics of the refugee groups indicate an unusually high proportion of young people, which suggests the entry into the labor market of a disproportionate number in a relatively short time.

There is little correlation between religious and ethnic grouping and occupation, the main exception being the concentration of Christians, who are more urbanized, in commerce, finance, and the professions.

Although the Jordanian Government has adhered to various international conventions regarding forced labor, to make a clear distinction between forced labor, as it is legally defined, and conditions similar to servitude or compulsory labor is difficult, because of the poverty of the population and the unorganized nature of the labor force.

In response to a questionnaire issued by the United Nations to member states in 1952 the Jordanian Government stated that no official laws or regulations provided forced labor for punitive, educational, corrective, or other purposes. Jordan has formally adhered to a

United Nations Middle East Seminar resolution regarding the treatment of prisoners.

Precise information is lacking as to the extent and character of compulsory labor in Jordan today, but it is clear that if it has not died out altogether it exists on only a minor scale.

Geographical Distribution

The majority of Jordan's industrial and professional workers are in Amman and Jerusalem; indeed, practically all the modern skills of Jordan are concentrated in those two towns. The slow though perceptible increase of the educated and skilled groups is largely attributable to the influx of the refugees, of whom it has been estimated that about one half can work with little or no supervision, and to the movement into the towns of discharged personnel of the Arab Legion who wish to continue to employ the skills they learned during their army training.

Two main occupational migration trends may be noted: permanent migration from countryside to cities, induced by higher wages and better living conditions, and seasonal migration—from country to town in winter and in the opposite direction in summer when some urban workers return to the country to help with the harvest. Other general trends helping to increase the supply of cheap labor are the sedentarization of nomads and the availability of semisettled tribal groups of the Jordan Valley for commercial agricultural enterprises and public works. Among the refugees, however, mobility is affected by a reluctance to leave the UNRWA relief system.

Employment

The Jordanian Ministry of Economy estimated recently that some 115,000 employable persons, about equally divided between East and West Bank dwellers, were totally unemployed. This figure represents nearly one fifth of the country's male labor force. Only international aid, which through the United Nations Relief and Works Agency brings direct relief to one third of the total population, has enabled the country to bear this level of unemployment without witnessing the actual starvation of some of its citizens.

Skilled workers, however, do not on the whole find much difficulty in securing jobs. Before 1948 there were very few workers with any modern skills, but the annexation of the West Bank and the influx of the more urbanized Palestinian Arabs have raised the general level in this respect. In Palestine, in 1944, some 60 to 65 percent of the Arab population was rural and 35 to 40 percent urban. Slightly over half of the Arabs were engaged in agriculture, livestock raising, fisheries, and forestry. One tenth were employed by the government and local authorities, and about another tenth were working in commerce, finance, hotels, and cafés; the remainder of the working population was made up mainly of soldiers, civilian employees of the British Army, and transport and communication workers. A survey taken in Palestine in 1943 among Arab workers showed that nearly two thirds of the skilled and semiskilled workers were in the following categories:

	Percentage of Total
Mechanics and Fitters	17
Carpenters	13
Shoemakers	8
Weavers	8
Blacksmiths	5
Tailors	5
Tinsmiths	3
Millers	3
	62

As regards professional skills, in 1952 there were in Jordan only 3,561 teachers, 194 physicians, 43 dentists, and 89 pharmacists.

One of the major trends in employment, at least until the middle of 1956, was the engagement of local labor in public works of an economic development nature. From 1954 until the middle of 1956 the United States development assistance program maintained an average monthly payroll of 10,000 workers, of whom 5,000 were employed on road construction. The British loan program and the Jordan Public Works Department also helped maintain the level of employment. The effect of these undertakings was widely distributed throughout the country as projects opened up in different locations, being particularly evident in 1955, when payments to persons normally engaged in agriculture helped replace the losses sustained during the bad crop year.

Productivity

The productivity of Jordanian labor is low, both in agriculture and industry; inadequate food, bad housing, and poor health are obvious causal factors. Except on a few modernized farms, agricultural equipment and techniques are those which have been employed for centuries, and general illiteracy, lack of capital, and force of tradition stand in the way of any rapid improvement. Such western-style industry as has developed in Jordan calls not only for skills but for attitudes toward work which are still alien to most Jordanians. Absenteeism and employee turnover are high among workers who are close to their rural origins and unaccustomed to factory discipline. Economic incentives are great enough to attract workers away from the subsistence conditions of the villages to the towns but so far not great enough to create any general determination to raise productivity. Efforts to raise the productivity level are further hampered by the poor condition of much of the plant equipment.

Industrial management, like the labor force, suffers from its ties with the past. Much management personnel was recruited from the old commercial class, whose notions of factory methods are not suited to modern industrial enterprise.

Wage Rates and Working Conditions

The dislocations caused by the Arab-Israeli war and the pressure of the refugees on the labor market have sharply reduced wage rates. On the other hand, the cost of living index has risen; figures compiled by the United Nations Relief and Works Agency show that from a base of 100 in 1950 there was a sharp rise to a peak of 172 in January 1952; by 1954, however, the index had stabilized around 90.

Table 3 shows wage rates in different towns in Jordan and in the various occupations. The variations from town to town are accounted for partly by the uneven concentration of refugees (of whom some 370,000 are in West Jordan and 110,000 in East Jordan), by substantial differences in the cost of living, and by the varying levels of economic activity in the different towns. In industry, unlike agriculture, wages are paid entirely in money rather than in kind, and this cash income is not augmented by such welfare devices as family allowances or old age pensions.

In agriculture day laborers earn from 15 to 20 piasters (42 to 56 cents) a day, while longer-term workers are commonly paid in kind at equivalents falling roughly within these limits. In the nonagricultural sector a clerk may earn anything from 15 to 40 Jordanian dinars ($42 to $112) a month. The influx of large numbers of educated Palestinian workers has greatly increased the competition for white-collar jobs and has forced many persons who normally would have entered this type of employment to move to manual work. Of the 1,500 persons employed by the Arab Potash Company, for example, 210 have secondary school certificates.

Legislation relating to hours of work concerns only women and children. For women in industry a maximum of 48 hours a week and eight and a half hours a day is fixed, and 52 hours a week and nine and a half hours a day in other employment; the maximum consecutive hours of work are four and a half and five respectively. In industry overtime is restricted to specific cases of necessity, while in other occupations it is limited to a maximum of six hours a week, or 100 hours a year. Night work is allowed only in hotels, restaurants, and similar establishments.

The minimum age for the employment of minors is 14 in industry and 12 in other occupations, but an exception is made by the Ministry of Social Affairs for approved institutions providing technical or professional education. For children under 14 who are attending school the maximum working day allowed is three hours; for juveniles from 14 to 18 a maximum of eight and a half hours a day and 48 hours a week is fixed. Night work is prohibited for all under 18 years of age unless authorized by the Ministry of Social Affairs. For those attending evening school the working day must end at 4 P.M. These regulations are widely ignored, particularly by the smaller employers.

For adult males the working week in the largest businesses is usually from 48 to 52 hours; in smaller establishments it may be considerably higher. The larger enterprises grant from 7 to 15 days paid leave a year in addition to sick leave of varying duration; such establishments also provide their workers with medical examinations and treatment.

In September 1956 it was reported that the Jordanian Government, in cooperation with the International Labor Organization, was drafting a law regulating working hours, holidays, compensation, and the settlement of labor disputes. A new governmental department would supervise labor conditions throughout the country.

Labor Relations and Organization

Economically, Jordan remains a typical Middle Eastern agricultural country in which the dominant pattern of labor relations is the traditional one developed between landlord and tenant. Mushaa tenure of land, under which certain villagers were able to acquire and alienate from the communal holdings sizable tracts, has lent itself to absentee landlordism. Such tenure is dying out but absentee landlordism and sharecropping remain a common although diminishing feature of the agrarian pattern (see chap. 14). Perhaps half of the cultivated land is worked under some form of tenancy, and this deeply rooted and generally accepted traditionalist pattern in the villages influences the attitudes of employers in the nascent industry of the towns. Employers and government officials both resist innovations which could give the workers a kind and degree of collective bargaining strength not possessed by tenants in the countryside.

Employer hostility to unionization is apparent in the cases of dismissal of workers on the ground that they have joined unions. Labor organization has also been hampered by the availability of the abundant and cheap labor of refugees and destitute tribesmen and most of all by the government's professed belief that unions are—or can easily become—instruments of Communist penetration. All unions must be investigated by the Criminal Investigation Department of the Ministry of the Interior, which has responsibility for identifying and combating subversive groups. Some unions have been denied the right to register.

Two Arab labor federations existed in Palestine before the West Bank was incorporated into Jordan: the Arab Laborer's Societies, consisting of 30 unions with a total membership of 20,000, and a rival left-wing group with a membership estimated at from 5,000 to 8,000. Both of these broke up during the Arab-Israeli war, but some of their members formed small unions in such West Bank towns as Jerusalem, Ramallah, and Nablus. In 1952 the Jordanian Government banned these unions and imprisoned some of their leaders, accusing them of communistic tendencies. Subsequently a few light industries were established, and the government, apparently realizing that unionization was inevitable, saw that regulatory legislation was needed. In 1953 the Union Formation Law, to be administered by the Ministry of Social Affairs, was adopted. The findings of the Criminal Investigation Department as to whether a union was subversive did not bind the Ministry. Under the new law a number of groups registered as unions. The tendency to penalize workers for joining unions was partly checked after a tailors' strike in 1954; workers who had been dismissed for joining the Tailors Union were rehired.

By 1956, 23 registrations had been accepted and 5 other applications were under consideration. Complete figures on membership are not available, but 16 of the unions had 3,940 members in February 1955. The membership of 11 of the unions increased from 1,755 in December 1954 to 3,090 in February 1955. The largest union is that of vehicle drivers (800 members), followed by those of hotel, restaurant, and café workers (350), construction workers (300), cement workers, railroad workers, electrical workers (250 each).

Individual union organization follows a uniform pattern in which a general assembly of all members elects a governing board. Until 1954, at least, the country had only one district federation of unions—the Central Board in Amman, consisting of member unions at the rate of one representative for every 50 members. Embracing unions covering some 4,000 workers, the Central Board elected its own officers; member unions contributed 20 percent of their revenue to it. Efforts were made to amend the Union Formation Law to permit the Board to become a national rather than a regional federation, and in July 1954 the Ministry of Social Affairs approved the formation of an all-Jordan federation of trade unions, but information is lacking as to the implementation of this action.

A Workers Compensation Law adopted by the Assembly has not yet been promulgated, partly because it fails to satisfy the labor leaders, who are pressing for amendments. The law relates to termination of employment and accident compensation. Under it, workers who are dismissed would be entitled to one month's wages for every year of service up to 3, and to one half month's wages for each of the following 3 years. Workers who are temporarily disabled by an accident are to receive half pay. In case of permanent and total disability the worker is to receive 500 days' wages plus one month's wages for every year of service. In case of death, dependents are to get 3 years' pay or 250 Jordanian dinars—whichever is more (the dinar is equal to one British pound or $2.80); if the worker had less than 3 years' service, the amount is to be 165 dinars. Children under 14 years of age are to get 1 dinar for each month of service of their deceased father. If there are no dependents the employer is to contribute a minimum of 30 dinars for funeral expenses.

As noted, the only legislation relating to hours of work concerns itself exclusively with women and children, and, as with other protective social legislation in the area, the degree to which this law is actually applied is questionable. The number of working hours of adult males is not regulated by law and reportedly averages between 48 and 52 weekly in the larger establishments but considerably more in the smaller ones. The labor unions have been agitating for laws to cover various aspects of working conditions and labor relations. Their greatest effort at present, however, is being directed toward increasing the number of unions and the size of the membership—in recognition of the fact that as long as union membership remains small and the supply of available labor (mostly from the refugees) continues to be large little can be done to improve conditions or to raise wages.

Up to now strikes have been few and of short duration. Members of the phosphate workers and shoemakers unions successfully carried out strikes to prevent lowering of wages. Another successful strike was conducted by employees of the cigarette company against the stoppage of wages during official holidays.

In general, the labor movement in Jordan is too weak to make its attitudes and desires felt. Increasing industrialization is bringing changes in the relations between employers and employees, but thus far little has been done to improve the rate and pace of productivity, and there is little to suggest that organized labor will soon achieve a strong bargaining position in relation to the employers. Nor is labor in a position to play any part in eventual decisions about the relocation of industry or the hiring of foreign laborers.

FINANCIAL SYSTEM

THE CONCEPT OF PUBLIC FINANCE AS AN INSTRUMENT OF THE modern state is new in Jordan. Officials and the mass of the people alike are only beginning to become familiar with modern fiscal operations. In the past, contact between the village and central government was largely confined to taxation and conscription; few tangible benefits came back to the village. The complex Ottoman tax system, which favored a wealthy minority, was revised by the British, and many of the characteristics of the tax laws promulgated under the Mandate are discernible today. For the people at large, however, taxes remain a burden to be avoided whenever possible, and attempts to collect taxes, especially new taxes, are usually met with evasion and hostility.

This traditional distrust is only partly overcome by the government's efforts to convince the people that tax revenues will be returned to them in the form of an improved standard of living brought about by economic development. The sudden and bewildering levying of new taxes on individuals unaccustomed to paying them has not alleviated the situation. As a consequence, legislative provisions and the available statistics conceal the actual conditions of public finance—the social resistance to taxation, the accepted practice of altering tax information, and the indifference of the government officers themselves.

The role of banks and of currency in Jordan also reflect the contrast between the old and the new—in this case the subsistence patterns of the village or nomadic encampment and the market economy of the city. While modern banking is playing an increasingly important part in the economic activity of the middle- and upper-income groups, their impact is only beginning to be felt in the countryside. The rapid growth of the towns since 1950, however, makes it difficult to draw as sharp a line as formerly between the new urban economy and the traditional pattern of the countryside because villages close to larger towns are being directly influenced by urban economic patterns, a process which is relatively more advanced on the more urbanized West Bank.

Public Finance

The precise attitude of Jordan's present leaders towards public finance and taxation is impossible to define. Political instability has bred expediency, and the severing of the financial relationship with Britain in 1957 left the central budget in a dangerous condition. Often, what appears to be government policy is no more than improper administration or the indifference of the responsible officials. Slightly modified western forms have been adopted, but administration practice lags and is still in the process of change from the old to the new.

The traditional Moslem concept of taxation as articulated in the Koran laid down the principle of drawing on the surplus wealth of the rich for distribution among the poor and needy. Ideally, *zakat* (almsgiving) was to be the means to this end. In the course of time *zakat* was imposed as a compulsory tax calculated at about 2.5 percent of capital. Two other taxes mentioned in the Koran are the *jiziah,* a levy on non-Moslems for exemption from military service, and the *kharaj,* a land tax on the unbeliever which might take as much as two fifths of his crop. Theoretically, only a small share of these taxes would be used for the traditionally narrowly defined operations of the government.

The fiscal ideal based on religious revelation and moral principle was, of course, only imperfectly realized. The burden of taxes often fell with disproportionate weight on non-Arabs and Christian Arabs; among the faithful themselves the poor and weak could not expect the same treatment commanded by the powerful. Even today there are complaints that, government pronouncements to the contrary, discrimination against Christians is still practiced by some officials in tax and other matters.

Some of the elements of the old Islamic system are still discernible, in spite of its corruption under the Turks and the changes made under the British. The old equitable basis for the land tithe, distinguishing between rain-fed and irrigated land, has remained applicable to this day, although the tax is now based on the capital value of the land rather than on crop yields. The government tax for social welfare has all the elements of the *zakat* fund, drawing on the traditional sources of capital and income, although the giving of *zakat* itself is today a voluntary individual act.

Under the four centuries of Ottoman rule, an aura of corruption surrounded taxation and public finance. Taxation could be described adequately as tribute or loot, collected more for the aggrandizement of the officialdom than for the amelioration of the condition of the population. The *zakat* fund itself was not immune from abuse. No distinction was made between public and private funds, the distribution and collection of taxes varied greatly from one area to another, and the tax collector's uncertainty of tenure increased his efforts to collect funds over and above the amount due the sultan.

The long experience of corruption and complexity in public finance left a legacy of suspicion which was not dispelled by efforts of the British to reorganize the tax system, nor has it yet been dispelled by similar efforts of the Jordanian Government. Moreover, the British reforms had two unanticipated and unfortunate consequences. The Transjordan land classification and tax laws of 1933 weakened the power of village headmen, introduced order into the levying of taxes, and guaranteed individual ownership through settlement of title, but they also enabled landowners, especially from Damascus and Beirut, to purchase village land with their war profits. Secondly, the villager in attaining ownership of his land had also to assume a more rigorous financial responsibility; as a consequence, he was burdened with indebtedness and mortgage in times of depression or crop failure. That the speculator did not acquire as much land as he might have and that it was difficult for a landlord to collect rents and taxes was largely due to the villager's suspicion of outsiders and his stubbornness. Further, since income tax laws did not, until 1951, apply to commercial and industrial groups, who were subjected to a trade license fee only, the authorities were unable to tap the great fortunes made during and immediately following World War II. In 1951 the income tax law was changed to apply to all incomes except farmers'.

Prior to the crisis which culminated in 1957 with the severance of the connection with Britain, the Jordanian Government was able to somewhat increase social and economic development while keeping expenditure on the army and police relatively stable. This emphasis suggests a genuine desire to channel available financial resources into economic rather than military development.

Encouragement has been given to private enterprise in the form of exemptions from import duties and corporate taxes. While the government is itself a direct investor, there is as yet no serious conflict between the public and private sectors. The Jordanian concept of a planned economy, vague as it is, does not include the practice of relieving the reluctant businessman of his profits for investment in government-owned enterprises.

Foreign assistance has been a major and integral part of all fiscal consideration in Jordan, and the budget itself is constructed on the basis of this source of government revenue. Thoughtful officials are aware of the extent of the country's dependence and continuing need for financial aid, but this awareness fades when they are confronted with the political implications of dependence. Definite reaction has occurred, however, only in Jordan's economic relations with Britain; no official criticism of Point Four activity has been voiced, but even the United Nations Relief and Works Agency for Palestine Refugees (UNRWA) has not escaped unofficial criticism. It is apparently difficult for Jordanians to conceive of aid without political strings. Thus the government finds itself in a dilemma, the seriousness of which will become greater as present funds run out and as it becomes necessary either to cut back development outlays or to find funds from less controversial sources to make up for the loss of British aid.

Expenditures

Although expenditures have risen (see Table 6), the budget pattern has remained substantially the same during recent years, but the loss of British aid, and the consequent shifting of funds which may be necessary, may alter that pattern.

Budgeted expenditures reflect not only the policy of a planned economic development but also the assumption by the government of social services which previously had been carried out by private and foreign institutions. These services have been increasingly demanded of the central authorities as a normal governmental function. The demand has come chiefly from the urban population, especially the Palestinians, who had become accustomed to such services in Palestine.

The past two years have witnessed a gradual shift towards more emphasis on education, health, and public works, while the share of defense in total expenditures declined in 1956 to under 50 percent from a former roughly 60 percent. The relative share allocated to the police has also declined. The government hoped to implement during 1957 a reclassification of a new wage scale for its own personnel, and had already distributed funds over all the departments to increase the salaries of the growing number of lower-grade civil servants.

A policy of economic development and the severing of the natural routes to the Mediterranean (due to the Arab-Israeli conflict) have resulted in increasing outlays for road and rail construction and improvements in the port of Aqaba, and it is expected that these expenditures will increase in the future. The government has also allocated funds to the development of new industries.

Budgeting practice has been to draw on the surplus account for deficits in fiscal operations. Because the budget has both overestimated expenditures and underestimated receipts, there has been an increase in the surplus account over the years. Foreign assistance does not enter into this account because receipts from these funds tally exactly with the expenditures. The reserve fund is used in bookkeeping as a balancing device. Increases in the fund are budget expenditures and decreases are budget receipts. The government feels that the surplus should be used for development projects.

The direct public debt is entirely external, directed chiefly to Britain. The Jordanian Government incurred several obligations upon the termination of the British Mandate, and by 1956 the total of British loans reached JD 6.35 million. All loans from Britain are interest-free, the capital of all but the first loan to be paid back in 15 installments.

Indirect public debt consists of a government guarantee of loans made by the Ottoman Bank to the municipalities, the expenditures of which have increased. (Theoretically, all municipal budgets must be approved and filed with the Ministry of Interior, but this rule is not closely followed.) The government has considered floating government bonds but apparently has not felt that such a step is yet necessary.

Prior to 1952 auditing of the budget was done by the Auditing Department of the Ministry of Finance. When this was found to be inefficient, the Bureau of Accounts was established; it is responsible to the legislative branch and independent of the executive. The Bureau audits all government finances and can investigate the accounts of private groups upon authorization by the Council of Ministers. In 1953 the practice of pre-auditing expenditures was instituted. Although the operations of the Bureau have been commendable, the disunity of the budget and the poor management of Treasury finances renders its work difficult. Furthermore, no clear distinction is made between Treasury funds and those of third parties held in trust by the Treasury.

Revenue

Government revenue consists of domestic tax and other receipts, as well as foreign grants and loans. Table 5 presents a breakdown of domestic revenue.

TAXATION. The principle of progressive taxation as a means of assuring equitable distribution of the tax burden is included in the 1952 Constitution of Jordan. In practice, however, although there are no discriminatory taxes leveled at particular groups, taxes have tended to be highly regressive, bearing heavily on low-income classes, and to reflect only to a limited extent changes in production and income.

Taxation on agriculture is light—if measured in terms of the share of agriculture in the national income—and relief is granted in years of crop failure. On the other hand, the poorer segments of the population, whether rural or urban, and to a lesser extent the middle-income group make a disproportionately large contribution to revenue through the payment of excise and customs duties on articles of popular consumption.

New direct taxes have been introduced in recent years but the regressive character of the system appears to have increased. A 37 percent increase in domestic revenue between 1951 and 1955 was achieved through the levying of new taxes and raising the rates on others. These years witnessed a decrease from 17.5 percent to 14.9 percent in the contribution of direct taxes, while 70 percent of the increase in tax income was gained from excise and customs duties. A liberalizing feature has been introduced in the imposition of very high duty rates on luxury imports but in general, progressive taxes have accounted for a decreasing proportion of government revenue.

The fact that so much of the tax load has been indirect may account for the absence of any great popular demand for tax reform. So far, proposals for re-evaluating the tax system have come from economists, international study missions, and other students of government operations rather than from the mass of the people.

No less than 60 percent of total tax revenue is derived from customs duties and other similar levies; only 15 percent is derived from property and income taxes. Excise taxes on popularly consumed commodities such as tobacco, matches, and salt, as well as numerous other fees, constitute the remainder.

Several exemptions are allowed to encourage the economic and social development of the country. Certain agricultural and industrial machinery and raw materials are exempt from import duties (see chap. 15), although this advantage is limited by the control of the government over the issuance of import licenses, which in some cases constitutes in effect an embargo on capital imports. The property tax on industrial sites is very small and can be deducted from individual income taxes. Deductions are permitted for children receiving higher education and for stock dividends if the issuing company is also taxed.

Differing rural property tax policies on the East and West Bank were equalized under the 1955 Land Tax Law. Agricultural taxes are determined on the basis of the presumed capital value of the land, differing according to the type of land and its use. The tax yields do not increase with rising crop output but only with the extension of the amount of taxable land. Under the present system, revenue from agricultural land is very small and the tax may be remitted in case of distress. Urban property is taxed on the basis of assessments made every five years. A lower percentage is levied on vacant lots than on buildings, encouraging unproductive speculation in vacant land.

Partly because of evasion and partly because of the present tax structure, which emphasizes other sources, income taxes constitute a very small proportion of total government revenue; despite rising personal and corporate incomes, the yields from income tax showed only an 8 percent increase in the five years ending 1955. The tax on personal income is levied progressively (to a degree slightly higher than under the Mandate) from 5 percent on incomes up to JD 400 to a maximum of 40 percent on incomes exceeding JD 2,800. According to the 1952–53 tax returns, 89 percent of the individuals taxed had incomes of less than JD 300 a year. Since farmers' incomes are not taxed, the few wealthy landowners are exempt. Corporations are taxed at a flat rate of 25 percent, with the exception that certain new industries are exempt from all taxes for the first three years. Other taxes and fees include a livestock tax, trade license fees, the tax for Social Welfare drawn from incomes, property, imports, and livestock, the National Guard tax, the Aviation Deposit tax, land registration fees, and traffic licenses.

Administration and Collection of Taxes. Administrative operations of the Jordanian Government have been characterized by a shortage of trained personnel, a low incentive on the part of subordinates, and a consequent shifting of responsibility from the lower to the higher levels of the bureaucracy. Interference by top officials, either because of the lack of confidence in lower-grade civil servants or because they wish to arrange—or conceal—favors, is also common. Low salaries do not encourage honesty or diligence among tax collectors, and when collection is in local hands the collectors function more as members of their village or clan than as agents of the government.

The resulting inefficiency in tax operations is evident in the high percentage of arrears. Roughly 40 percent of the tax forms are never returned, and of those returned, only half are satisfactorily completed. It has been estimated that with tighter administration yields of the income tax could be increased by 50 percent and of the property tax by 20 to 30 percent. The government has shown little disposition to employ fines and other punitive measures for tax evasion.

Although there has been some increase in returns on urban property taxes, the actual yield in 1954–55 was only 70 percent of the amount assessed. The Amman municipality alone was responsible for more than two thirds of the uncollected amount. Arrears in rural property taxes have increased. The classification of land and the collection of these taxes in partly cultivated areas under Desert Administration is in the hands of village committees appointed by the district commissioner. The low yields undoubtedly can be attributed in part to the leniency of these committees toward their fellow villagers. No precise information is available on the collection of taxes in settled areas—so classified by the government for tax purposes—or as to whether village communities are permitted to deduct for community needs a percentage of the tax collected.

The livestock tax, one of the few taxes which can be applied to nomad tribes, is collected by local committees appointed by the Ministry of Finance. Here too there undoubtedly exists a strong bias in favor of the community in the levying and collecting of these taxes.

NON-TAX REVENUE. Domestic non-tax revenue has come chiefly from postal, telegraph, and telephone service fees and from oil company pipeline royalties. A recent substantial amount has been obtained from stock dividends from the cement factory which enjoys a monopoly over all cement production in Jordan (see chap. 15). Very little revenue is gained from sales of state domain.

FOREIGN ASSISTANCE. From 1951 to 1955, no more than 40 percent of government budget revenue came from domestic sources; foreign grants accounted for more than 50 percent and foreign loans for 8 percent of the total receipts. It has been estimated that almost one third of the national income of Jordan formerly was provided by British assistance alone. A further large amount of foreign aid, such as that from UNRWA and Point Four funds, is not included within the budget itself. Almost two thirds of the expenditures for the economic and social development of Jordan have been covered by foreign assistance (see Table 4).

In the budget alone (see Table 6) half of the "extraordinary expenditures," which include development projects, are met by foreign loans. Furthermore, the normal expenditures do not include defense costs. Before 1957 the military establishment was financed by British grants, except for nominal amounts contributed by the Arab states and the Jordanian Government. Clearly, any large-scale development program will require substantial amounts of foreign assistance; domestic revenue is increasing but is not yet large enough to cover total budget costs.

Banking and Currency

Farmers in Jordan, both tenants and landholders, generally turn to relatives for assistance or contract loans with village moneylenders; loan repayments are often made in kind rather than in cash. The basic security required by the moneylender is a major share of the borrower's crop—based on a high interest rate. (Attitudes toward banking and interest-taking have been changed as a result of reassuring, twentieth-century interpretations of the Koran.) The strong bonds attaching the farmer to family and village make it very difficult for an external institution to penetrate village economic activity (see chap. 6). While loans have been extended to farmers through credit institutions such as the Agricultural Bank, they have so far reached only a minority and have been small in amount. The Jordanian Development Board also offers agricultural loans but poses strict security requirements which most farmers cannot meet.

The Jordanian peasant with any surplus has traditionally hoarded it in the form of gold or jewelry or used it to buy land; he views paper currency with suspicion and does not readily trust his money to a faraway bank. Nomads place a high value on livestock and precious metals. Except for a few of their wealthy leaders, they have little contact with the banking system. Trade within the village is conducted largely as an exchange of goods, only occasionally with currency as a medium, and during the harvest season traveling peddlers frequently take away cereals in exchange for products needed by the farmer. Villagers mainly use currency in transactions that relate to ceremonial occasions such as weddings, in dealings with the village moneylenders (though often repaying in kind), and for the purchase in the towns of articles unavailable locally. In all such cases, however, goods of recognized value in the local community may still be used as a medium of exchange. The continued practice of barter at the village level indicates the continued widespread self-sufficiency on a subsistence level of the rural community. The self-sufficiency is also revealed by the relatively small amount of indebtedness secured by mortgages held by outsiders. It is, of course, in sharp contrast with the economic dependence of Jordan as a whole, with its growing towns and its burden of refugees.

In the urban centers the policies of credit institutions play a significant part in determining the industrial and commercial profile of the nation. Loans are advanced particularly to encourage the development of the import trade, the growth of small- and large-scale industry, and the production of commercial agricultural crops. Currency has become the sole medium of exchange used by the upper levels of the commercial and industrial community, and it is used increasingly even by the poorer segment of the urban population.

Monetary System

Jordan has belonged to the sterling area. The Palestinian pound, which had served as the legal tender, was replaced in July 1950 by the Jordanian dinar, like its predecessor equal to one pound sterling.

A Jordan Currency Board is authorized to issue currency, provided that an equivalent amount in pounds sterling is paid in advance in London. Thus the currency has 100 percent backing. This regulation, however, drastically reduces the influence of the currency-issuing organization on the supply of money and credit in Jordan. In effect, the balance of payments determines whether the currency can be contracted or expanded, and the dependence of the economy on foreign aid is increased. It has been suggested by the International Bank for Reconstruction and Development that more flexible currency regulations should be adopted, policies that would permit the Jordanian Government through the Currency Board to meet changing economic conditions with appropriate fiscal measures. According to these recommendations, the Currency Board should be permitted to use a certain quantity of domestic securities for currency backing.

Commercial Banking

Successful commercial banks must possess assets which may be sold on the open market for ready cash at their full value. There are few securities in Jordan for which there is a strong market and which can be rapidly converted into cash, and the Jordanian banks must therefore depend on liquid assets held in their head offices, principally in London; as a result interest rates in London determine Jordanian interest rates. Commercial banks in the country are accordingly not free to charge rates to attract customers nor to adapt their loan policies to the particular credit needs of the economy. In 1952–53 the legal maximum interest rate was 9 percent. In 1957 it was reported that actual interest rates were averaging 5 percent. Private loans, on the other hand, have brought rates as high as 50 percent a year.

Merchants and industrial entrepreneurs are the main customers of the commercial banks. Advances to private enterprise are mainly short term and consist primarily of overdrafts against personal guarantees and loans against mortgage security. Although commercial banks formerly followed conservative policies in extending loans, since 1954 slightly more liberal policies have been initiated. Importers may now secure letters of credit with a 25 percent deposit, and merchants may receive loans on the basis of anticipated income from accounts receivable. In spite of these new developments the commercial banks, operated on western lines, tend to emphasize the collateral possessed by the individual rather than his personal record or the potential of his business.

Since 1952 public deposits have increased rapidly; in 1955 they represented half of the total deposits of commercial banks. Although banking activity is restricted to a small part of the urban population, the growth of a new middle class, the expansion of industry, and recent developments in the import trade have all contributed to a slow but steady increase in savings accounts and private demand deposits, as well as in institutional loans to the private sector of the economy. In March 1955, currency in circulation totaled 12.6 million Jordanian dinars, while private demand deposits reached only JD 4.8 million, a further indication that most private monetary transactions occur without recourse to banks.

Major commercial banks operating in Jordan are the Arab Bank Ltd., the British Bank of the Middle East, and the Ottoman Bank. In addition there are Barclays Bank, with a branch in Nablus, the Arab National Bank Ltd., the Jordan National Bank (Banque al-Ahli), and the Cairo Bank of Egypt. The last two organizations received a charter in 1955 and were opened for business in April 1956. The Ottoman Bank operates as the government's fiscal agent.

Other Credit Institutions

Designed to complement commercial banks, other credit institutions have been set up in Jordan to meet particular needs of the economy. The capital for most of these credit facilities, ranging from government-managed institutions such as the Agricultural Bank to semiofficial organizations such as the Development Bank of Jordan and the cooperative societies are derived directly or indirectly from foreign sources.

The Agricultural Bank in 1954–55 had an estimated capital reserve of JD 416,500, and it is anticipated that by 1960 capital reserves will reach JD 700,000. The bank has had a rather limited usefulness for the small farm tenant and sharecropper because it does not provide short-term credit at low enough rates. Very conservative in its loan policy, it advances loans on pledges either of real estate or joint security. It is significant that 75 percent of its loans have been for small amounts estimated at an average of JD 50 each. It has had great difficulty in collecting repayments, and arrears are a serious problem. Although it was originally intended to reach all agricultural districts, in practice its activity has tended to be centered around Amman. Its effectiveness also has been impaired by the influence of political considerations upon its loan and personnel recruitment policies.

USOM (United States Operations Mission) Loan Projects were designed to meet special needs, including community demands for development funds, the loan requirements of individuals on the basis of the potential of their businesses, and the demands for capital for investment in agriculture, marketing, tourism, and small industries. In 1955 the outstanding loans totaled US $581,055. Rates of interest were generally very low, and in special cases, such as municipal loans, funds were advanced free of interest to the community. It is difficult at the present time to evaluate the impact of these United States loans on Jordan's economy (see chap. 10; chap. 14; and chap. 15).

The Development Bank of Jordan relies principally on international agencies such as UNRWA (United Nations Relief and Works Agency for Palestine Refugees) and the Jordanian Government for its capital. In spite of its offer of a guaranteed dividend of 5 percent annually, it has not attracted large funds from commercial banks. Its objective is to raise the standard of living of the population, particularly that of the refugees. It is reported that 67 percent of its loans have been in agriculture; the remainder were advanced to industry in such fields as flour milling, olive oil production, dairy farming, and marble quarrying. Eighty percent of the loans have been of substantial amounts, each averaging more than JD 10,000. The criteria used by the bank in advancing loans appear to be rather conservative; almost all loans are made on the basis of substantial security. The entrepreneurial ability and earning potential of the business does not appear to be given significant emphasis. The bank presents, however, an excellent record in the prompt repayment of its loans.

The Jordan Development Board grants loans to the Rural Credit and Thrift Cooperatives at an interest rate of 4 percent. The cooperatives advance loans to their members at an interest rate of approximately 7 percent. By March 1955 the capital and reserves of the cooperatives totaled JD 19,812, and their loans to members reached JD 67,552. With such meager resources they can play only a relatively minor role in the rural economy as a whole; however, they have recently been active in West Jordan, where it is reported that some 50 new societies have been formed (see chap. 14).

The Arab Land Company was established by the Arab League with an authorized capital of one million Egyptian pounds (of which £E 640,000 have been paid up). Originally designed to buy Arab lands in Palestine which might otherwise have been sold to Jews, the Land Company now finances agricultural and construction projects in Jordan and the Gaza Strip. From 1951, when it started operations, until March 31, 1955, it granted 817 building loans for a total of JD 827,000, and 212 agricultural loans for a total of JD 134,000.

AGRICULTURAL DEVELOPMENT

AGRICULTURE DOMINATES JORDAN'S ECONOMY. SOME 75 PER-
cent of the nonrefugee population depends on agriculture or animal
husbandry for livelihood and the greater part of domestically produced income is derived from those two sources. Most of Jordan's
few industries process locally grown products, much of the transport
system is engaged in moving them, and the commercial and banking
systems deal largely with agriculture. Agricultural produce in 1955
accounted for about 58 percent of Jordan's exports.

Some livestock is raised by Jordan's settled cultivators, but the
bulk of it is produced by the nomadic and seminomadic bedouins.
The nomads, largely concentrated in eastern Jordan, make up only
some 200,000 of the total population of 1,440,000. It is estimated
that the bedouin group is about equally divided between partly
sedentary tribesmen who complement livestock-breeding with cultivation and those who still pursue a purely nomadic pastoral existence.
Among the various factors that enter into the acceleration of nomad
sedentarization, the scarcity of watered grazing lands and the higher
yield which can be realized from cultivation are especially important.
Some tribes have acquired large tracts of arable land which they have
put into cereal cultivation, employing migrant laborers from the villages and sometimes poorer tribesmen. The al-Huwaqah, for instance,
which is a subdivision of the Beni Sakhr tribe and ranges over about
30 percent of the land area of Jordan, has large landholdings, among
them a 25,000 acre tract of grainland which it works with migrant
labor and modern equipment.

Jordan's villagers make up the majority on both the East and
West Banks. Typically, the small Jordanian cultivator has limited
financial means; he is at the mercy of the village merchant or money-
lender for the means to produce his crop and for the sale of his
produce; and his position in the village depends today, as it has for

generations, upon the relative importance of the kin-group—extended family or lineage—to which he belongs. He is deeply attached to his land, arid and uneconomically small though it may be, for the ownership of land is identified with prestige and power. A few fortunate farmers may enjoy the security of an irrigated farm, but most are at the mercy of a scanty and unreliable rainfall. The rigors of the physical environment are matched by the hardships and dangers of a society not only threatened from without but also internally in explosive transition. Most often a Moslem, the villager faces these difficulties with a fortitude in part inspired by a sense of the inexorability of God's will.

Cultivated Areas

The amount of land under cultivation in Jordan has increased appreciably during the last thirty-five years. Improved domestic security under the British Mandate made it possible to shift the margin of cultivation eastward, and improved transport and the proximity of the rapidly expanding Palestinian market made it profitable to increase the output. During World War II high prices and shortages of goods and of shipping encouraged the further expansion of the crop area by about 10 percent. After 1948 the influx of some 470,000 Palestinian Arab refugees greatly increased the pressure on the country's resources and led to a 15 percent extension of cultivation (see Map, Agricultural Regions.)

According to the 1954 agricultural census, the total cultivated area in Jordan is a little less than two million acres. Under the prevailing system of crop rotation, however, only about two thirds of this is actually cropped in any one season, the remainder lying fallow. About 120,000 acres are irrigated. There are about one and a half acres of nonirrigated land and a tenth of an acre of irrigated land per person, including refugees. About five sixths of the nonirrigated cropped area and the bulk of the irrigated area are on the East Bank; most of the orchards are on the West Bank.

Except for the small amount of irrigated land, the greater part of agricultural production, approximately four fifths of the total value, results from dry farming. The soil varies greatly in quality, but much of it is good, particularly for the cultivation of vegetables and tree crops. The greatest physical limitation is the scarcity and irregularity of rainfall. It is estimated that about 16 inches of rainfall a year, relatively concentrated in the autumn and spring, is the minimum required to produce adequate yields of most Jordanian crops grown in winter and summer rotation; 8 inches of rainfall marks

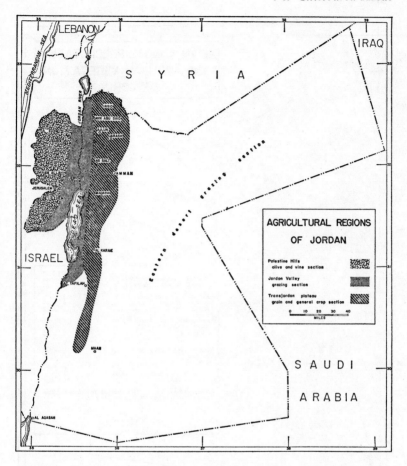

the limit of regular cultivation. The Palestine Hills and the northern Transjordan plateau receive the most abundant rainfall, and each produces approximately half of the major portion of the total agricultural production of the economy. With irrigation, the Jordan Valley where rainfall is low, could contribute much more substantially to Jordan's agricultural production than it now does. (See Map, Mean Annual Precipitation and Natural Vegetation.)

The high rate of evaporation, the irregularity and lack of concentration of rainfall, and a negligible dewfall reinforce the effects of scarcity of rain in Jordan. The combination of these factors greatly increases the chance of crop failures, and a delay or shortage of rainfall in spring or autumn can be disastrous.

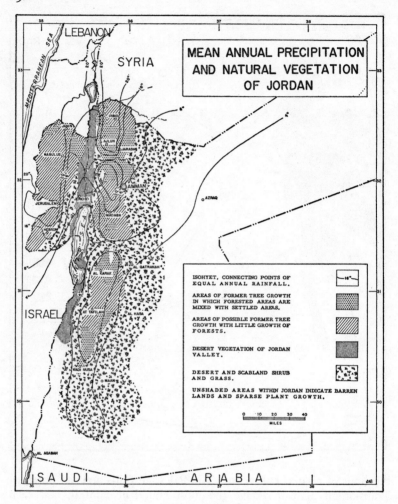

Land Ownership

Land is the most prized possession of the villager. He takes pride in his holdings and in his ability to work them. Ancestral land is especially prized and is the last to be relinquished if the farmer must sell.

The size of landholdings varies regionally. In the northern part of eastern Jordan small landholdings predominate. In the fertile district of Ajlun, for example, where annual rainfall is between 20 and 26 inches, the average holdings in 1938 ranged from 14 to 20 acres.

A decade later in the Jordan Valley, where rainfall is lower, the average holding was slightly more than 23 acres. Such averages are deceptive, however—in the Jordan Valley 22 percent of the holders own less than a half acre each, 50 percent own about 4 acres each, and fewer than 2 percent own over 250 acres each.

Land in Jordan is usually held in several parcels, which may be inconveniently distant from each other. It has been estimated that the average holding in the Jordan Valley is divided into 2 or 3 separate pieces of land, while estates of 100 acres or more may consist of as many as 14 pieces. Land settlement legislation may have encouraged some consolidation of holdings, particularly in Ajlun, but the laws governing the inheritance and sale of land contribute to further fragmentation.

Joint ownership of land, once more common than now, still predominates in some areas. It is estimated that out of 5,071 holdings in the Jordan Valley only 46 percent are in the hands of single owners, 54 percent being jointly owned. Although the title of a joint owner may be separately alienated or inherited, it does not appear that much village or tribal land has been transferred to urban creditors and buyers. Apparently village and nomad resistance to encroachment by town dwellers remains strong, while the role of the city money-lender in many rural areas is still comparatively unimportant.

Land Tenure and Credit

In Jordan land tenure is less of a problem for agricultural development than it is in neighboring states. The country was surveyed after 1928, boundaries were demarcated, and titles to the greater part of cultivated lands were settled. As a result, long-standing disputes were terminated, land tax was assessed equitably, and some consolidation of fragmented holdings was achieved. More important, land settlement meant the termination of the traditional mushaa system of communal holdings under which, varying with the particular custom of the village, the landowners redivided the land between them at fixed periods ranging from two to nine years. Under that system division was made in proportion to the number of shares held by each; each farmer tilled the plots he was allotted, knowing that at the end of his tenure he would have to cultivate a different tract of land following customary redistribution. One authority has observed "it is doubtful if a tenure more inimical [than mushaa] to good farming could have been devised by any community."

New problems, however, have arisen with the influx of refugees and the consequent increased demand for land. Tenancy (on which statistics are lacking) is another area of difficulty. Leases are short—usually not more than one year—and prevent the incentive to invest and improve. Where field crops are grown, if the tenant has borne all the expenses of cultivation he returns to the landowner 33 percent or more of the produce; if the landowner plows the land and provides half the seed the tenant returns 50 percent of the crop. Another problem is that the small landowner lacks adequate credit facilities for needed seasonal loans. Confronted with the seasonal need for seed, fertilizer, or implements, he is obliged to borrow from the village shopkeeper, the landlord, or the moneylender—in many cases one and the same person. In borrowing he is usually required to pledge either his land, his crops, or his movable property to receive an interest rate which may vary between 20 and 50 percent; without such security, interest may mount as high as 300 percent. Compelled to spend a large portion of his income in paying interest on such loans, the farmer has little left for amortizing them, much less for building up a reserve. In the spring of 1955, largely as a result of several years of low rainfall, total registered agricultural indebtedness reached JD 3,389,000.

Attempts have been made to improve credit facilities to the farmer through various organizations. The government has established an Agricultural Bank, which specializes in medium- and long-term loans. A Development Bank with a capital of JD 500,000 was founded in 1951 by the United Nations Relief and Works Agency, the Jordanian Government, and some private banks, to finance agricultural and industrial development. The government has also offered fruit trees at 50 percent of cost, with payment spread over three years, and direct loans to villagers near the Israeli frontier for terracing and tree planting. Attempts have been made to revive the credit cooperatives which existed in western Jordan and to found new ones in eastern Jordan; by 1955 there were 57 registered Rural Credit and Thrift Cooperatives with a membership of 2,684, about three quarters of which were in West Jordan. Some of these, aided by government loans, specialize in short-term credit for seasonal needs. The credit facilities developed so far are still inadequate, but it is expected that the cooperative societies will play an increasingly important role in meeting the pressing short-term credit needs of the small farmer on a local level.

Methods of Production

Jordanian farming methods are conditioned primarily by uneven water distribution, wide variation in the quality of the land, and the differing needs and capabilities of farmers. The farmer on the West Bank appears to be more enterprising and resourceful in utilizing his resources than his compatriot on the East Bank. Except for commercial wheat farming in the areas of adequate rainfall, and intensive vegetable and fruit farming in irrigated districts, Jordanian agriculture is characterized by the application of little capital and labor to the land.

The practice of rotation depends largely upon the presence of a regular and relatively adequate water supply. Where water and soil conditions are favorable, two crops may be grown: a winter crop (mainly wheat and barley) and a summer crop (such as maize, tomatoes, melons). With rainfall of less than sixteen inches, only a winter crop can be raised. In much of the cultivated area rainfall is so irregular that 50 percent of the land may be left fallow. A dry year may yield almost no production in even the most fertile wheat districts of Jordan, whereas a wet year may yield a production in excess of the requirements of the economy.

Grain is commercially produced in the neighborhood of Amman and around Irbid and Madaba, where on some of the larger tracts modern methods of production are employed—as in the case of the wheatland held by the al-Huwaqah subtribe. This project is directed by efficient managers and is equipped with modern agricultural machinery.

On inferior land, subsistence farmers use light plows drawn by oxen, mules, or donkeys; they harvest with sickles and thresh with primitive flails. Livestock raising is also of a subsistence nature. Animals receive insufficient nourishment and care, and little systematic effort is made to control their breeding.

There are many obstacles to the full utilization of the agricultural resources of Jordan. Methods of production are often inefficient; there is no mixed farming, and almost no forage crops are planted; animal husbandry is not integrated with crop production in that most of it does not occur among settled village cultivators. Mechanization is handicapped by the high cost of fuel, by lack of skills for operation and maintenance, and by the abundance of cheap labor, while inadequate transport facilities impose an excessive cost factor on the marketing of agricultural produce.

Attempts to intensify production include government distribution of improved seeds and selected livestock; some agricultural research is being carried out. A shift to more intensive crops for export is also being encouraged, and it has been suggested that nearly half of the area to be irrigated in the Jordan Valley should be devoted to such perennials as bananas, citrus fruits, grapes, and fodder, and that of the remainder, which would be planted to annual winter crops, one half should be double-cropped, bearing both spring and summer yields. Some 185,000 acres of open scrub or denuded forests are being reforested, and conservation measures are being taken on the 173,000 acres of state forests—steps made imperative by the high price of timber and the need to halt soil erosion.

Irrigation and Water Control

The conservation and utilization of a limited and unreliable water supply are of critical importance, and irrigation possibilities set upper limits on agricultural development. Those limits, however, have by no means been reached. According to what may be a conservative estimate, the perennial flow of Jordan's springs and streams is sufficient to increase the production of irrigated crops by one third.

Irrigation is making possible the development of highly specialized large-scale vegetable and fruit farming which, with the simultaneous growth of urban markets, promises to bring into existence a new middle-class farmer employing modern methods and producing cash crops for distant markets. Irrigated fruit and vegetable cultivation is highly intensive, involving a heavy application of capital and labor to the land to produce maximum yields. Water is brought through concrete and masonry conduits and flumes. Vegetables, planted in terraces, are double-cropped and intercropped. Bananas and citrus fruits are produced to be marketed throughout the year and receive intensive care under skilled management. The biggest of the irrigated orchards are near Jericho, where the Arab Development Society, a private philanthropic body, has succeeded in irrigating and cultivating 6,200 acres of salt desert land. The project includes an agricultural and crafts training center for Palestinian refugee orphans.

The Jordanian Government has been active both in planning and implementing irrigation and water-control schemes. Of the twelve small irrigation projects proposed by the government's Department of Irrigation, five, totaling 12,800 acres, have been carried out. The others have been abandoned, either because they could not be implemented successfully or because it was found advisable to consider them as integral parts of an over-all Jordan Valley development scheme.

Government plans have also been made for terracing some 150,-000 acres on mountain slopes in both eastern and western Jordan, at an average cost of $112 an acre. Since an acre of terraced land planted to olives or grapes has a gross annual return of about $67, the proposition seems well worth while. Other government schemes include American-assisted projects for the provision of increased grazing through proper water runoff control—an undertaking of major significance in view of the ever-present hazard of drought. By 1955, twenty million gallons of water for livestock had been provided in areas in which water had not previously been available.

Under Moslem law the major streams and springs are under private control. Water may be sold with or without land. This system creates problems relative to the availability of water where it is most needed.

Production and Consumption

Winter cereals have occupied by far the greater part of the cultivable area in Jordan—an annual average of 900,000 acres for 1952, 1953, 1954. Wheat, the major cereal, averages in value about one third of the total agricultural produce. Average annual wheat output, however, is insufficient to meet the annual consumption needs of the nation, which have been estimated to be approximately 190,000 metric tons. Owing to shortage of rainfall, unscientific methods, and the prevalence of pests and diseases, wheat yields have averaged only about 750 pounds per acre in good years and may fall as low as 350 pounds in a poor year such as 1953. (The yield figure for good years is less than half that of several western European countries.) Irrigation not uncommonly brings yields up to 1,000 pounds per acre. The national crop has varied from the low of 69,000 tons in 1951 to the 230,000 tons harvested in 1954. These extreme fluctuations in Jordan's wheat production present a major problem in stabilizing agricultural income, and they subject many farmers to loss, through the speculation which occurs in November and December while the outcome of the harvest is still in doubt. Barley is usually grown on poorer land than that planted to wheat; its yield approaches 800 pounds per acre in good years but falls below 400 pounds in years of drought.

Fruits and vegetables are rapidly increasing in importance. Between 1952 and 1953, for example, the production of fruits other than grapes doubled, and the area planted increased by over 40 percent; the area in vegetables increased from 75,000 acres to 98,000 with a slight decrease back to 94,000 acres in 1954. Jordan was essentially self-sufficient in most vegetables in 1951 and produced a surplus of sesame, grapes, bananas, beets, and olives. The value of fruit and vegetable exports increased steadily from $600,000 in 1951 to $2,800,000 in 1955; in the latter year these crops constituted Jordan's major agricultural exports in terms of value. The leading varieties are tomatoes, cucumbers, squash, artichokes, grapes, bananas, melons, figs, apricots, and almonds, most of which provide an export surplus. If packing, grading, and transport were improved, most of these could be sold to Europe out of season.

Another major agricultural surplus is olive oil, with an average annual output of 35,000 metric tons and an average annual surplus of 7,000 metric tons exported in most recent years. Under present processing the acid content of the oil remains too high to meet world standards but improved techniques could remedy this defect. It has been estimated that olive oil production could be raised by 25 percent.

Tobacco is a relatively major industrial crop. There are two varieties: *hishy* and Virginia. The former is grown by small individual operators for local consumption. Virginia is grown on large plantations owned and operated by the cigarette companies.

Animal husbandry is the main source of livelihood of the nomadic and seminomadic segments of the population. Decisions pertaining to the general utilization of grazing lands and watering places are made by the tribal sheikh and his council of elders, but the effective economic management unit is the extended family. This group, consisting of a number of closely related males and their families and usually headed by the eldest male, jointly owns its herds and flocks and moves about on the tribal range on an annual cycle. The actual wandering units, which may consist either of a few or of many extended families, vary considerably in size but are ultimately restricted by the harshness of a natural environment which narrowly limits the number of men and animals a particular piece of territory can support at any one time. During the dry summer months these groups, regardless of size, converge on the margin of the cultivated land, where there is water and forage. Whereas camel herds can survive for extended periods without water, sheep and goats have to be watered more frequently and their mobility and radius of movement is much more limited (see chap. 6).

It was estimated in 1955 that outside of the zone of rainfall adequate for farming about 250,000 sheep and over 50,000 camels were grazed by the nomads and seminomads. These figures (which do not include the larger part of the camels of the Rwala tribe, since its wandering range extends outside of Jordan) indicate a slight increase in the numbers of camels and sheep since 1952, when the reported count was 42,000 camels, 226,000 sheep, 358,000 goats, and 81,000 cattle. It is reported that since 1952 Jordan has become an importer rather than an exporter of sheep and goats because of the increased need for milk, milk products, and meat resulting from the trebling of the population after annexation of the West Bank.

Development Schemes

A number of large-scale irrigation schemes have been drawn up for Jordan. All of them, however, continue to be blocked by the tension between Jordan and Israel and the difficulty of reaching an agreement regarding the allocation of the waters of the Jordan River and the Yarmuk. Of the numerous plans formulated by the governments of Jordan and Israel and by various international organizations, the two most important are the Bunger Plan and the Main Plan.

The Bunger Plan was prepared in 1952 for the Jordanian Government by the United States Point Four program. It calls for a high dam on the Yarmuk River and canals fed by subsidiary dams. It would make possible the irrigation of approximately 109,000 acres in Jordan (as well as 6,000 in Syria) besides providing 28,500 kilowatts of hydroelectric power for use by Jordan and Syria. Total costs were estimated at around $60 million; the time required for completion was estimated from five to eight years.

The Main Plan was prepared in 1953 under the supervision of the United States Tennessee Valley Authority. Its principal features include storage dams, canals, and powerhouses on the Jordan's headwaters in Lebanon, Syria, and Israel; the use of Lake Tiberias for storage of Jordan and Yarmuk waters; irrigation canals on the eastern and western rims of the Jordan Valley; an irrigation canal above Lake Hula (for Israel); and a powerhouse at Al Adasiyah. This plan was studied by the Arab countries concerned and by Israel; each country made various counterproposals in its own favor and there the matter rests.

INDUSTRIAL DEVELOPMENT

INDUSTRY PLAYS AN INSIGNIFICANT ROLE IN JORDAN'S ECONOMY. In the past such industry as existed in the area developed along the Mediterranean coast of the Palestine Mandate, where a labor market and raw materials were available. Inland, within the boundaries of present-day Jordan, there were before 1948 practically no factories and even handicrafts were little developed. Since then a few modern enterprises have been established, largely by Arab refugees from Palestine, among whom were a number with industrial skills or a certain amount of liquid capital.

Some recent gains in industrial production have resulted from the increased output of existing industries and some modernization of technique. There has been government activity in the exploitation of minerals, and there appears to be a slight trend away from the processing of agricultural materials and toward development of consumer goods such as textiles. Despite these signs of progress, however, there are many obstacles confronting the expansion of industry. Available raw materials are limited, and there is already evidence of competition for resources. When local industry has looked abroad for raw materials, it has usually shown itself unable to compete either in price or quality with the imported finished commodity. Among the few exceptions are a number of textile and clothing manufacturing establishments which have been able to compete effectively with imported goods.

Jordan's domestic market is at present too limited to support the employment of modern techniques and heavy machinery. Social resistance to modernization is relatively insignificant, however, especially in the towns, where people no longer question the use of new methods and machinery and are responsive to efforts made to raise their standard of living. Nevertheless, there are large sectors of the population still untouched by new trends and ideas. In its simplest terms the problem is one of bridging distances made greater by poor transportation and of finding appropriate methods to raise the quantity and quality of small-scale production on which Jordan must rely.

Lack of capital has been another obstacle. The Palestine refugees brought large amounts of liquid capital, almost doubling the amount of currency in Jordan, but the boom thus generated has leveled off. The relatively few wealthy individuals prefer to invest in residential housing and merchandise, and the exorbitant interest rates charged on private loans inhibit long-term investment.

Other obstacles to industrialization are those common to most agricultural economies. There is a lack of skilled labor, of adequate transportation facilities, and of a developed market. The business community, traditionally composed of wealthy merchants, is very small, although recent increases in government loans indicate that the number of investors is growing. The government, itself an industrial leader, seeks to encourage the flow of private capital into new industries.

Composition

Notwithstanding the stimulus of a sharp increase in population and the expansion of the domestic market, industrial growth has been minor; of a total labor force estimated at 370,000, only 55,000 workers were engaged in "urban enterprises," a classification which includes commercial as well as industrial jobs. The 1954 industrial census of the Jordan Ministry of Economy listed 424 mining and manufacturing establishments employing 5 or more workers. These enterprises employed a total of only 7,461 persons (not including the figures for employees of shoemaking and leather tanning establishments, statistics for which are unavailable but which would probably raise the total not more than a few hundred), and their 1954 production was valued at JD 6,929,177 (the Jordanian dinar equals an English pound, or $2.80). Table 7 gives figures for the major industries, the number of workers employed in each, and their gross value output.

Industry is concentrated largely in the urban areas; 60 percent of the country's industrial establishments employing 44 percent of the industrial labor are on the West Bank. At Amman, which furnishes a ready and growing market and more advanced transport facilities, there are several large enterprises, many of them new, which contribute 52 percent of the gross industrial production of the country. The cities of Nablus, Jerusalem, Bethlehem, and Irbid are other centers of industrial activity. At Rusayfah, northeast of Amman, where

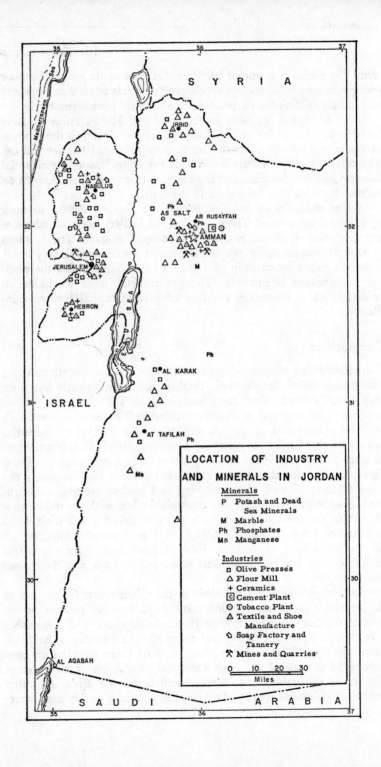

LOCATION OF INDUSTRY
AND MINERALS IN JORDAN

Minerals
P   Potash and Dead
    Sea Minerals
M   Marble
Ph Phosphates
Mn Manganese

Industries
▫   Olive Presses
△   Flour Mill
+   Ceramics
C   Cement Plant
O   Tobacco Plant
▲   Textile and Shoe
    Manufacture
⌂   Soap Factory and
    Tannery
✕   Mines and Quarries

0   10 20 30
     Miles

a large phosphate plant is in operation, is developing into a major industrial center. (See Map, Location of Industry and Minerals.)

The 1954 census excluded such establishments as olive presses, commercial and noncommercial quarries, and repair shops, as well as the thousands of subsistence cottage and handicraft industries. These small undertakings owned and operated largely by families, still constitute the bulk of Jordan's industrial establishments. Their techniques are often primitive, and the output is of poor quality. A large family shop employs as many as a half dozen assistants, usually related at least distantly to the employer. Carpet embroidery and lace handicrafts are common family endeavors, and particular skills are handed down from father to son. Even in mechanized industry the hiring of kin and friends is encouraged by the tiny supply of skilled labor: it is as easy to train a relative as it is a stranger.

Of the roughly 1,000 establishments employing four or more workers (excluding cottage industry), approximately half are engaged in the processing of agricultural products. Such industries as olive-pressing, soapmaking, leatherworking, grain milling, and vegetable processing are directed mainly to a small domestic market. The major mineral assets of the country—phosphates, building stone, and the mineral salts of the Dead Sea—are only partly exploited. There are no known oil or coal deposits in Jordan and the high cost of imported fuels represents one more factor in the low level of the country's industrial development.

Raw Materials and Power

Minerals

The paucity of metallic minerals and sources of fuel restricts the extent to which industry can expand. Jordan possesses very few mineral resources, most of them of a nonmetallic nature. Abundant high-grade phosphate deposits are found at Ar Rusayfah. The small company which had previously operated there was reorganized by the government in 1952 into the Jordan Phosphate Mines Company; since then production has increased sharply, more than doubling between 1953 and 1956. The government hopes to exploit other deposits at Hasa, possibly establishing a superphosphate fertilizer plant which would considerably widen the existing market.

Jordan owns two thirds of the Dead Sea, which contains great quantities of mineral salts. The British plant that carried on potash extracting operations during the Mandate was destroyed in the 1948 conflict, and its Jordanian concession was abolished in 1954. In 1956 an arrangement was made with other Middle Eastern countries (Syria,

Iraq, Saudi Arabia, Lebanon, and Egypt) and the Arab Bank to help finance the reopening of the works. Up to early 1957 no definite report on the plans had been announced, although the government stated that it would proceed on the basis of its own funds and public subscription.

The search for oil in Jordan has so far proved a failure. An American company has a concession to explore, with extensive extraction rights if adequate deposits are discovered (see chap. 16).

There are widespread deposits of building stone, including fine marble. Quarrying is most active in the vicinity of Amman because of the construction demand in that city. Many villages have their own quarries. All ingredients for cement production are present. Ceramic clays and silica sands are found in many areas. Iron ore deposits are not large enough to warrant large-scale mining operations, and it is at present technologically impossible to exploit the country's manganese deposits.

Agricultural Raw Materials

The agricultural base for Jordan's industry has consisted chiefly of olives, tobacco, grain, and fruits and vegetables (see chap. 14).

Many olive oil presses are found in the olive-growing areas of the country; because of the range of operations, from the small primitive shops to the larger plants, it is difficult to judge their contribution to the national economy. Although crude olive oil is exported for refining, its quality is not uniform and much of it is too poor to be sold other than locally. The government has participated in the construction of an olive oil refinery at Nablus; most of its output is expected to be consumed domestically.

The soap industry is one of the oldest and most primitively organized in Jordan. Its products are not attractive enough to compete with imports, although some of the larger establishments, located mainly in Nablus, are carrying out studies to improve their competitive position.

There are many small flour mills in eastern Jordan, reflecting grain production patterns. Six or seven of the large commercial mills are the only ones using motor-driven machinery. They have facilities for modern packaging and grain storage and can produce several grades of flour. Statistics gathered by the Ministry of Economy in 1954 indicate that flour milling is the largest contributor to gross output value, with 32 percent of the total. Although flour milling remains a profitable industry, the field is already overcrowded under present conditions. Since 1950 it has been necessary to import wheat to supplement the low domestic crop production.

Power

The lack of domestic fuel sources is one of the most serious handicaps faced by industrial enterprises in Jordan. With virtually no development of water power, the country has been dependent upon imports of coal and oil. The inadequate capacity of public utilities and the high cost of electricity have forced a number of factories to install their own generators.

The government is attempting to offset these difficulties through two projects. A petroleum refinery is planned in the Az Zarqa–As Sukhnah area, where an increasing demand for fuel is being felt. The crude oil will be obtained from the Trans-Arabian Pipeline Company (Tapline) in place of royalties owed to Jordan as a right-of-way rental. The operations of the plant should substantially benefit Jordanian consumers, whose requirements are expected to double over the next ten years. The second project is the power plant of the Jordan Central Electric Company begun in 1955 in the Az Zarqa–Ar Rusayfah area. Expected to be in operation at the end of 1957, the plant will also utilize oil from Tapline.

Generous estimates have been made of the power potential of the Jordan, Yarmuk, and Zarqa rivers and the larger wadis. A number of development schemes have been proposed and considered by the government, mainly in connection with irrigation plans. The feasibility of a project including both irrigation and power is handicapped by economic considerations and by present relations between Jordan, Israel, and Syria.

Manufacturing

Cement manufacturing contributed 11 percent of the gross industrial output value as estimated by the 1954 census. This relatively high percentage is remarkable in that Jordan's single cement plant began operations in 1954 (previously all cement was imported). Taking advantage of the domestic abundance of all the ingredients for cement, the government organized the Cement Factories Ltd. in 1951, and three years later prohibited imports of cement. The factory was built near Amman, where the greatest demand for cement exists and where there is an available labor force. Its high quality output is expanding rapidly and may be doubled over the next five years.

Cigarette and tobacco production is the third largest contributor to industrial output value, at 9 percent of the total. There are five factories operating in Jordan; one of them controls 70 percent of the market.

No silk and little cotton is produced domestically, and the textile industry is based on raw material imports. There are a number of successful textile and knitting enterprises and clothing manufactures, and the government is considering the construction of a large textile mill. Local wool is used by some small hand-weaving establishments but in general is of too poor a quality for large-scale manufacturing. The sheep raised by the bedouin tribes are used primarily for meat.

Organization and Ownership

Jordanian industry is highly decentralized and evidence indicates that this traditional pattern will prevail. The numerous small enterprises, however, are less important in terms of number of persons employed and total output than the fewer larger establishments: the 1954 census shows that about 60 firms employ half of the industrial labor force and produce more than half of the total gross value of goods.

Because of their dominant position in the industrial field, the large firms have secured near-monopolistic control over certain sectors of the market. Two tobacco and cigarette companies satisfy 95 percent of the national demand and a single cement factory fills all of Jordan's requirements; one phosphate plant controls all production and export. These big concerns, producing for a reliable market and in most cases protected by high tariffs, are able to make a generous margin of profit. Even the small firms enjoy relative security; each produces for an isolated, local market in which supply and demand can be kept in close relationship.

These apparently monopolistic conditions are somewhat misleading. The few large companies, foreign or domestic, have not been established long enough to wield significant political influence, although there is some correlation between industrial and political leadership (see chap. 16). Nor do there appear to be any arrangements among firms to decide prices, divide the market, and eliminate competition, although there is ample opportunity for such practices. The monopolistic feature of vertical integration or ownership of the various stages of production and supply by one company is also lacking. Credit and support for improvements in railroad and trucking facilities have been offered by the phosphate plant, but such examples are rare. Because industrial development has begun so recently, there has not been time for more than a few large firms to appear; limitations of resources, market, and capital, rather than restrictive business practices, appear to account for such monopoly as exists. Furthermore, official encouragement is being given to invest in those fields over which public-owned companies now exert monopolistic control.

Foreign capital has never been attracted to Transjordan or to Jordan as widely as to neighboring countries. Under the Mandate a number of British firms did come in and some of their establishments, destroyed or seriously damaged during the Arab-Israeli conflict in 1948, have been repaired and put back into operation under public ownership. In line with current development plans, the government is attempting to encourage foreign investment. A German firm has assumed a small part of the ownership of the country's sole cement plant.

Corporate ownership is a recent development, introduced chiefly through government efforts. Public sales of stock in new companies have received a favorable response, though undoubtedly many of the stock purchases are being made by the relatively small group of persons whose wealth and modern education open the door for them to such investment. Recently established industries—the olive oil and petroleum (proposed) refining plants, the proposed manganese mine, the phosphate and cement factories—had little difficulty in finding public support. The government participates in these enterprises through Jordan Industries Ltd., which owns from one third to nearly one half of the stock. Jordan Industries now has control over the market for its products, but the cement plant is the only case where an exclusive concession (for fifty years) has been granted for the extraction and production of cement. In other fields now dominated by these public monopolies the government is encouraging further private investment.

The shortage of capital in Jordan is reflected in the high cost of credit. Interest rates as high as 50 percent on long-term loans have not been unusual, although the legal maximum is low. The presence of some liquid capital in the hands of refugees and the liberal credit terms offered by the government in cooperation with UNRWA (United Nations Relief and Works Agency), Point Four (United States Operations Mission), and the Arab Bank Ltd. have no doubt tended to lessen the difficulties. Such imperatives of sound industrial practice as technical improvements, reinvestments, and modern personnel procedures must, however, compete with an indifference to technical efficiency and a tendency to distribute a maximum of profits and to employ relatives and friends—patterns still common in the Middle East.

Role of Government

Government policy as expressed in laws and regulations is aimed at planned industrial development. The Jordanian Government has outlined basic projects of its own and participates in industrial activity through part ownership of various enterprises. It further attempts to direct private domestic and foreign investments through legislation, import licensing, and credit facilities. Formal protective measures against imports have been a basic element of government policy since 1951.

The agencies that plan and supervise development are decentralized. Individual ministries implement their own programs and arrange plans with foreign aid organizations. The Ministry of Economy draws up its projects without necessarily consulting other groups, although its Economic Planning Division carries out studies and advises the whole government on request. The organ which most closely approximates an over-all supervisory and policy group is the Development Board, established in 1952. Legislation introduced in 1956 would strengthen the Board through changes in its membership and by granting it powers to approve all projects proposed by foreign and international groups.

In 1953 the British Government participated in drawing up a Five-Year Plan which was financed during its first year by British loans. Subsequently both expenditure and funds dropped far below the original estimates. The industrial plans now being carried out by the government include the installation of a potash plant, expansion of the phosphate industry, and improvements in transportation and port facilities. Additional projects in which the government hopes to participate include a sugar refinery, a brewery, and a textile mill.

There are various government loan projects: village loans and a Jerusalem City Loan program, both directed mainly to the West Bank and carried on by the Development Board; the Development Bank of Jordan set up in agreement with UNRWA in 1951 to extend long-term loans to industry and agriculture; the Economic Development Fund, which in 1954 began to grant industrial loans through the Arab Bank Ltd., backed by United States technical assistance funds; the Individual Grants Program, initiated in 1954 by UNRWA, through which grants up to JD 150 are made to refugees. A loan project for the development of small industries was being discussed with Point Four officials in 1957. The repayment conditions for all of these loans are very favorable, the interest rates for even long-term loans being as low as 4 to 6 percent. The loans and grants are made after a careful review of the applications and usually a study of market conditions. Many loans have been made covering every type of industry, and often there are more applications than can be handled by the funds available.

In 1955 two important laws were approved by the National Assembly for the purpose of directing and encouraging domestic and foreign investment. The first, the "Law for Encouragement and Guidance of Industry," listed a number of industries and fields for which special exemption from taxes and import and export duties would be granted. These included potash and other Dead Sea minerals, refining of natural oils, textiles, chemical fertilizers, sugar, canning, leather goods, and ceramics. The tourist industry is also listed for special exemptions; the country as a whole contains many sites of religious and historical significance, and great hopes are entertained for the successful redevelopment of this trade and its related industries. The second, the "Law for the Encouragement of Foreign Capital Investment," granted similar exemptions and also favorable rights of transfer and withdrawal of capital to projects approved by the government. Political instability and the undeveloped economic environment, however, may prove to be strong barriers to foreign investment.

An Industrial Education program is being implemented by the government, in cooperation with the Point Four program, through the Amman Trade School and through supplements to the curricula of several secondary schools. Both UNRWA and UNESCO have set up vocational training and handicraft schools in Jordan. Earlier, applicants often were youths unable to secure white-collar jobs; they entered vocational training as a somewhat despised second choice. Recently there have been many more applicants with a primary interest in electrical, mechanical, and construction work. The average Jordanian is eager and quick to learn; efforts made in technical and vocational training will undoubtedly yield good results.

DOMESTIC AND FOREIGN TRADE

DOMESTIC TRADE IN JORDAN IS JUST BEGINNING TO SHOW THE dichotomy which, to one degree or another, has characterized the internal commerce of the Middle Eastern countries since the entry into the area of western mercantile patterns. Egypt, Lebanon, Syria, and Turkey have been strongly influenced by western marketing, banking, and exchange practices for half a century; by contrast, the Jordan area had until recently preserved almost untouched a simple pastoral and marginal farming economy. Such changes as took place stemmed mainly from British initiative, and even today Jordanian marketing patterns are basically as they were in Ottoman times. Only in the rapidly growing capital city of Amman and those urban areas where Palestinian influence is strongest do the forms of domestic trade resemble those familiar in the West.

In the cities a money economy has taken shape, and the taste of the wealthier and better-educated Jordanians for western goods has resulted in the growth of a sizable import business. This trade, though limited by the availability of Jordanian products for export and by the small number of persons with enough buying power to absorb any considerable quantity of imports, is lively and expanding. The urban development has so far had only a limited effect on the countryside, although the villagers, through the sale of animal and agricultural products, are receiving some small quantities of imports from the towns. Generally speaking, village business is conducted in long-established market centers where various types of middlemen move the scanty village surpluses to the urban areas. The rural market centers remain relatively isolated from the towns and from each other, and turnover is limited to the sale and purchase of such essentials as foodstuffs which cannot be produced locally, household utensils (enamelware, hurricane lamps, etc.), and textiles. The bedouins, who once appeared in settled areas as raiders, now come to the town and village markets to trade for clothing, tent cloth, and other articles which they formerly produced themselves or took by force.

In foreign trade, Jordan's dependence is reflected in a chronic deficit in the balance of payments and in the balance of trade. The growth of the import trade, which far overshadows export activity, and the increase of the national product from 1952 to 1955 have depended for the most part on foreign aid. Basically, Jordan lacks sufficient resources to provide for an increase in the standard of living of the population, cover refugee requirements, or take care of the expenditures of the armed forces.

Nomad-Village Trade

Until the end of World War I the more powerful nomadic tribes had always exploited the settled cultivators who lived on the borderland of the desert and the sown area. This exploitation involved periodic raids on the more exposed villages or the exaction of crops and goods from them in return for "protection." In this way the nomads supplemented the resources of their herds and obtained items which they themselves did not produce.

The increasingly successful effort of the British and later the Jordanian authorities to protect the settled borderland against the inroads of the nomads has largely eliminated the old vassal-protector relationship. The nomads, once able to demand what they wanted from the villages by the right of power, have had to come to terms with the necessity of paying for their needs with the products of their own animal husbandry. New barter and commercial relationships have developed; the nomads exchange animals, milk and milk products, hides, skins, and a few handicraft products for foodstuffs and other consumer goods produced in the villages and towns.

The exchange of merchandise between the settled and the nomadic economy is carried out through two main channels: direct buying and selling in both the village market places and the town bazaars; and visits to the nomadic encampments by merchants.

Bargaining

Most consumer buying in Jordan, outside of that which takes place in a few of the major stores in the cities, is still mainly carried on through the medium of bargaining. Bargaining in the Middle East is a highly ritualized procedure sanctioned by long tradition. Though both parties are aware of a fair going price for an article or consignment, each endeavors to bring the deal to a close on terms which he considers to be in his favor. Following the opening moves of a bargaining encounter, margins between asking and offered price narrow as the deal develops, and, when agreement is reached after a series of proposals and counterproposals, dealer and client, even in large transactions, generally signalize their understanding with no more than a verbal commitment. To the western observer the amount of time spent on these bargaining discussions is out of all proportion to the margin of profit gained, but for the Middle Easterner bargaining not only is taken for granted as the "natural" way to do business but also brings more than purely economic satisfaction. A sharp and persistent bargainer gains in social prestige, while to refuse to bargain is apt to be taken as an insult or gratuitous breach of convention. Western patterns are undoubtedly making inroads, and a few European-type stores in the largest towns have introduced—apparently not altogether successfully—the fixed-price system. As marketing methods develop, however, the old ways will probably lose more ground.

Retail Trade

Retail trade in Jordan, on both urban and village levels, has the same general characteristics as elsewhere in the Middle East. Even today most of the stores in Amman are small, one-room establishments exhibiting a very high degree of specialization, and it is not unusual to find shops which sell, for instance, pickles and preserves only or cheese and milk, or even those which stock only enamelware. In Amman there are a few small department stores, but in other Jordanian towns the small specialty store is the only type.

The sook (traditional market) is the center of retail commerce in all towns of any size. In the sook there is no compromise with westernization; the narrow streets are crowded from dawn to dusk with throngs of people bargaining noisily with the proprietors of the small, open-front shops and canvas-covered stalls. In addition to those at Amman and Jerusalem, sizable markets are to be found at Maan, the railhead for southern Jordan, Az Zarqa, the chief military center, Ramallah and Nablus, both of which depend largely on a generalized trade in agricultural produce, and Al Mafraq, which was previously a pipeline station of the Iraq Petroleum Company and is now an emergency landing field of the British Overseas Airways Corporation.

In smaller towns such as Kerak there are no stores of the luxury type and a good proportion of the establishments may best be described as trading posts where local produce is bartered for staples. In the villages there are often at most only two shops, carrying a very limited range of goods; a coffeehouse and a gasoline station perhaps complete the "business center."

Marketing

Farm Products

An appreciable part of Jordan's farm output is still disposed of at fairs and local markets through a network of wholesalers, retailers, and other middlemen. The marketing structure, which differs in detail for various products, suffers from serious weaknesses. First, there is the multitude of middlemen between the producer and the consumer. A poverty-stricken small producer ignorant of any alternatives to existing arrangements, the average Jordanian farmer is at the mercy of middlemen, who understand and take advantage of market conditions as he cannot. The farmer's position is worsened by the undeveloped state of agricultural credit. The many farmers who are forced to borrow from middlemen commonly find themselves required to sell their produce only to or through their creditors at an agreed price, usually lower than market price.

Lack of proper storage facilities, especially for cereals, is another serious problem and results in much wastage and financial loss. The lack of rapid and regular transport services connecting the producing centers with the main markets limits the expansion of production and works a particular hardship on the many cultivators whose output is too small to enable them to hire, much less buy, a truck. Many wholesalers or commission agents are now sending trucks around the country to collect produce.

Jordanian commerce also suffers from the lack of proper standardization and grading practices. Good quality is generally mixed with bad, and little attempt is made to classify products according to variety and size. This makes buying by description almost impossible and tends to limit the market for and depress the prices of agricultural products. Consumers are apparently not educated to appreciate the advantages of graded commodities, and a good-quality grade does not command higher prices; middlemen seem to have a definite preference for present practices, which give them greater latitude in manipulating prices paid to farmers or received from consumers. Efforts are being made, however, to meet the demand of the export market for standardized and graded products.

Cereals, which make up the greater part of the country's crop, move to the domestic market in several ways. A common one is by barter with the peddlers who tour the countryside during harvest time, carrying a variety of goods needed by the farmers; the peddlers resell the cereals to wholesalers. The wholesalers, however, often deal directly with the farmers through agents who buy cereals on the threshing floor or at local fairs. Some wholesalers also acquire grain through commission merchants in the towns. Large landlords occasionally sell directly to flour mills.

Perishable vegetables and fruits are sold in towns through commission merchants who have offices in the terminal market and sell the produce they receive from the farmer on a commission basis. Less perishable vegetable products may also be disposed of in this manner, but more commonly, especially when the product is to be exported, the wholesalers send their representatives to the countryside to buy directly from farmers.

Livestock is sold at animal markets held on specific days or at the fairs; dairy products are usually bought from farmers by peddlers and resold to city shopkeepers. Recently there has been an increase of direct selling by farmers to large city distributors.

Industrial Products

Little exact information is available concerning the marketing of industrial products, but it is known that most domestic goods are sold through wholesalers and retailers to consumers. Imported items may pass through the same channels, or else be sold directly by importers to retailers. Except for handicraft products, no direct sales to consumers are made, and few sales are made by manufacturers to retailers. Manufacturers have not been able to enforce fixed prices on either wholesalers or retailers, among whom competition is intense and profit margin narrow.

Manufacturers and traders do little advertising. There is a tendency, due to the marked consumer preference for foreign goods, to adopt brand names which suggest that a domestic product is imported.

Transportation

Railroads and Ports

The only railroad in Jordan is the Jordan Royal Hashemite Railways, a section of the Hejaz line, running from Damascus in the north through Amman to Ras An Naqb, 15 miles to the southwest of Maan. A former spur line, which branched westward at Dara on the Syrian side of the border, giving access to the port of Haifa, has been closed since the Arab-Israeli war. Aqaba, Jordan's only port, has no railroad facilities, but a highway connects with the railway at Ras An Naqb. Service on the Hejaz is infrequent and slow; the locomotives are of the oil-burning steam type, and the loads they haul are usually light.

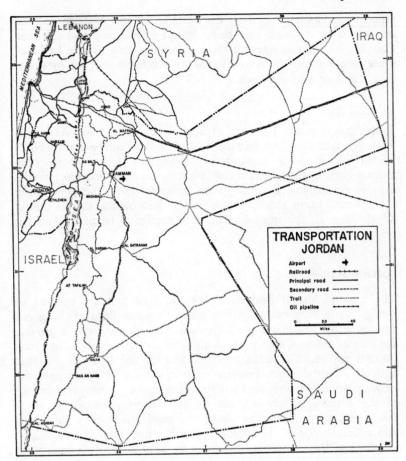

**TRANSPORTATION
JORDAN**

Airport
Railroad
Principal road
Secondary road
Trail
Oil pipeline

0   20   40
Miles

Highways

Jordan's main roads, constructed by the British, run northward from Amman to Damascus, westward to Jerusalem, southward through Kerak to Aqaba. Another road runs northeastward to Al Mafraq where it joins the Haifa-Baghdad highway. On the West Bank the road system is better developed, linking the centers of Ramallah, Nablus, Tulkarm, and Janin.

Jordan's so-called secondary roads are in very poor condition, and it is estimated that four out of every five villages in the country are inaccessible to motor traffic. On the main roads, however, bus transportation is developing very fast; the buses are always overcrowded and are loaded on top with everything from firewood to crated chickens. Carrying between villages off the highways is done usually by ox or mule cart; the most remote villages are accessible only by means of foot travel or pack animals.

Air Transport

Jordan has one passenger and freight air transport line (Arab Airways, Jerusalem), which uses the Amman airfield and operates services within Jordan and throughout the Middle East. Other international airlines have landing facilities at Amman. Local air transportation is slow in developing, but Air-Jordan operates charter services within the country, using mostly the air strips laid by the British during World War II. Air transportation is a negligible factor in domestic trade.

Foreign Trade

The most important business activity in Jordan is the conduct of foreign trade. It is estimated that more than one third of the goods consumed by Jordanians are imported. Agricultural exports provide the major source of foreign exchange for Jordan's imports, but food imports are equal in value to approximately one half the domestic agricultural production. Imports provide, outside of agriculture, the major portion of goods required for consumption or for maintenance of the economy. They account for the means of transport, most machinery, all petroleum products, and nearly all textiles, chemicals, and pharmaceuticals. The trade deficit has increased since 1952, as the demand for imports has increased far beyond Jordan's capacity to expand exports; the deficit was about $45 million in 1952, and had grown to $68.5 million by 1955.

The current foreign trade policy of the Jordanian Government is to relax somewhat the previously rigid import controls, and to encourage foreign investments within a well-defined framework.

The government in 1955 permitted the use of the free-money market, thus releasing previously concealed earnings and opening the way to trade with hard-currency areas. It also made official foreign exchange available upon the importer's request. Import controls (which in effect constitute import embargoes on industrial equipment), tariffs, and other protectionist measures continue to be applied particularly to imports the government regards as competitive. Import duties are not unduly high compared to those in neighboring states but, despite some liberalization, taxes and fees add considerably to the burden.

Import Trade

In 1955 the United Kingdom maintained its position as the leading supplier of Jordan, furnishing approximately 19 percent of the country's total imports; the United States ranked second with a little over 10 percent of the total (see Table 8). The United States and West Germany made the greatest gains in expanding their Jordanian trade: the United States went from third to second place in 1955; West Germany doubled its Jordanian imports between 1954 and 1955, largely as a result of the exceptionally easy credit terms and the competitive prices offered by German exporters.

Although the total imports of Jordan increased from 1953 to 1955, particularly between 1954 and 1955, the general nature of the goods imported did not change appreciably. Recently there has been a proportionately greater demand in the Jordanian market for transport and equipment goods and industrial and agricultural machinery and parts; this however has been more than offset by a reduction in the demand for foodstuffs, textiles, clothing, and building materials, owing to the accumulation of these goods in the internal market. Major increases in total trade in 1955 also widened the selection of goods available in the domestic market. (The classification "Other" in Table 8 has recently been used to include military goods not previously listed.)

The large increase in imports during 1955, $75.7 million as against $55 million in 1954, indicated both exceptional developments and new trends in the import pattern of Jordan. The exceptional elements were a substantial increase in wheat imports necessitated by the poor wheat harvest of 1955 and the arrival of large quantities of United States aid project equipment which had been ordered during 1954. The new trends in order of importance were the liberal import policies instituted in 1955, the addition of free-market reserves to trade transactions, the improvements in purchasing power due to development programs, progress in over-all commercial activity, and the opening of credit facilities on better terms both within Jordan and from foreign exporters.

Export Trade

Jordan's exports in 1955 were, in order of importance, vegetables and fruits ($2.8 million), phosphate rock ($1.7 million), and olive oil ($1 million)—see Table 9. These are also, for the present at least, the products with the greatest export potential.

Among agriculture exports in 1955, vegetables accounted for nearly one fourth of the total. Vegetable production in Jordan has increased steadily, reaching a total value of $1.7 million in 1955 (compared with $1.14 million in 1953), but serious handicaps to the expansion of fresh vegetable exports exist in the inadequate transportation system and poor marketing facilities. The greatest possibilities for expanding Jordanian agricultural exports in the long run rest in the cultivation of olive trees and other rain-fed fruit trees. The full potential of Jordan's fruit production will take at least ten years to realize, since it depends largely on extensive terracing and long-term research.

In the immediate future the export of Jordan's high-quality phosphate may provide one of the major sources of foreign exchange. In 1955 it was anticipated that by 1956 phosphate production for export would reach $2.8 million. It was reported that the production of phosphates could be raised from 164,000 metric tons in 1955 to one million metric tons in 1960.

Balance of Payments

The deficit in Jordan's balance of payments, excluding foreign grants, ranged for the period 1950–54 from a low point of JD 10.41 million in 1950 to a high of JD 13.76 million in 1953. Imported goods account for a little over three fourths of Jordan's international payments. On the credit side of Jordan's balance of payments, besides gifts and capital items, the most important items in 1954 were services ($13.8 million)—of which tourism ($6.08 million) and payments from foreign oil companies ($4.03 million) were the major components—and exports of merchandise ($8.5 million). There was a marked improvement in the foreign exchange earning capacity of Jordan between 1950 and 1954. Export earnings increased by one third, earnings for services almost doubled, and, within the latter category, payments from oil companies quadrupled and payments for tourism more than doubled. Aid from foreign governments in 1954 totaled $34.9 million, and private gifts and donations reached $4.6 million—an amount about equal to half of Jordan's total export income.

The most important transfers of foreign exchange for meeting Jordan's deficit in 1954 and in previous years were allocations from the United Kingdom in support of various arrangements for aid to Jordan. UNRWA grants have gradually increased in importance, the high point of $15.40 million being reached in 1954, which was almost equal to United Kingdom grants for the same period.

Trade Agreements

Jordan's recent trade relationships have moved toward closer inter-Arab cooperation. Preferential treatment with respect to customs duties on specified commodities was granted in recent agreements concluded in 1953 with all the Arab League powers, and the list of goods receiving preferential treatment was extended in 1956. A separate agreement with Iraq in 1953 extended the most-favored-nation treatment and provided that most agricultural goods from either country would be exempt from import duties and import licenses. Prior to federation closest economic cooperation had been achieved with Lebanon and Syria, agreements with both of which provide free transit in the territory of the other party, exemption from duties for agricultural and livestock products, and customs-free entry for many industrial products.

Trade talks outside of the inter-Arab community in 1956 led to an agreement providing for Yugoslavia to import Jordanian olive oil, tobacco, phosphates, and other goods.

Two major oil pipelines run through Jordan—the Trans-Arabian Pipeline Company line (Tapline) originating in the Arabian-American Oil Company (Aramco) field operating in Saudi Arabia and ending at Sidon in Lebanon, and the Iraq Petroleum Company (IPC) line from Kirkuk, Iraq, to Haifa in Israel. Only the first line is in operation, but both provide a source of revenue to the Jordanian Government; Tapline payments reach an average of $840,000 per year and the IPC agreement requires a minimum payment of $168,000 per year. The Tapline agreement permits Jordan to purchase 200,000 tons of crude oil for domestic purposes at a preferential rate.

Foreign Capital

The entry of foreign capital is discouraged by political uncertainty, the scarcity of raw materials, and the small size of the Jordanian market. The outstanding instance of foreign capital participation is the Arab Potash Company. In June 1956 five Arab nations—Syria, Iraq, Saudi Arabia, Lebanon, and Egypt—agreed to subscribe individually to founders' shares in this company, the remaining shares to be offered through public subscription in the Arab countries. By the end of 1956, Jordan had received Iraq's contribution of JD 125,000 and Syria's of JD 62,500.

Foreign investments in other industries appear to have been minor. In the Jordan cement industry, for example, a German company, which supplied most of the machinery, owns only 5 percent of the total shares, valued at 5 percent of the total capital invested. Foreign oil companies have indicated an interest in investing capital in a petroleum refinery but most of the shares of this proposed enterprise (costing JD 4.9 million) have already been subscribed by the public and the government.

Following the termination of the Iraq Petroleum Company agreement for petroleum prospecting, a concession agreement was signed in October 1955 between the Jordanian Government and E. W. Pauley Association of California. The agreement, running for fifty-five years, concedes substantial exploration rights, requires drilling operations within twenty-four months, and provides for a fifty-fifty sharing of profits plus recovery of Pauley's original investment.

To encourage foreign investment, laws have been passed providing for exemptions on taxes and import dues and guaranteeing profit transfers and capital withdrawals. The opportunities available to foreign investors, however, are strictly circumscribed by regulations on importing industrial equipment and by other government policies aiming at a planned economy.

PUBLIC HEALTH AND WELFARE

JORDAN'S ECONOMIC PROBLEMS ARE REFLECTED IN THE GENERAL living standard of its population. Standards of living in turn reflect a considerable disparity between the Palestinian segment of the population and the East Bank residents. Relatively better educated, to a greater degree urbanized, and more prosperous, West Bank Jordanians enjoy living conditions which are generally superior to those of their compatriots to the east. Many welfare problems are, however, shared by both groups, and the situation of the refugees has severely strained the meager food resources and welfare facilities of the country as a whole.

Overcrowding is a major problem. Steady internal migration to the towns in recent years, coupled with the tendency for those skilled refugees who have been absorbed into Jordan's economy to concentrate in urban areas, has given rise to sharp urban population increases: Amman, for instance, grew from a town of 30,000 to a city of nearly 200,000 in only five years. Such spurts have resulted in an acute housing shortage throughout Jordan. In 1952 nearly a third of the people were housed in tents or other nonpermanent structures; over three quarters of the total reported dwelling units had only one or two rooms, only about 9 percent had running water, and slightly less than 4 percent had electricity.

The high level of unemployment and the low income of the population at large (see chap. 12) combine to keep many Jordanians at a bare subsistence standard. The refugees, who receive rations from UNRWA (United Nations Relief and Works Agency for Palestine Refugees), are actually better off than many of the original inhabitants.

Other welfare problems revolve around the almost total lack of effective legislation regulating conditions of work. Apart from certain specified limits to hours of work for women and children, the only labor legislation in Jordan concerns the formation of unions, termination of employment, and accident compensation. Agricultural workers, who form the bulk of the labor force, are not covered by such provisions. Child labor is common, not only under parental supervision in the fields or in traditional crafts but increasingly in factories.

Conditions of health and sanitation also clearly reveal a disparity between the West and the East Bank segments of the population. While the over-all state of public health is far from satisfactory by western standards, the health of the former Palestinians is considerably better than that of East Jordanians.

The incorporation of the Palestinian Arabs into Jordan has resulted in considerable overcrowding in the towns, with attendant consequences to public health, but the medical facilities gained through the annexation of Palestinian territory provided a valuable supplement to East Jordan's meager medical resources. UNRWA has furnished additional medical facilities, and the nutritional level of present Palestine refugees is higher than that of many of the original inhabitants of Jordan.

Traditional Institutions

Welfare activities in Jordan, as in other Middle Eastern countries, traditionally have been carried on by the family, through the deeply felt mutual obligations of its members, and by Islamic and other religious institutions of charity. Historically, little has been expected from the government in terms of social welfare. Modern conditions, however, have created new welfare problems and given rise to unprecedented demands for remedies on a broad scale. Although most of the efforts aimed at relief and improvement of health and social conditions are still conducted under religious and private auspices, an incipient national public welfare program is underway.

Public welfare in the Islamic tradition is based on the principle of mutual responsibility of all members of the community. While recognizing inequalities of talent and prosperity among men, Islamic theory imposed a moral obligation on the wealthy to assist the less fortunate members of the community. One of the Five Pillars of Islam is almsgiving, regarded not as charity but as a religious duty (see chap. 5). In time it came to be institutionalized in the form of *zakat*, collected as a government tax, the proceeds of which were used for charitable purposes and the building of mosques. The exact amount of the imposition varied, but generally it averaged 2.5 percent of an individual's annual earnings. Additional voluntary offerings brought prestige to the donor, who was thought to acquire special merit in the eyes of God.

In Jordan the *zakat*, as a government imposition, no longer exists, but its underlying principle continues to be reflected in voluntary contributions to charity and in the government's social welfare tax. Collected from the same sources as the old *zakat,* this tax revenue is derived from levies on sheep, goats, camels, and cows, a land tax, and a tax on the value of imported goods. Funds from the tax are distributed to needy families, travelers, and students and are also allocated for the upkeep of mosques and for salaries of imams (prayer leaders) and teachers in religious schools. No information is available on the method of distribution.

A major role in traditional Middle Eastern charity was also played by the institution of wakfs, or bequests. Under this system a man could establish a family trust for his heirs or a religious endowment for charitable purposes. The property (usually real estate) made into a wakf could not be sold or otherwise alienated; it had to be held in perpetuity with only its yield used by its beneficiaries. In some Moslem countries the institution is gradually dying out, but in Jordan, although increasingly centralized under government control, it has been left relatively intact. Since only a small proportion of the population benefits from them, however, wakfs cannot provide an adequate substitute for modern public welfare programs and may eventually become obsolete.

Supplementing, but at times conflicting with, religious charities, is the traditional role of the family in taking responsibility for the welfare and social security of its members. Firmly established in the Arab world before the advent of Islam, the sense of family solidarity and mutual obligation is stronger than the interest in community welfare. Thus bequests in the form of wakfs were frequently made with the stipulation that the income could not be used for charitable purposes until after the donor's line had become extinct.

Government Health and Welfare Efforts

The Constitution of 1952 contains elaborate provisions for public welfare that amount, in effect, to a proclamation of a welfare state. Among the various provisions enumerated are the state's obligation to protect labor, to provide for minimum wages and maximum hours, and to establish unemployment insurance and other types of social insurance. In addition, health conditions in industry were to be regulated and trade unions were to be allowed freedom of action "within the legal limits." To date, however, these stipulations have proved more of a statement of principle than a realistic blueprint for government action. The labor legislation and social insurance program have so far not been enacted. Because of limited financial resources, as well as reliance on traditional welfare agencies, the government administers directly only a handful of institutions—several reformatories, orphanages, and homes for the blind, beggars, and illegitimate children. The Ministry of Social Affairs encourages and to some extent subsidizes the work of various voluntary organizations on which it relies for the major part of the country's welfare program. With the gradual emancipation of women in Jordan, women's societies have been increasingly active in social work, but their efforts are restricted largely to the towns. In many rural areas, particularly in East Jordan, traditional forms of charity and family aid are still the only sources of assistance, the prevalence of beggars attesting to the inadequacy of welfare services.

The introduction of modern medical techniques into Jordan dates only from the last few decades. Neither medical facilities nor personnel are adequate to meet the country's growing needs, and preventive medicine is still in its infancy. The shortage of trained medical personnel is aggravated by the tendency for Jordan's urban-oriented doctors and nurses to concentrate in the towns. Westernized by education, they share the townsman's distaste for village life. The availability of hospital care is almost entirely restricted to the larger towns, Amman and Jerusalem in particular, and some remote rural areas in East Jordan have access to virtually no medical facilities. With the aid of the Point Four administration and UNRWA, the government has managed to establish an incipient national public health organization. It has begun an extensive malarial control program and campaigns against tuberculosis and other major health menaces. So far, however, most of these efforts have benefited the Palestine refugees rather than the population as a whole, and East Jordan lags far behind the West Bank in standards and availability of medical treatment.

The impact of the recently absorbed Palestinian Arabs on the country as a whole has confronted the Jordan Government with the necessity of furnishing many social services which the original Jordanians had never known. The situation has been aggravated by the tendency of the refugees to spread discontent. Popular demands for improved living conditions and readiness to request and accept help from local, national, and international welfare agencies are much more widespread in West Jordan than on the East Bank, but both segments of the population are becoming more vocal in pressing for modern social legislation. From rural areas, too, increasing numbers of delegations to the government are demanding schools, clinics, health centers, and welfare services.

Nutrition and Diet

Jordan has a serious problem of inadequate food resources; inadequate transportation facilities, particularly in East Jordan, aggravate the situation, and near-famine conditions sometimes exist in isolated areas.

On the whole, the Jordanian diet is lacking in vitamins and by western standards is deficient in proteins, particularly animal proteins. The relatively high percentage of calories derived from the consumption of cereals is explained not only by actual shortages of meat but by traditional eating habits and attitudes. The presence of herds, for example, does not necessarily indicate frequent consumption of meat, for the possession of cattle brings prestige to the owner. Similarly, vitamin deficiency often stems from the peasants' distaste for growing vegetables as major crops. Except for onions, few vegetables are grown. There is, of course, considerable variation in the nutritional levels and dietary habits of nomads, peasants, and townspeople, and between those of the rich and the poor.

Camel's milk, drunk either fresh or sour, supplies the main nourishment of the nomad population. During the winter months, when camping in the interior of the desert, the bedouins live on milk and dried dates supplemented by boiled cereal (wheat, rice, or white sorghum), wild plants, and on occasion roasted locusts. Meat is a rare luxury. Supplies are replenished in the summer, when the tribes are near settled areas and can sell their surplus animals and buy foodstuffs. Coffee drinking and smoking the narghile (traditional water pipe) help to offset the monotony of the bedouin diet.

The basic diet of the settled rural Jordanian consists of bread and fermented milk supplemented by fruit in season, olives, and cheese made from the milk of sheep and goats. Onions and lentils are almost the only vegetables eaten, and meat, regarded as a great delicacy, is too scarce to be consumed regularly. Goat meat is generally preferred to mutton.

The townsman's diet is far more varied and of greater nutritive value. It includes vegetables, fruit, and beef and various other meat. The well-known Middle Eastern dishes—such as stuffed grape leaves, *kibbah* (a kind of meat ball made of ground meat, cracked wheat, and seasoning), *hummus* (a paste made of chick-peas and sesame oil) —are all available to the town dweller but seldom eaten by the peasant.

Sanitation

Sanitation in the western sense is almost nonexistent in the villages and large parts of the towns. The majority of the people, especially on the East Bank, accustomed to living in the midst of dirt and refuse, are ignorant of the elementary principles of personal hygiene and have no understanding of the connection between disease and the prevalence of flies or the contamination of water.

A typical rural dwelling consists of one or two rooms which are often shared with the livestock at night. Many village houses are without sanitary installations of any kind; housetops, yards, and irrigation canals serve as latrines. Garbage is disposed of simply by tossing it into the streets or fields.

Such sewage and sanitary facilities as exist in the towns are for the most part antiquated and unsatisfactory by modern health standards. Piped water supplies are found only in the larger towns, and only recently in Amman, the capital, has water been purified. In the countryside water may be transported considerable distances by human carriers, donkeys, or camels and is often polluted in the process.

Sources of food contamination are innumerable. Food is not protected from flies or handling, and inspection of conditions in markets takes place only irregularly and only in the larger towns. Amman has a pasteurization plant for milk, but no such facilities exist in rural areas.

Incidence of Disease

Weakened by malnutrition and living in unsanitary and crowded conditions, a large part of Jordan's population is susceptible to a number of preventable diseases. Statistics on disease, generally inaccurate in most Middle Eastern countries, are especially unreliable in Jordan. Even in the principal towns the reporting of illness and death is incomplete and diagnosis frequently faulty. The presence of various diseases may go unnoticed by health authorities unless severe epidemics occur.

Ailments arising from general lack of sanitation are most prevalent. It has been estimated that 90 percent of the population is infected with different types of intestinal parasites. The beef tapeworm is common throughout the country; the pork tapeworm is a problem in Christian communities, although many indigenous Christians share the Moslem aversion to pork. Transmitted by contaminated food and water, typhoid fever is endemic.

The incidence of tuberculosis has increased in recent years, especially among the bedouins and the refugees. Veneral diseases are most prevalent in the urban population, but bejel, a disease resembling syphilis, is common among nomadic and seminomadic tribes of the East Bank. An estimated 40 to 70 percent of the population is affected by trachoma; generally more widespread in East Jordan, its incidence among children in elementary schools ranges from 10 to

58 percent. Malaria, prevalent in the Jordan Valley, is less common farther west.

Infant mortality is high, particularly on the East Bank. In recent years there seems to have been some improvement in the situation, but estimates indicate that whatever decline there may be in infant mortality is taking place more slowly in East Jordan than in formerly Palestinian territory. Within East Jordan the rates have been consistently higher in villages than in towns, ranging in certain districts to nearly 300 per 1,000. Here, as in many other parts of the Middle East, a large proportion of deaths occur during the first five years of life. Infant mortality is particularly high among the bedouins, who take no precautions whatsoever in maternity and among whom women frequently deliver their own children unaided.

Attitudes Toward Medical Treatment

The disparity between levels of sanitation and health conditions in West and East Jordan not only reflects the early difference in administration of the Palestine and Transjordan mandates and the subsequent concentration of UNRWA projects on the West Bank, but also highlights the contrast between the two areas in economic circumstances, education, and popular attitudes. For the most part conservatively Moslem in their orientation, rural and nomadic Jordanians on the East Bank tend to cling to traditional notions about sickness and its treatment. Ignorance and superstition remain serious obstacles to the introduction of modern medical techniques. The relation between sanitation and health is hazed over. Jordanians, like other Middle Easterners, have traditionally regarded illness as a manifestation of God's will, and hence a natural misfortune to be borne with resignation. Sickness is also seen as the work of evil spirits, and in this case the usual method of treatment consists of ceremonies performed by a religious or other practitioner who has power to exorcise or control the spirits. There is still widespread objection among Moslems to women being examined and treated by male physicians. Such attitudes are an important factor hampering the effectiveness of Jordan's extremely limited medical facilities.

In recent years, however, Jordanian attitudes have been changing under the impact of the Palestinians and of modern techniques. Resistance to innovation is encountered less often than formerly and is more easily overcome. News of the beneficial effects of sanitation or preventive medicine travels by word of mouth, and it has been found that once a health center or a clinic, for instance, is established in a village and its advantages become manifest neighboring villagers come clamoring for similar services.

FAMILY

THE FAMILY IN JORDAN, AS IN OTHER ARAB COUNTRIES, NOT only provides its members with support and social orientation in childhood but remains throughout their lives the primary agency for economic cooperation, social control, and mutual protection. The first loyalty of the individual is to his family—on whose wealth, welfare, and reputation his own depend. Prescriptions relating to family obligations, marriage, and the defense of family honor are binding, and there is a strong tradition of kin solidarity which antedates the advent of Islam. Relatives may quarrel but in the face of any outside threat the family displays a fundamental cohesiveness.

Deep family loyalty manifests itself in business and public life no less than in those domestic matters which in the West are regarded as the appropriate area of family concern. The mutually protective attitude of relatives is taken as a matter of course, and kinsmen are to render to each other special favors and services. Taken for granted, the widespread practice of securing employment and favored treatment for relatives—and the friends of relatives—bears no stigma of nepotism.

Western influence and the general process of modern technological and social change are affecting the family as well as other aspects of Jordanian life, especially in the cities. New forms of economic activity are modifying the old self-sufficiency of the family, and a nascent Jordanian nationalism may, given time, transcend the once exclusive loyalty to kin and local group. Among the villagers and nomads, however, the family essentially has preserved its traditional character.

Structure and Dynamics

The basic principle determining membership in the Jordanian family is kinship reckoned in the male line. The typical household of an extended family in the traditional pattern consists of a man and his wife and their unmarried children, along with married sons and their wives and children. It may also include the father's widowed sister or daughter, his parents, a paternal orphaned niece or nephew, or a paternal cousin. His married brothers and their wives may also live in the same house or nearby and cooperate in economic activity. The essential bond is blood relationship to the father. In the event of a quarrel between the families of the father and mother, a son is expected to stand by his father against his mother's father or brothers.

Upon marriage, a girl leaves her own extended family and becomes a member of her husband's. She is supposed to relinquish loyalty to her own father and brothers and to identify herself completely with the extended family of her husband; in practice she often retains ties and contacts with her own blood relatives.

The Arabic terms for uncle and aunt differentiate paternal and maternal relatives, keeping the two lines distinct. The father's brother is called *amm;* his sister, *ammah.* The mother's brother is *khal;* her sister, *khalah.* Similarly, different terms are applied to cousins on the mother's and the father's side.

The various branches of the large family live under the same roof or in adjoining houses or, in the case of nomads, in a number of tents pitched close together. Statistics are not available for nomads or for villagers, but the average urban household ranges in size from 5.5 to 6.5 persons—considerably larger than households of western Europe or America. Native Christian households tend to be smaller than those of Moslems—owing in part to a lower birth rate among Christians.

The economic role of the extended family is no longer as great as it once was, and in the towns, under the impact of western influences and new economic activities, there is a growing tendency for married sons to set up separate residences. Despite the loss of some of the functions of the extended family, however, the mutual ties and obligations of its members remain to a large degree intact.

Beyond the single extended family, kinship ties reach into the group of related extended families, the lineage, which traces descent through the male line back to a common ancestor. In small villages everyone is likely to trace his descent from the same male ancestor, but in larger villages there may be two or more lineages. Rivalry between lineages is common, but tempered by economic cooperation and intermarriage. The fullest extension of this principle of kinship organization is seen among the nomads, who are organized in a complex series of units increasing in size from the family through the sublineage and lineage to the tribe.

Individuals have certain obligations to other members of their lineage, the most important of which is assistance against outsiders. Primarily important among the nomads, these larger kin-groups are fading out in the settled population of the villages and towns. They tend to be evident mainly on public and formal occasions and in important matters of family discipline or mutual defense.

Authority

For Moslem families the code covering personal and group conduct is laid down in the Koran or sanctioned by religious tradition. Jordanian Christians have their own codes of behavior. But in both communities the family is the paramount social unit; in both, family authority is vested in the father.

Paternal authority is particularly emphasized among Moslems. Ideally, the senior male as husband and father is master of the household and exercises absolute control over wife and children. The personality factor is of course important here; a strong-willed wife can, and generally does, dominate a weaker husband. Moreover, the wife in her later role of mother-in-law exerts considerable authority and influence over her sons' wives and children.

Ultimate authority in the extended family generally rests with the oldest male, but personality, ability, or wealth may bring about the selection of a younger man. Matters of family policy, honor, and relations with other families are determined by the head of the family in consultation with other ranking male kin. On the level of the lineage, the authority of the senior member dwindles to a more or less compelling advisory power.

Respect for masculine authority and seniority is carefully ingrained in children, much attention being paid to the formal deference owed to the father. Sons of rural families, even after marriage, are expected to obey their fathers strictly. A son may accompany his father to work in the fields or to deliberations of the village council, but he must remain in the background and listen quietly to his elders. Only when he himself becomes a father does he begin to gain any prestige or authority; even then he is expected to consult his father and respect his decisions.

In keeping with the respect and awe the family ideally accords him, the father rarely becomes intimate with the children; in their presence he maintains a formal demeanor with his wife. Affection between father and children exists, but the tendency is to suppress its expression.

Children

Koranic injunction, economic motivation, and considerations of prestige and family strength all contribute to the traditional high value placed on large families. The greater the number of children, especially sons, the greater the prestige of the father and, through him, that of the family as a whole. Children are regarded as economic assets by most Jordanians; the cost of their maintenance is small, and they begin to contribute to the family income at an early age. The subordinate and sometimes servile position of the daughter-in-law in the household of her husband's family provides an additional motive for having many offspring, for the young wife, unless she is from a more important family than her husband, gains prestige and position only with the birth of children. A childless woman—often said to be cursed by God—is afforded a commiseration mixed with contempt. Failure to bear children may frequently result in divorce or in the husband's taking a second wife.

Strong emphasis is placed on teaching a child to conform to the patterns laid down by his elders and to be an obedient member of the family group. Family solidarity is stressed and the child learns early that his wishes are subordinate to the interests of the family. Corporal punishment is frequently employed except when children are very young.

Children know much greater intimacy with their mothers than with their fathers, and maternal influence, although less formally sanctioned, is very great. Responsibility for the training of boys gradually shifts to the father, who starts preparing them for the economic tasks of adulthood at an early age. At the age of four or five a girl has already been given some simple household duties and has begun to help her mother tend younger children. From this time on the mother prepares her for her eventual role in her husband's household, explaining to her that she will serve not only her husband but also her mother-in-law.

Marriage, Divorce, Inheritance

Marriages in Jordan, as in other parts of the Moslem world, customarily have been arranged by the parents of the young people. The parental decision was considered binding, and except among the more westernized of the townspeople this is still the case. Marriages contracted within the large extended family are preferred, and those between first cousins are considered ideal. Among the nomads and villagers, marriage with a paternal uncle's daughter came to be regarded as a man's right and a father was not allowed to give his daughter to anyone else without the consent of the girl's cousin.

Such marriages within the family are favored for a number of reasons. A girl married to her cousin remains in the same extended family as her parents and thus conflicts of loyalty are less likely to arise; both sets of parents are satisfied that the match is socially suitable, since the young couple are of the same descent; the bride's father acquires the support of a son-in-law who is also his nephew; and a girl's inheritance from her father remains in the family, since her husband is also her cousin.

Recent investigations indicate that, although a man's right to marry his first cousin is no longer insisted upon, the preference for such marriages persists in the countryside.

A girl from the same village ranks next to a close relative as a desirable marriage partner. Marriages between lineages are also favored because they strengthen village solidarity and help either to prevent or settle differences between families. Marriages to women from other villages, however, are not uncommon; in such cases the wife's efforts to acquire daughters-in-law from among her own relatives is apt to be a source of friction in her husband's family.

Statistics on the average age of men and women at marriage are not available. In the countryside early marriages are still the rule, but increased educational opportunities and western influences in the towns are bringing about later marriages there.

Polygamy, permitted in Islam to the extent of four wives, is regulated by strict rules of tradition and Koranic prescriptions that surround the institution with difficulties. Polygamy is also expensive, and it has been estimated that only one out of ten Jordanians has two wives and that very few have three or four. The King and the leading families of Jordan have set an example of monogamy which undoubtedly has an effect on the society as a whole.

Marriage Ceremonies

Among the Moslem majority, marriage is concluded as a civil contract between the families of the bride and groom. In the villages and in conservative urban circles two ceremonies precede marriage: the *khutbah* (engagement) and the *katb al-kitab* (signing of the marriage contract). For the *khutbah* a few relatives and friends are invited to the prospective bride's house, where the parents of the couple announce the forthcoming marriage. The ceremony of *katb al-kitab*, held sometime later, is attended by an official of a sharia court as well as a large gathering of friends. Written into the contract is the amount of dowry to be paid by the bridegroom. A portion of the dowry is payable only in the event of divorce. The father of the bride customarily spends all or most of the dowry for clothes, jewelry, or land for his daughter. The actual marriage, which may take place immedi-

ately or up to a year or more after the signing of the contract, is accompanied by feasting and dancing.

Among the nomadic tribes the wedding ceremony is likely to be
a simpler affair, the principal formality being the escorting of the
bride into the groom's tent.

The marriage practices of the native Christian minority are governed, of course, by Christian prescriptions; but Christians share in
the underlying view that marriage is not merely the private affair of
the bride and groom but a major concern of the families involved.
Prohibited by Islam, marriages between Moslem women and Christians
are extremely rare in Jordan.

Divorce

Under Moslem law a husband can divorce his wife at will by pro-
nouncing the traditional formula "I divorce you" in the presence of
two witnesses. The wife does not have the right either to oppose the
divorce or to initiate it. Dissatisfaction with the law has been increasing in recent years, particularly in the towns where western influences
are strongest.

A divorced woman usually returns to her father's or brother's
household and can claim that portion of the dowry reserved for divorce. If a wife leaves her husband on her own initiative and he subsequently agrees to divorce her, she forfeits this part of the dowry.
After a divorce a man may remarry at once, but a woman must wait
for three months to make sure that she is not pregnant. Should she
be, she may not remarry until she has borne and weaned the child;
during this time her former husband must support her and the baby.
Under Moslem law the children of divorced parents are in the custody
of the father, but they generally remain with the mother until the
age of seven in the case of boys and nine in the case of girls.

Inheritance

Inheritance of property is regulated in Jordan, as in other Middle
Eastern countries, by the laws of the religious community to which
the family belongs. Inheritance for Moslems is governed by a Koranic
prescription which stipulates that when a man dies his estate first pays
his debts, then certain shares of the estate go to his wife and other
members of his family besides his children, and finally the remainder
is divided among his sons (each of whom gets a full share) and his
daughters (each of whom gets a half share). Among the nomads
certain pre-Islamic customary rules of inheritance persist: bedouin
women, for example, are excluded from inheritance, and a man may
dispose of his property as he chooses, whereas Moslem law allows
him to dispose of only one third of his property in this manner.

FORMAL EDUCATION

UNTIL THE ADVENT OF WESTERN INFLUENCE, EDUCATION IN THE Middle East was almost entirely in the Islamic tradition with its emphasis on classical and religious learning. The curriculum of elementary schools was based on memorization of the Koran, with secondary emphasis placed on reading and writing. Such higher education as existed was concerned largely with Islamic theology and mastery of classical Arabic. The Christian minorities and foreign missionaries maintained their own counterparts of the Koranic schools, with a comparable emphasis on religious training. Today the traditional village school, the *kuttab,* has almost disappeared, but the original pattern of rote learning persists in secular education and frequently conflicts with teaching and experimental methods borrowed from the West. Similarly, the traditional value placed on facility of verbal expression has left a deep imprint upon present-day education. Eloquence and the ability to quote from the Koran or to marshal proverbs in argument are still the marks of an educated man.

It was not until the reforms at mid-nineteenth century that a secular system of public education was established throughout the Ottoman Empire. In what is now eastern Jordan, however, which was then administered as a subordinate part of the province of Syria, the Turks maintained only a handful of elementary schools for boys in the larger towns, and formal schooling for girls was nonexistent.

With the establishment of the Emirate of Transjordan in 1921 and the British Mandate in 1922, a small public school system began to develop under British influence. Far more extensive and westernized, however, was the educational system—both public and private—set up under the direct British administration of Palestine. This difference in educational opportunities is reflected today in a conspicuous disparity between the educational level of the former Palestinians and that of East Bank Jordanians. It has also affected the attitudes of the two groups toward one another. The East Bank residents resent the fact that Palestinians, because of their superior qualifications, have been able to assume coveted positions in government, business, and the professions; the Palestinians regard the East Bankers with disdain as backward and ignorant people.

There is also a disparity between the educational level of Moslem Jordanians and that of Christian Jordanians, especially pronounced for the women of the two groups. A survey in Palestine, for instance, revealed that more than 95 percent of a sample of Moslem Arab women were illiterate as compared with 55 percent among Christian Arab women. (The over-all literacy figure for Jordan is estimated to be in the neighborhood of 20 percent, but the figure is undoubtedly higher among the more urbanized Palestinians.) This reflects in part the tradition among Palestinian Christians of sending girls as well as boys to European and American mission schools (see Table 10); also, Christian Jordanians are largely urban dwellers, with access to more and better educational facilities. The Christians tend to look down upon their less literate and generally poorer Moslem neighbors.

The Present Educational System

Schools are maintained in Jordan by the government, private groups, foreign missions, and UNRWA. The administration of public schools is highly centralized under the Ministry of Education, which controls appointment and dismissal of teachers, conduct of state examination, and setting of curricula as well as inspection of schools. The Ministry also licenses private schools and has supervisory responsibility for them.

Jordanian law provides for compulsory education for seven years, but the law is not enforced. The demand for education has greatly exceeded the availability of educational facilities, and the large refugee population after the Arab-Israeli war put an added strain on the school system. Funds at the disposal of the Ministry of Education have never been adequate to provide for universal education.

Government primary schools in the villages offer four years of the seven year elementary course. The program of studies for the elementary course comprises Arabic, religious instruction, English (introduced in the fifth year), arithmetic, Arab history, civics and geography of the Arab world, hygiene, nature study, and physical training; Arab studies are increasingly emphasized. The curriculum of the Palestinian schools has been altered to conform to this program in the interests of inculcating a uniform loyalty to the new state; the government is attempting to unify the school systems of the West and East Banks.

Beyond the elementary level is a two-year intermediate course which offers further instruction in Arabic, English, and religion, mathematics, social and natural sciences, as well as vocational and physical training. Full secondary schooling leading to a state education certificate requires still another two years.

The disparity between the numbers of boys and girls enrolled (see Table 11), characteristic of Moslem countries, is decreasing steadily in Jordan under the impact of western influence. Even conservative Jordanians are now demanding education for their daughters as well as their sons. Coeducation is common in rural primary schools, since facilities are usually too limited to permit separation of boys and girls; in the towns, unless necessitated by physical circumstances, it is not sanctioned by public opinion.

In primary schools a nominal tuition fee is charged those who can afford it; free places amounting to half the enrollment are reserved for poorer pupils. Secondary school fees are JD 2, but exemptions are granted to 30 percent of the students.

Private schools, for the most part sponsored by religious organizations, follow the government curricula and examinations fairly closely. They are required to teach Arabic and the history and geography of the Arab world. The relative distribution of students in public and private schools is shown in Table 10.

There are also a number of schools administered by UNRWA for Arab refugees. In 1956 it was estimated that 94,000 refugee children were receiving free education in UNRWA schools. Without this United Nations assistance the government of Jordan would have been totally unable to carry the tremendous educational burden entailed by the refugees. UNRWA's educational program has steadily expanded and includes elementary and secondary schooling, vocational training, granting of university scholarships to exceptional students, and basic education for illiterate adults.

There are no facilities for higher education in Jordan. Traditionally, sons of the wealthy have been sent to universities in neighboring countries or overseas. Recognizing the need for higher education on a broader scale the government now offers a number of scholarships for study abroad. Other grants are available through UNESCO, the British Council, and United States Government exchange programs. Increasing numbers of Jordanians are going to the United States for study.

Educational Problems

The primary educational problem faced by the Jordan Government is the need for over-all expansion of the school system. At present educational facilities are available to only about 40 percent of girls and

60 percent of boys of school age, and schooling among the nomad population is still in its infancy. Frequent requests for more schools indicate that the people of Jordan are eager to accept as much education as the government is able to provide.

Apart from financial limitations, a major impediment to expansion of the educational system is the lack of teachers and teacher-training facilities. Although the teaching profession enjoys considerable prestige, it is poorly paid. Moreover, a teaching post in rural areas offers little incentive to the typical urban-oriented government teacher, who tends to look down on village life. The quality of teaching is in general poor because the majority of teachers have never had professional training. In recent years, however, Jordan has received financial and technical assistance from the United Nations and the United States in dealing with this problem; several institutes for the training of teachers have been established.

There is also a serious lack of vocational training. A school of arts and crafts and an agricultural school provide the only technical vocational instruction other than that given in regular secondary school courses. For this type of education to be greatly expanded, however, basic attitudes toward the goals of education must change. Despite the country's pressing economic need for technical skills, education in the eyes of most Jordanians is still primarily a path to urban life and to white-collar positions, especially in government. Like other Middle Easterners, Jordanians tend to look upon manual work with disdain and aversion. The government, conscious of this problem, is trying to give education a more practical orientation.

ART AND INTELLECTUAL EXPRESSION

GIVEN JORDAN'S RECENT EMERGENCE AS A DISTINCT NATIONAL entity, it is not surprising that its traditions of artistic and intellectual activity are less its own than those general in the Moslem Arab world. Distinctively Jordanian styles in the arts or approaches to the concerns of the intellect have barely had time to evolve. Their absence is, or until very recently has been, a matter of indifference to the anything but nationally conscious Jordanians. The country has no art galleries, no art schools, no budget allottment for the purchase of art works.

In the Arab world generally the most elaborate and highly valued forms of artistic expression have been those of literature—especially poetry—while philosophy and theology have been the principal concern of the intellectuals. The traditional Islamic injunction against the portrayal of human and animal figures has channeled the visual arts into architecture, abstract decorative design, and handicrafts. Painting and sculpture have made their appearance only recently, with the penetration of western influence and the weakening of the proscriptive force of religion. The artistic rendering of living creatures has been done mainly by Christians or as a result of influence from Persia through Syria.

In Jordan, as elsewhere, works of the imagination and the intellect, have always been interests of the town rather than the countryside. Excellence in craftsmanship became possible with the concentration of wealth in the cities, and the development of written literature has been dependent on education. The demand of wealthy urbanites has stimulated the recent emergence of painting and sculpture.

Another recent aspect of urbanization has been the emergence of a number of women poets, prose writers, and artists. Jordan has no organized feminist movement such as those which have developed in Egypt and Lebanon, but a few women, especially among the more westernized Palestinians, have been successful in achieving recognition in these traditionally masculine fields. This is particularly notable in literature, less so in the visual arts. It can be expected that the number of women in the arts will increase.

The gulf which separates the town from the country has been widened by the adoption of western tastes by the wealthier urban groups, although this gap in turn becomes less marked as the influence of urban life spreads out to the villages. The extension of urban influence may add wholly new media of expression and appreciation—such as radio broadcasting; on the other hand it has undoubtedly discouraged old crafts through the introduction of imported and mass-produced articles.

Poetry

Popular speech in the Arab world is heavily embroidered with vivid imagery and proverbial usage. A complex rhetorical style denotes the effective speaker, and even a commonplace conversational exchange is apt to be marked by loudness and apparent emotional reinforcement which, to the western ear, would be appropriate only to impassioned argument. Used in this way, ordinary language takes on some of the qualities of the formal poetry which Arabs at all social levels so greatly admire: in the hierarchy of the arts the poet occupies highest place.

The late King Abdullah was himself a poet of considerable standing. The former Jordanian Ambassador to the United States Abdul Moneim ar-Rifai composed the Jordanian national anthem. Classical poetry is still taught and committed to memory in schools throughout the Arab world. High praise is heaped on the student who can compose poetry, and the accomplishment is widely cultivated. A number of schools have revived in one form or another an institution similar to the pre-Islamic Sook Ukaz, a fair held in Mecca at which poets from all parts of Arabia assembled to compete for prizes.

The subject matter of traditional Arabic folk verse and song is the individual—his loves and hates, deeds of valor and cowardice, and experience of beauty and ugliness. A major theme is the description of a beloved woman, her beauty and virtues. Usually sung, folk poetry is an almost inevitable accompaniment of weddings, harvests, and other festivals. Another form, the ballad, often provides an evening's entertainment; the hearers are transported back in time to David and Solomon and to the early Arab warriors. An oral literature in colloquial Arabic, folk poetry is transmitted from generation to generation. Ignored and somewhat disparaged by educated urban dwellers in recent years, it is again being cultivated in the towns and a movement is gathering force to revitalize it and put it into written Arabic.

Jordan has not yet produced a writer of formal poetry of major stature, although a number of Jordanian poets have some following. The best known is the late Mustafa Wahbah at-Tell. He served the government in various capacities, among them that of private secretary to King Abdullah, by whom he was admired and patronized. Anecdotes about him and the sovereign have passed into folklore. After his death, his poems, which included many bedouin and gypsy love songs rendered into classical Arabic, were published in a collection entitled *The Nights of Wadi al-Yabis*.

Mustafa Zayd al-Kaylani is the oldest of the living poets. His work has been collected under the title *Spirits and Songs*. Fadwa Tuqan, author of *Alone with the Days,* is a young woman of Palestinian origin whose imaginative and lucid verse is becoming known beyond the confines of Jordan. Other poets include Khalid Nasra, Mohammed Said al-Jundi, Thurayya Malhas, a graduate student at the American University of Beirut and lecturer on Arabic literature at the Beirut College for Women, and Kamal Nasir, a young revolutionary poet of Palestinian origin, now in political exile.

Before World War II Jordanian poetry concerned itself very little with political, social, or economic subjects. Mustafa at-Tell often criticized King Abdullah, but the point of view was personal rather than political and the blame was often followed by praise. Unlike the Syrians, Lebanese, and Palestinians, the Jordanians in the three decades after World War I enjoyed relative peace and security. The British, although the political masters, remained in the background, and the Jordanians were on the whole left free of the direct or onerous government pressures which might have bred a literature of discontent. After World War II, however, political and social issues became the most usual subjects of poetry. Nationalism and an awareness of national political and social problems were stimulated by extensive contacts with foreigners, by education, and by increased information about political developments in the Arab states and in the world at large. The Arab-Israeli war was a profound psychological shock to the whole Arab world and brought in its wake not only intense anti-Israeli feeling but a readiness to blame all those, whether Arab or foreign, who might be regarded as in any way responsible for the debacle. Jordan received the largest number of Palestinian refugees. More politically and socially conscious than the rural population of the East Bank, they tended to enrich and develop Jordan's intellectual, political, and social life; they also spread discontent. In this atmosphere Jordanian poetry is increasingly political, exploiting satire, invective, and patriotic sentiment in a manner familiar elsewhere in the Arab world.

Prose

Local developments in prose—the novel, biography, and works in the humanities and sciences—date almost exclusively from World War II and are predominantly political in character. For contemporary reading matter the Jordanian townsman also has looked to Egypt and, to a lesser extent, to Syria, Lebanon, and Iraq. Books from these countries—in Arabic, in other languages, or translated into Arabic—make up most of the stock of the bookshops in Amman and Jerusalem. The literate minority is predominantly interested in works on political, social, and economic topics—such as the internal problems of the Arab world, relations with the West and with the countries of the Soviet bloc, and the Palestinian question. There is considerable demand, too, for publications dealing with Arabic and world literature, and young students may be heard discussing the relative merits of such figures as Shakespeare, Voltaire, or Tolstoy with the excited interest of discovery. Third in popularity are translations of contemporary European and American novels.

A personal contribution to Jordanian literature was made by the late King Abdullah in the form of his memoirs, which have been translated into English. Of the few professional writers, Asma Tubi ranks high; she has contributed to magazines in Egypt, Syria, and Lebanon, and has often been heard on the radio. Amin Malhas, a writer of short stories, reflects the reaction of the young generation to events in Palestine. Ruks Uzayzi, a self-educated teacher at a Christian school in Amman, wrote a biography of Father Anistas al-Karmili and collected and transcribed bedouin folk stories. Isa Nauri, a short story writer and literary critic, has written mostly about Palestine. He founded a weekly magazine, *al-Qalam al-Jadid* (The New Pen), but it has now ceased publication. Arif al-Arif, historian, folklorist, and literateur, is widely known and highly respected.

Music

Both classical and folk music are constructed on a seventeen-note scale different from the western scale (though originally the notes corresponded roughly to the tones of the western chromatic scale). Extremely complex rhythms are characteristic. In the Arab tradition such music appears as background for lyrics, the content and poetic style of which occupy the center of attention. In recent years a number of Jordanian composers have sought to adapt the Middle Eastern mode to new popular forms. Classical western music has an extremely small audience in Jordan, almost exclusively concentrated in the two largest cities of Amman and Jerusalem. Popular music consists chiefly of Arab ballads.

Peculiar to Jordan is the folk music known as *hajin,* sung by the nomads to the rhythm of the camel's gait; during long treks across the desert, the camel driver sings and improvises verses to a monotonous and melancholy chant. Another style, called *chrouqi,* which probably was brought in from Lebanon, serves as an accompaniment to folk dances. Among the extensive bedouin repertoire of songs there seems to be one for every routine activity of daily life and the average man or woman knows and sings a large collection of them.

The *taqsim,* which came from Turkey, is an improvisation on various instruments. Originally concerts were opened with a *taqsim,* which was supposed to express the state of mind of the performer. Today, the name is used for any such improvisation. At rural celebrations of holidays each member of the village orchestra plays a *taqsim* and any vernacular poet present sings an improvised poem called *ar-raddah,* after which the best musician and poet are chosen.

Instrumental music is forbidden in the mosques but services begin with the chanting of set passages from the Koran and songs may be sung dealing with the life of the Prophet. The music of other religious rites represented in Jordan is of varied origin—Byzantine, Syriac, Latin, and Arab.

The most frequently played musical instrument in Jordan is the *qasabah,* a short reed flute. The *rababah,* a very old instrument used by the bedouins, is a one-stringed violin with narrow body and straight neck, fitted with two keys. The *buzuq* (bezok) is a long-necked mandolin with two strings bound with five bands of sinew; it is used by vagabond entertainers. The *ud* is a large pear-shaped lute with a short neck. Its five double strings are plucked with the quill of an eagle's feather. The *qanun,* or harp, is a trapezoidal box somewhat resembling a grand piano in miniature; its 78 strings are played with both index fingers to which are fastened metal plectra. The *daff* or *riqq* is a circular tambourine; the *darabukka* is a long clay drum with a skin drumhead.

Jordan has no important schools giving instruction in either occidental or oriental music.

Theater and Dance

The contemporary theater, a borrowed western form in the Arab world, has developed slowly in predominantly rural Jordan. It has been further handicapped by the preference of the small number of potential theatergoers—largely western-educated—for works in the English language. Very few translations or adaptations of foreign plays have been made by Jordanians; even fewer plays have been written by them. Such plays as are produced are generally chosen from the repertoire of the Egyptian theater, often adapted to the Jordanian Arabic vernacular; sometimes partly sung, they resemble operettas more than dramas. Until recently, at least, no regular theatrical company existed in Jordan. A few amateur groups perform in the larger towns, mainly Amman and Ramallah. No formal theatrical tradition exists in the countryside; however, enlisted men of the Arab Legion sometimes entertained themselves with spontaneous skits mimicking the characteristics of the officers—a possible indication of similar village pastimes based on the countryman's penchant for mimicry.

Recently there have been signs of a growing interest in the theater. The broadcasts of the government-owned radio stations in Ramallah and Amman are creating an audience for short, semi-musical sketches. The West Bank population is contributing to the evolution of popular tastes, and it is this group which is stimulating the production of political sketches and plays with such titles as *The Tragedy of Palestine*. There are no well-known Jordanian actresses; women's parts are played by men or by actresses imported from Egypt or Lebanon.

Dancing remains for the most part a folk activity. Most of the traditional dances are of foreign origin, such as the *dabkah* from Lebanon, the Coffee Dance from Iraq, and the Sword Dance from Damascus. Any acquaintance with western styles of the modern dance and the ballet is limited to an educated urban minority.

Handicrafts

There is a centuries-old tradition of handicrafts in the area, and such skills as tapestry weaving and the making of pottery and glass still occupy numerous craftsmen in the villages and towns. The bedouins have a less highly developed handicraft tradition than the settled population, but notable among bedouin skills is the leather work and weaving done by the women. Rug and textile designs are passed from mother to daughter, and particular patterns have become identified with the tribes which have produced them for generations.

Handicrafts in Jordan are much the same as those of neighboring Arab countries, except for the distinctive shellwork and peasant embroidery produced increasingly for the tourist trade in Ramallah and Bethlehem. Silk and wool are embroidered in varied colors and motifs. Decorative forms are combined in intricate meshwork, with a high quality of workmanship. A large number of women and girls make silk tablecloths, curtains, lace, scarves, and altar coverings decorated with religious motifs or with leaves and flowers. Frequent exhibitions are held of embroidery work in girls' schools and clubs in Amman; some of this output is sold on the local market, some exported. Brocades for ecclesiastical vestments are executed in silk and velour, with delicately and gracefully contrived religious inscriptions and stylized figures of saints in gold thread.

Wood inlay is used in the decoration of private homes and of pulpits and Koranic inscriptions in the mosques. Animal and vegetable forms are executed in wood inlay on knives, daggers, expensive boxes, and wardrobes—a craft apparently brought from Persia via Syria.

The pottery produced includes terra cotta pitchers, jars, flowerpots, and vases in traditional shapes; most of it is used for domestic purposes. Metalware vases and trays, highly polished or engraved in arabesque patterns of leaves, are used in interior decor. Glasswork is a Phoenician craft brought to Jordan centuries ago. Syrian influence is seen in the candelabras and lamps made of enamel glass for mosques. Oval glass jars decorated with flower motifs in a variety of colors, are produced in quantity for daily use.

Richly colored tapestry has been woven for centuries on single-wheel looms. Common motifs are hunting scenes and arabesque ornament derived from Syrian handicraft. The tapestry made today by mass production methods has poor colors, but there is a superior type woven of goat and camel hair in black and white, sometimes with ocher tones added.

Painting and Sculpture

There has been little development in Jordan of painting and sculpture, and the Ministry of Education does nothing to encourage these artists. Painting and sculpture—for the most part by foreigners—are displayed in the reading rooms and club rooms of American, English, and Jordanian institutions. Jordanians, particularly of the upper classes, are not only acquiring a taste for such works but are buying them to decorate their homes. Foreign artists are being commissioned to do decorative paintings and bas-reliefs for the public rooms of city hotels, night clubs, and the better restaurants. A few Jordanians also have received such commissions—among them several women.

Motion Pictures

Jordanians have made no films of their own. Motion pictures have attracted increasingly large audiences in Jordan in recent years: in 1950 the annual attendance figure was about 1 million; in 1956 it was 2 million. By 1950 about 700 films were being shown annually, of which 45 percent came from the United States, 30 percent from Egypt, 15 percent from the United Kingdom, and 10 percent from France, Italy, and India. At that time there were 24 motion picture theaters (of which 6 were open-air and operated only during the summer) with a seating capacity of approximately 12,000.

Exhibitors order films from Cairo or Beirut, where the Arabic subtitling is done. All films must receive the approval of a censorship board appointed by the prime minister; the under-secretary of state is chairman, and the two other members represent the Ministry of the Interior and the police. The board sometimes asks the advice of various Moslem organizations when there is a question as to whether a film might give offense to the religious feelings of the public.

VALUES AND PATTERNS OF LIVING

IMPORTANT DIFFERENCES IN OUTLOOK AND WAY OF LIFE DIS-
tinguish the nomads from the villagers of Jordan, and the largely
tradition-bound rural population as a whole from the more westernized town dwellers. The peasants and the desert bedouin might almost
be said to live in another—and earlier—time than the educated urban
elite. The world of the peasant revolves around the land he works,
his family, and his village. Although the nomad is accustomed to considerable freedom of movement, his interests are similarly restricted
to family, clan, and tribe and to the unremitting struggle for subsistence in the desert environment.

A further disparity exists between the degree of westernization of
the East Bank population and that of the former Palestinians which
is reflected in differences in their beliefs and social patterns. By and
large better educated, more prosperous, more urbanized, and less conservative in their outlook, the Palestinians of the newly annexed West
Bank have given impetus to the forces making for change in the
country as a whole. In particular, the growth of the urban centers,
which had been going on at a steady pace as more and more rural
Jordanians migrated to the towns, was spectacularly increased by the
Palestinian influx. Thus the disruption of traditional values and ways
of life, always a consequence of urbanization, has been accelerated. In
the face of western influences—both direct and emanating from the
West Bank—traditional values remain relatively intact among the nomads and to a lesser extent among the villagers of eastern Jordan.

Although the customs and beliefs of nomads, villagers, and townsmen differ in important respects, the trend toward the sedentarization
of the bedouins, coupled with an accelerating flow of the settled rural
population to the towns, has brought about considerable interaction
among the three groups. In this process the dominant forces are those
of town and village, but Jordanian life as a whole continues to be

colored by the nomadic values injected into it through the absorption of tribal elements by the villages. Similarly, village beliefs and attitudes are carried into the growing cities, and western patterns radiate from the towns back to the surrounding countryside.

Traditional Values

Man and the Universe

Except for the Christian minority, Jordanians—nomads, villagers, and urban dwellers alike—share a common heritage of Islamic values. The Koran and the Hadith, together with their interpretation by religious leaders, form a comprehensive guide for life which has given coherence to the mosaic of local, family, and tribal exclusiveness. Survivals of pre-Islamic practices among the nomads and villagers have undergone a process of unconscious reinterpretation and have come to be regarded as native to the Islamic tradition. Islam presents man as inherently good, but weak and subject to the temptations of Satan. A major function of Islamic society was to protect its members from their frailty, teaching and disciplining them to submit themselves to the will of God.

In traditional Islamic society, social life was so minutely regulated by religious precepts that social values were largely indistinguishable from religious values. Moreover, in the settled population strict observance of religious obligations early became a means for the attainment of social prestige. Similarly, the nomadic virtues of generosity and courage acquired sanction in the Koran and value in the eyes of the people as a whole.

An important consequence of the traditional Islamic regulation of virtually all aspects of life has been the tendency for Jordanians, like other Moslems, to adjust to and accept life rather than to attempt to manipulate it or experiment with it. The commonly quoted Koranic phrases "it is written" and "it was willed by Allah" symbolize attitudes toward the value of human endeavor which Arabs have held for centuries. Man exercised no ultimate control over events in a world in which all things were ordained by God. Success was the manifestation of God's benevolence; failure was simply God's withholding of benevolence. Among the peasants this outlook has been reinforced by generations of subservience, to landlords and persons in political authority, which conditioned them to a degree of submission not found among the bedouins.

Religion and religious observances loom large in village life, and rural recreation focuses on religious feasts or ceremonies occasioned by circumcisions, weddings, or funerals. Traditionally, recreation patterns in the towns—until recently in Jordan hardly more than large villages—were similarly oriented.

Among the nomads specific Koranic prescriptions and rituals occupy a much less important place. Sedulous in affirming their faith, they pay scant attention to the other four of the Five Pillars of Islam (see chap. 5). Many nomadic social values, however, such as that assigned to hospitality, closely parallel virtues enjoined upon all Moslems by the Koran.

Man and Society

The primary role of the family in Jordan in the lives of its members, not only in childhood but throughout life, puts it at the center of some of the most deeply felt values and loyalties. The type of occupation to which a man may aspire, his standing in the community, and his range of choice in selecting a wife are all determined by the relative wealth, power, and prestige of the family. The individual in dealing with other groups finds his only firm security in loyalty to his family, and this attachment is a factor in the many blood feuds that mark Jordanian tribal and village life. Family honor must be safeguarded, even at the risk of life. Strong family loyalties also enable the Jordanian, like other Middle Easterners, to adhere to separate standards of conduct and morality in dealing with relatives and outsiders. Within the family certain norms of obedience and industry are required; outside the family different standards of behavior and honesty may prevail.

Among the nomads mutual obligations and loyalty extend to larger kin-groups and the tribe as a whole; for settled Jordanians larger kin ties are less binding, but they may come to the fore in the face of outside threats.

SOCIAL PRESTIGE. Wealth, traditionally one of the principal avenues to privileged social status and a sign of divine favor, is still correlated to a high degree with leadership. The possessor of wealth, as one who had received the blessing of God, was once—and to a degree still is—expected to display and use it in a manner designed to glorify God by benefiting others. If most often in practice this meant luxurious living, it also took the form of almsgiving and hospitality. One of the severest criticisms a tenant can level against his landlord is lack of generosity—an offense against both God and one's fellow men. Even the poorest peasant strives to provide for his guests, and nomad hospitality is surrounded by elaborate rules concerning the entertainment and protection of guests.

Land early became a prized form of wealth, coveted by peasant and townsman alike. Although urban dwellers look with disdain upon agriculture and other forms of manual work, they are eager to acquire land to be farmed by others. Land and landownership are the abiding preoccupations of the villager, and plots of land often have long, specific histories and frequently are given names.

The bedouin, in addition to the status acquired from membership in an important tribe or from wealth (measured in terms of camels or sheep and, increasingly, land), derives social prestige among his fellows from a reputation for courage. Although the settled population traditionally has looked down on the nomad as a predatory raider and robber, a somewhat romantic stereotype of the desert Arab— brave, generous, independent—has persisted, and townsmen and villagers are quick to claim ancestry in one of the noble bedouin tribes. Although the *ghazu* (bedouin raid for booty) has been outlawed by the Jordanian Government, the value placed on courage and prowess is still reflected in the mock battles and other recreational activities of the nomads.

Jordan's relatively few urban dwellers traditionally have placed great value on learning and looked down upon both nomads and villagers as backward and ignorant. The prestige attached to learning was enhanced by the fact that the learned man, as a person trained in Islamic theology, often functioned as a religious leader, teacher, or judge. Religious knowledge coupled with a mastery of classical Arabic was considered the highest achievement of learning, and educated Moslem Jordanians looked to al-Azhar, the great institute of Islamic studies at Cairo, as the intellectual center of the Arab world. Learning is regarded with similar veneration by the small Christian minority.

ATTITUDES TOWARD AUTHORITY. Governmental authority—historically arbitrary and distant—has long been distrusted by the bulk of the Jordanian population. For the villager the image of the government official has been an intrusive agent sent to extort rents and taxes. The nomads for their part tend to identify the government with the settled population—the traditional target of their contempt. Although driven increasingly by economic and political pressures in the direction of sedentarization, the bedouins still nourish old grievances against the settled population and retain their feeling of superiority.

The allegiance to the kings of Jordan sworn by the chiefs of the principal tribes appears to be more a declaration of personal loyalty to a kind of superior sheikh than any real acceptance of government jurisdiction over their affairs. Jealous of their independence, the tribes have resented what they deem unwarranted government interference, particularly when it runs counter to the values and practices embodied in their customary law. For a nomad to submit to state law (whether Moslem law or the recently adopted modern secular law) may often be tantamount to disgrace. A family which delivers the murderer of one of its kinsmen to the governmental authorities instead of taking its own vengeance may be dishonored in the eyes of the tribe.

Despite traditional distrust of the government, official position carries high prestige and a government appointment remains the primary goal of education for many Jordanians. Those in positions of authority are expected to make a forceful display of their power, and it is generally taken for granted that they will use it for their own advantage and that of their families.

Man and Man

It would be difficult to exaggerate the importance of personal relationships among all segments of Jordanian society. The individual tends to be identified and rated in terms not so much of a notion of his own qualities and attainments as of his place in a network of personal and kin relations. A man is important if he has powerful relatives and friends, and his relationship with them is one of mutual obligation. This pattern—with its emphasis, in matters of preferment, on whom rather than on what one knows—has placed a premium on personal acquaintance and personal interaction between individuals. The relatively impersonal patterns which in the West are regarded as appropriate in business and governmental affairs find little response in the Jordanian, whose tradition tells him that security and success are to be obtained only through personal relations and the claims of personal acquaintance.

This preference for highly personalized relationships is nowhere more evident than in the bargaining process. Bargaining is the traditional and (despite the appearance of the western style *prix fixe* store in the cities) the dominant way in which goods are bought and sold in Jordan as elsewhere in the Arab world. More, the bargaining pattern is applied in a wide variety of non-economic situations. A Jordanian finds it "natural" to bargain in almost any situation calling for agreement between two parties; he finds security and aesthetic satisfaction in the give and take of the bargaining process. Bargaining provides the opportunity for the parties concerned to demonstrate their virtuosity and to exchange gossip and opinions as well as to arrange a transaction. To refuse to bargain in the numerous situations in which it is normal to do so is regarded as a discourtesy.

The emphasis placed on the personal relationship is also reflected in the tendency stemming from the bedouin Arab tradition to rely on oral rather than written agreements. Written agreements are employed, but there is a finality about them which is distasteful to Jordanians. Furthermore, insistence on a written contract is regarded not only as implying distrust of the individual's word but as potentially prejudicial to the kind of personal adjustments to which most agreements in the Middle East are subject.

The Sexes

Although the social segregation of the sexes is part of the Islamic tradition, the veiling and seclusion of women has always been confined to a small segment of Jordanian society, centered in the upper classes of the towns. Nomad and village women as a rule are not veiled. While their sphere of activity is largely confined to the family circle, they may help their husbands outside the home; they also participate in the traditional forms of bedouin and peasant hospitality, a considerable amount of social contact between men and women not related to each other having long been accepted. The position of working-class women in the towns is similar in many respects to that of rural women, although the former are more likely to be veiled in imitation of the middle and upper classes.

Until recently a mark of social status—a sign of belonging to the coveted upper reaches of society—the seclusion of women is becoming restricted to the most conservative urban families. The impact of western influences, directly and through the relatively emancipated women of the West Bank population, has greatly speeded this process. Educational and professional opportunities for girls have been increasing, and the royal family has set the lead in promoting emancipation of women. However, even the mixed social life (in the western sense) of the small segment of the educated urban population is inhibited by traditional restrictions. A girl is generally chaperoned by her brothers or other relatives, and even engaged couples are seldom allowed to be alone.

Traditional Islamic codes governing sexual behavior are rigid, and among villagers, nomads, and conservative elements in the towns they are still adhered to. Sex is never a subject of discussion in mixed company, and physical modesty is strictly required of young people. Premarital sexual relations and adultery are regarded with violent disapproval. Among the nomads a woman guilty of adultery may be severely punished and even put to death by her father or brothers, who are considered responsible for her moral conduct, and in the villages the attitude toward sexual laxity in women is almost as severe. Urban

society is in a state of transition in this as in other aspects of social life
—there are indications of some slackening in observance of the traditional sexual code.

Westernization

Western thought and technology have affected different segments of the Jordanian population in varying degrees and ways. The strongest impact has been felt in the towns, particularly those of the former Palestinian territory, and the most conspicuous reactions have been those of the educated urban groups. While some conservative Jordanians—religious leaders in particular—have persisted in a fundamental opposition to western values and institutions, most upper- and middle-class townspeople have accepted western technology and educational methods and have tended to espouse many of the western, especially the secular, patterns of thought. Consciously imitating western social patterns, they verge on a rejection of much of their value heritage and traditional social controls—without any real assimilation of the competing western ideas. This is evident in the typical Jordanian product of foreign schools abroad or of western-modeled education at home. In the face of western curricula, teaching methods, and texts, Middle Eastern patterns persist—in particular, the practice of rote learning with its repressive effect on initiative and original thinking and the tendency for eloquence and diction to take precedence over substance. Moreover, western notions of academic honesty are apt to have little relevance for the Jordanian student, whose tradition tells him that cheating is clever rather than morally reprehensible.

Nor has exposure to western patterns necessarily produced pro-western sentiments. Those who have been quickest to adopt the outward trappings of western culture and to identify themselves with the West—often as a means of enhancing social prestige—have frequently harbored feelings of inferiority, envy, or hostility in the face of western power. This ambivalence is reflected to some degree in the mixed attitude of East Bank Jordanians toward the more westernized former Palestinians—the urge to emulation being coupled with resentment and jealousy.

Western influence in the towns has affected business, industry, the professions, and general patterns of life in matters ranging from recreation to dress. The highly personalized business dealings of the past are showing signs of yielding to the more impersonal methods usual in western countries, and individual accomplishment vies increasingly with wealth and family affiliation as an avenue to success and social prestige.

The secularizing effect of western influences is reflected in recreation patterns. In the towns new mass-produced media of entertainment modeled on western prototypes are gradually replacing traditional forms of recreation centering on family activities and religious ceremonies. Urban recreation revolves around coffeehouses, clubs, societies, and films.

In the countryside traditional patterns persist but are being affected to some extent by the forces of change. The influence of the towns on surrounding areas is considerable and the old isolation of the village is breaking down. Increasing numbers of peasants are drawn to the towns either as visitors or for education and temporary or permanent employment. With the transition to urban life, the new townsman tends to shed some of the older family controls and his once exclusively local loyalties compete with a feebly developed but growing consciousness of belonging to a larger society.

Although still relatively untouched by the influence of modern education or western ideas, Jordan's nomads have not been immune to the new forces at work in the area. The coming of the airplane and the oil pipeline has altered their vistas, and the gradual displacement of the camel by the truck has set into motion far-reaching changes in their customary living patterns. Service in the British-led Arab Legion gave many tribesmen experience in a highly disciplined, westernized military organization in which they gained new values and wider loyalties.

NATIONAL ATTITUDES

THE JORDANIANS SHARE WITH NEIGHBORING ARAB PEOPLES THE religion of Islam, the Arabic language, and their history up to the end of World War I. A feeling of relatedness and of a certain community of fate persisted during the period of the British Mandate. The idea that the Jordanians in common with the other Arab peoples had certain shared interests and aspirations was implicit in the country's joining the Arab League. But on the establishment of the Emirate of Transjordan a deliberate effort to foster among the Jordanians a sense of separate statehood and nationhood was made by the royal family, the government leadership, and all groups whose interests were served by statehood. It was an effort which had to overcome serious handicaps and which even now has not fully succeeded; what effect federation will have in this area, only time will tell.

In the territory which constitutes the present state of Jordan the very idea of nationhood in the modern western sense was unknown a generation ago. If the British had not carved the Transjordanian Emirate out of Syria, the present inhabitants, or at least the city dwellers among them, of the region east of the Jordan River might have developed the feeling that they were Syrians. As a matter of fact, some Jordanians today speak of themselves as South Syrians. It is highly questionable whether Jordanian national patriotism has struck deep roots in the consciousness of the people, especially those former Palestinians who became Jordanians after the accession of the region west of the Jordan. Many Jordanians feel that the state was created artificially, primarily in order to serve the political aims of Great Britain; that a foreign princely family was superimposed over it as the ruling house, and that *de facto* the state has not achieved complete independence or real sovereignty. The national and patriotic movements—of very recent date in every Arab country—are in Jordan complicated by factional struggles. While the royal family, the bedouins, and the propertied classes of the region which was formerly Transjordan may repudiate the idea that there is no justification for the separate existence of a Jordanian state, the feeling is especially strong among the former Palestinians that a small, weak country whose very name had to be artificially created would better serve the interests of its people by merging with other Arab nations to form a truly independent, large, strong state.

The idea of merging Jordan and Syria had originally more general popular support than any other scheme of unification. It became, however, the special thesis and passionately supported political theme of the former Palestinians after their leaders rose to position and power; it also became the unavowed but obvious goal of dominant elements in the Egyptian and Syrian governments. Consequently, many former Transjordanians who favored it tended to turn away from it and toward other plans, previously favored by the political leadership, for unification of Jordan with neighboring countries. Of these the most important, aside from the Greater Syria Plan, were the various schemes, now brought to fruition, for merging Jordan and Iraq, both ruled by the Hashemite House. Such plans have been the specific Jordanian development of an idea and movement found in many circles in many Arab countries: Pan-Arabism, based on a community of language, religion, history, and world outlook.

Jordanian Nationalism

In Jordan, as in Iraq, Pan-Arabism came into conflict with the nationalism of the political leaders, whose vested interests demanded the perpetuation of the kingdom and who resisted the domination of the Arab world by Egypt. Thus, two different varieties of nationalism compete with each other in Jordan: on the one hand, an all-embracing Pan-Arab nationalism strongly influenced both by Colonel Nasser's Egypt and by Moslem leaders willing to use—and be used by—international communism to serve the goals of a professedly anticolonial supra-nationalism; on the other hand is a particularist Jordanian nationalism bent on preserving the existence of the nation, willing to strengthen the ties of the nation with those of its neighbors fully committed to resist the inroads of international communism into the Middle East, and also willing to accept the help of the United States.

On the issue of Israel, however, there is no true difference: both varieties of nationalism are committed to the destruction of that state. Pan-Arab nationalism, derived from the old consciousness of being part of a large Arab community, has been colored, changed, and given new, more militant form by the growth of Colonel Nasser's power and influence, by the strengthening of Syria's ties with the Soviet world, and above all by the connivance of some of the Palestinian-Jordanian leaders with both Egypt and Syria. Jordanian nationalism, relatively new, has drawn upon older, conservative elements, particularly in former Transjordan, elements increasingly alarmed by the role of international communism in the Middle East. Pan-Arab nationalism seemed until recently to have a more assured place within the traditional hierarchical structure of loyalties than the newer Jordanian nationalism, but the pattern now seems to be changing under the impact of the two mergers, with its final arrangement not yet foreseeable.

The strength of the personal loyalties within the old established hierarchy has been greatly modified by a decisive change in the Moslem world. The peoples have been divided into separate states; they have been formed into or emerged as separate nations, at times with conflicting interests and attitudes; the cohesive force of a common religious tradition and way of life has tended to fragmentize. The new states have claimed a national loyalty not only new in itself but of a type previously unknown in the Moslem world. The situation of Jordan, however, was unusual: unlike most of its Moslem Arab neighbors, it could not easily support a claim to the patriotic fealty of its people by the evocation of an historic tradition stemming from ancient statehood or empire; Jordan had never before been a separate state or nation. Necessarily, therefore, national patriotism had to assert itself with difficulty against the opposing claims, on the one hand, of loyalties to family, kin-group, and tribe, on the other, of a Pan-Arabism which pronounced itself the full and logical extension of the old hierarchy of loyalties.

In the towns, especially in the capital, Amman, efforts to foster the people's loyalty to the state were helped by the sense of participation in political events which develops in a population living in spatial proximity to the king, government, parliament, and those leading families whose members fill important political and administrative positions. Moreover, both in the towns and in the countryside mass communication propaganda methods were used, although on an extremely modest scale; the people were drawn into the atmosphere of national patriotism by radio broadcasts reaching into every town and almost every village, by the newspapers, which though few in number included several speaking for the government, and by the increasing activities of the political parties. In the campaign for the 1947 elections several candidates used airplanes to drop leaflets over villages and bedouin camps. The developing school system became a means of spreading national consciousness among young people. For the first time in Jordan, pupils of the higher grades participated in street demonstrations, following the example of students in Cairo, Damascus, and other Arab capitals.

The efforts of Jordanian nationalists were at first directed toward channeling some of the force of family and local loyalty into national patriotism. After Jordan's acquisition of the West Bank region, however, the leaders of the former Palestinians became a powerful force of national disintegration; passionately eager, above all, to wrest all of Palestine from the Israelis and convinced that only the absorption of the state of Jordan into a larger and more militant Arabic political entity could accomplish their aims, they symbolized and embodied the transformation of the old Arabism into modern Pan-Arabism. It soon became the major task of the Jordanian nationalists not so much to win over the people from the ancient local loyalties to the cause of national loyalty as to defend the nation against those who sought to subvert it. The official use of mass communication quickly appeared weak and puny when contrasted with the resources applied in the same field by the supporters of Pan-Arabism in Cairo and Damascus. Further, the Palestinians could make better use of the organized mob than the government could of its bedouin supporters. Above all, following the dismissal of the British officers from what was then the Arab Legion, the entry of the Soviet Union with its mighty propaganda apparatus into the Middle East as the supporter of Colonel Nasser and his version of Pan-Arabism, the absorption of Syria by the terms of the United Arab Republic, the Jordanian national patriots were put on the defensive; the final doom of the Jordanian nation seemed only a matter of time.

But in the spring of 1957 there was a change in both the international climate and that of Jordanian politics. The young King Hussein dared to assert his personal authority in an effort to save both his throne and his nation. He was helped by the emergence, particularly among the people on the East Bank of the Jordan, of a significant change in attitude: many Jordanians saw the willingness of Pan-Arabism, as symbolized by Nasser, to associate itself with some of the goals of international communism as a threat to traditional Islamic values and a challenge to the hierarchical pattern of loyalties. They felt that their society was being invaded and corrupted by alien influences; that the assistance professed to be given freely by international communism was a harbinger of future bondage; that the help of the supposedly anticolonialist Soviet Union might be more damaging than the harm wrought by the old colonialists of the West; that the sympathy of the United States, the leading nation in the western world, was worth having. Thus Nasser's Pan-Arabism lost some of the support which, through the ancient local loyalties, had traditionally been given to Arab nationalism. The new Jordanian nationalism gained by that loss, and an opportunity was presented for presenting an alternative form of Pan-Arabism.

The attitudes of Jordanians toward their own country, then, are conditioned by the convergences and conflicts within several sets of influences, principally the social and the political, the traditional and the contemporary. The Jordanians lack the kind of unity as a national people which might have been created by a common historical evolution long enough to fuse disparate elements; they are indeed less a people than a congeries of local and kin groups, and their attitudes both to the nation and to their role in it are necessarily varied.

In general, the traditionalist elements tend to make themselves most felt in the context of personal orientations and social patterns; but, whereas they might have reinforced the political impulse toward a single great Arab Moslem nation, they had been deflected by the growth of Nasser's Pan-Arabism into support of a Jordanian nation. On the other hand, the strong contemporary influence, specifically political, tended to invoke the older values of Islam as a justification of a merger of Jordan with Syria, the modern Arab state most closely tied with international communism.

Attitudes toward Jordan's survival are closely linked with those toward the ruling royal house, and these in turn reflect the attitudes of the various local groups and kin-groups toward one another. Those Jordanians who are loyal to King Hussein favor independent statehood, and those who prefer nationalism to Pan-Arabism have in many cases shifted their loyalty to him. The bedouins of the East Bank are now more passionately loyal to the King by reason of the fact that the Palestinians are against him; the Palestinian townsmen, who despised the nomads, are most committed to the destruction of the throne. Yet when Abdullah was established in Transjordan by the British soon after the end of World War I, the suspicion and distrust of all government, habitual in the Moslem world, was most markedly directed against him by the bedouins and the other traditionalists. He was seen as a prince from remote Hejaz imposed by an even more remote infidel power. Abdullah worked hard for the better part of his lifetime to be accepted as the head of a nation and to make all of the people—the bedouins, the villagers, the townsfolk—see that their interests were identical with those of his House. His grandson, the present King, has been hindered in following a similar course by the Palestinian townsmen who see him as a traditionalist obstacle to the triumph of their modernist version of Pan-Arabism.

The Jordanians are thus too divided among themselves to accept a national as distinguished from an Arab ethnocentrism, the feeling and conviction that their own country, nation, and culture are always right and that their own ethnos—people, race, or ethnic group—is the center of culture and the locus of the highest cultural achievements. The former Transjordanians, especially the bedouins, regard the settled townsmen and primarily those of former Palestine as less manly, softer, less Arab than themselves; they oppose intermarriage and disdain all urban occupations. Yet, though young King Hussein seeks to be a modern monarch and is willing to take advice and even help from the West, they are loyal to him and, because of that loyalty, they are national patriots.

The villagers, most of them living in what also was Transjordan, regard with suspicion both the nomad bedouins, who used to raid and rob them, and the townsmen whom they associate with the King's government and whom they hated as extorters of rents, dues, and taxes. Their loyalty to the King has increased, however, as Palestinian townsmen bent on removing the King have more and more taken over positions of power in the government. Similarly, as the townsmen of former Transjordan have been displaced from positions of power by the former Palestinians and treated as no better than the other East Bankers—the bedouins and villagers traditionally regarded as backward and ignorant—some of them have moved toward greater loyalty to the royal house. Other Transjordanians, however, have already gone so far in rejecting all connection with the old traditions without at the same time absorbing western democratic values, that they have tended to succumb to the influence of communism.

The Role of Religion

The traditional hierarchical structure of loyalties in Jordan is deeply influenced by Islam. In the Moslem outlook the world is divided into two parts: the *dar al-islam,* House of Islam, is the realm of peace within which all Moslems are equal and live in harmony under the law of Islam; the *dar al-harb,* House of War, is outside the Islamic realm and hostile to it. To conquer the House of War and to pacify it in the sense of subjecting it to Islamic law and rule is sometimes regarded as the Sixth Pillar of Islam.

The House of Islam is divided into sects, of which the most important are the Sunnite and Shiite; into language groups, such as Arabs, Persians, Turks; and, most recently, into states. In Jordan the House of Islam is identified with the Sunnite Moslem Arab world.

During the Ottoman regime the presence of different religious and/or linguistic communities in one and the same locality was taken care of by the millet system, based on a concept of protected, separate groups. Into this order there was introduced after the end of World War I the new concept of nation-state. With this innovation the several coextensive millets were abolished, their place was taken by the nation. Thus, after the establishment of the Emirate of Transjordan all the inhabitants of the new political entity became officially members of the new Jordanian (Transjordanian) nation, irrespective of their religion, language, or ethnic origin. The official Jordanian view in recent years has been completely to deny even the existence in Jordan of "those groups of inhabitants who have national, religious, linguistic, and special characteristics which make them different from the rest of the population."

This official attitude notwithstanding, members, and especially leaders, of the ethno-religious minority groups still feel it necessary from time to time to emphasize their oneness with the nation. For instance, in neighboring Syria, where the Christian ethnic groups occupy a position closely parallel to that of the Jordanian Christians, Monsignor Houbbi, the Latin Archbishop of the Jazirah province, issued a statement in which he said: "We are all one Syrian Arab people, we live under the Syrian sky as brothers in the Arab sentiment. We denounce energetically any separation propagated by foreigners and their agents." Other Christian notables of Jazirah issued a similar statement.

Attitudes Toward Other Arab States

Jordanian attitudes toward the other Arab states reflect the variations in the political orientations within the country's population. Syria and Egypt were highly regarded by most Jordanian city dwellers and some villagers during the early years of Jordan's existence as a state. Recently, however, Syria and Egypt, though intensely popular with many West Bankers, have come to be viewed with increasing suspicion and distrust by the East Bankers, and some West Bankers have come to feel that Syria, Egypt, and even the whole Arab world are responsible for their misery in not coming effectively to their aid against Israel. For the average bedouin, Egypt, Syria, even Jordan, are only vague concepts; the United Arab Republic and the Arab Federation are vaguer still.

Iraq, like Jordan, is ruled by a member of the Hashemite dynasty: King Faisal is a second cousin of King Hussein. Although there has been a certain affinity between the royal courts of the two countries, the Iraqi Government was until recently unpopular in Jordan; it was considered pro-British or even British controlled (see chap. 10). But attitudes toward Iraq have more recently conformed, in reverse, to the changed pattern in relation to Syria and Egypt; those who were against Syria and Egypt found new virtues in Iraq.

In the past, Jordanians generally had been critical of the lavish display of luxury and the personal conduct of members of the Saudi royal family. Later, however, the political conduct of King Saud tended to become the criterion of judgment; Saudi Arabia was popular with the East Bankers insofar as it seemed to support King Hussein's cause, unpopular with the West Bankers for the same reason.

Attitudes Toward Israel and the West

The attitudes of the Jordanians toward foreign countries, peoples, and ideas have undergone great changes in recent decades. Until the early nineteenth century, foreigners from western countries in general were considered simply infidels whose ideas were sinful. In Transjordan, with the establishment of the Mandate, the foreigner gained the prestige which Moslems accord the citizen of a conquering nation. At the same time, however, he incurred the dislike and resentment stemming from his role as an invader or interloper, for there was no desire that the rule of the Ottoman Empire should be replaced by that of other empires, not only colonialist but also infidel.

Nevertheless, some ideas and ways were emulated, at least superficially. Beneficial measures introduced in such fields as sanitation and education impressed the Jordanians, and such evidences of western luxury as the automobile attracted them. The rudiments of freedom, never enjoyed under Turkish rule, whetted the Jordanians' appetite for more of the same but also increased their resentment against foreign domination. The aura of British and French political prestige in the Arab communities during the period between the two World Wars extended also to the superficialities of British and French culture, and of western culture in general. With the waning of the political prestige after World War II the aura began to vanish. In recent years, particularly following the creation of Israel, the rise to power of Colonel Nasser, and the Israeli-Franco-British foray into Egypt, whatever has seemed a vestige of western domination has been regarded with more and more open hostility, and accordingly some aspects of western influence have waned, although the process of westernization goes on.

In Jordan the change in attitude became most marked after the creation of the state of Israel. The Jordanians share with the other Arabic peoples the view that Israel is an aggressive foreign state planted in their midst by Britain and the United States. The Jordanian attitude of bitter antagonism toward, mixed with fear of, Israel is stronger than that of the other Arab peoples, partly because Jordan has a longer common frontier with Israel than has any other Arab state, but also because a majority of the present population of Jordan is made up of former Palestinians.

The presence of the former Palestinians is one of the factors which prevent simple and easy generalizations about the attitudes of Jordanians as a whole toward foreign countries, peoples, and ideas. There are in fact several different types of attitude: that of the Jordanians of the West Bank of the Jordan in territory formerly part of Palestine; that of the town dwellers of the East Bank; that of the villagers and of the bedouins on the East Bank. Even these distinctions are not adequate to suggest the actual complexities. The degree to which the present population of Jordan has been attracted and influenced by western ideas, cultures, and habits of living is greatest among the former Palestinians, and diminishes in descending scale among the townsfolk of the East Bank, the villagers, and, finally, the bedouins among whom it is virtually nonexistent. On the other hand, the amount of resentment against the West is smallest—if it exists at all—among the bedouins and rises in ascending scale to passionate intensity among the Palestinians, largely because of their hatred of Israel and their assumption that the western nations block their hope for the destruction of the Jewish state.

Suspicion has been a long-standing characteristic of Arab intergroup relations. Although the amount of suspicion toward foreign nations, governments, and institutions varies in nature and degree among the different elements of the population of Jordan, it is omnipresent. Newspapers, for example, tend to be quick to give an anti-Jordanian interpretation to completely harmless or well-meaning acts undertaken by foreign governments, institutions, or individuals. Once hostile sentiment is aroused against a foreign country any individual or group from that country is regarded with suspicion. During the rioting fomented and carried out by opponents of the Baghdad Pact, for example, mobs attacked and damaged the American hospital in Ajlun, several American technical assistance projects, and a small Quaker-sponsored community project in the village of Dibbin (see chap. 10).

The steep decline in the prestige and popularity of the western countries has been accompanied by a rise in the esteem accorded the Soviet Union. But here, too, simple generalizations tend to be distortions because of the variety of attitudes in the different parts of the Jordanian population. Insofar as the Soviet Union has seemed to support the whole Arab world against colonialism, it has gained Jordanian respect in all quarters; insofar as it has supported Colonel Nasser against Israel, provided him with military weapons, and threatened to come to his aid against the British and French in the Suez campaign, it has won enthusiastic gratitude. Conversely, the British and French lost enormously in prestige because of their association with Israel in the military campaign; and the United States shared in the loss of popularity because it was considered lukewarm in condemning Israel. While such attitudes have been most marked among the West Bankers, they have been present everywhere in Jordan.

But Jordanians of the East Bank, who welcomed the Soviet stand on Israel, tend to be vigorously opposed to international communism and to welcome United States help in restricting its inroads into Middle Eastern affairs. Loyal to King Hussein, determined to prevent any serious alteration in the status of the nation, they are in effect and indirectly the allies of the West against all the enemies of Jordan's continued existence—ranging from the pro-Soviet or neutralist leaders of the Palestinians, to the supporters of Egypt and Syria, and finally to the local and foreign Communists. In this frame of reference, the bedouins are diametrically opposed to the Palestinian leaders and willing to fight them to preserve their way of life under their sheikh and the throne.

Loyalty

Given the ambiguity of Jordanian concepts of the nation, it is necessary to look elsewhere for the fundamental context within which the Jordanian views himself. The important distinctions made in Jordan between men are made on the basis of local and kinship affiliations, coupled with religion, wealth, and occupation.

The traditional Middle Eastern family is the center around which the individual's loyalties revolve. For its members the family still takes precedence over any other larger social group, including the state. Next in order of loyalty comes the lineage, the kin-group composed of several related families; then the larger descent group to which the lineage belongs; and so on up the scale of size, with the intensity of loyalty diminishing as the distance increases. The Moslem Arab community is conceived—particularly in the Pan-Arab view—as a huge kin-group. Related, but more distant, are the non-Arab Moslem communities which fill out the mosaic of the Islamic world.

TABLES
RECOMMENDED READING
INDEX

Table 1. Population of Jordan by Districts and Subdistricts, 1954

District and Subdistrict		Population
AMMAN		202,313
AL BALQA		97,533
As Salt	68,278	
Madaba	29,255	
AJLUN		227,607
Irbid	149,023	
Ajlun	28,519	
Jarash	28,424	
Dayr Abu Said	21,641	
AL KARAK		63,088
Al Karak	43,158	
At Tafilah	19,930	
MAAN		29,801
Maan	24,829	
Al Aqabah	4,972	
JERUSALEM (AL QUDS)		316,928
Jerusalem	89,833	
Ram Allah	115,548	
Bethlehem (Bayt Lahm)	59,069	
Jericho (Ariha)	52,478	
NABULUS		332,696
Nabulus	161,807	
Janin	84,555	
Tul Karm	86,334	
HEBRON (AL KHALIL)		132,661
DESERT ADMINISTRATION		----(a)
Total		1,402,627

(a) No settled population figures available.

Source: Adapted from working papers prepared under contract
with the Human Relations Area Files at Dropsie College
under the direction of Raphael Patai; citing from Jordan
Ministry of Economy: Department of Statistics, Annual
Statistical Yearbook, 1954.

Table 2. Jordanian Labor Force, 1955

Agricultural

	Refugee	Indigenous	Total
Full-time Employment	negligible	131,000	131,000
Part-time Employment	50,000	10,000	60,000
Unemployed	42,000	40,000	82,000
			273,000

Urban

	Refugee	Indigenous	Total
Full-time Employment	10,000	43,000	53,000
Part-time Employment	16,000	4,000	20,000
Unemployed	20,000	13,000	33,000
			106,000

Table 3. Average Daily Wage in Principal Towns in 1952
(in Jordanian piasters)[a]

Industrial Group	Average All Areas	Jeru-salem	Hebron	Amman	Irbid	Nabulus
A. Adult Workers						
Average All Groups	22.4	22.1	17.7	25.2	20.8	20.9
Building	22.9	22.1	20.2	24.7	22.7	18.6
Food Industries	23.5	24.1	16.7	26.8	17.4	23.3
Transport	25.9	24.0	21.4	29.9	25.9	25.2
Other Industries	22.7	18.5	18.8	26.8	16.5	21.8
Crafts	23.5	25.1	17.6	27.3	20.1	19.8
Services	20.4	19.5	13.5	22.9	17.5	20.3
B. Young Workers						
Average All Groups	6.1	8.3	4.3	8.5	6.2	5.5
Building	---	---	---	---	---	---
Food Industries	8.1	14.8	3.9	7.4	9.0	4.2
Transport	3.7	4.3	3.8	5.7	3.4	2.9
Other Industries	7.4	5.0	7.8	8.7	4.2	5.5
Crafts	6.1	5.9	3.2	9.6	5.2	4.8
Services	6.8	7.9	6.4	---	6.3	6.6

[a] One piaster equals 2.8 United States cents.

Source: Adapted from working papers prepared under contract with the Human Relations Area Files at Dropsie College under the direction of Raphael Patai.

Table 4. Development Expenditures, Jordan

(JD 1,000)

	1950-51	1951-52	1952-53	1953-54	1954-55	1955-56	Total
Regular Ministries Expenditure on:							
Economic Activity	484	601	534	661	964	1,052(a)	4,296
Capital Items	892	1,624	1,106	924	1,673	1,693(a)	7,912
Development Board Expenditures	--	--	570	1,192	1,221	1,414	4,397
Point Four Contributions	--	1,678	1,134	3,882	2,691	2,806	12,191
UNRWA Expenditures	--	248	339	818	1,208	1,060	3,673
Total	1,376	4,151	3,683	7,477	7,757	8,025	32,469

(a) Estimated.

Source: Adapted from United Nations Relief and Works Agency for Palestine Refugees, _Bulletin of Economic Development_, No. 14, Special Reports on Jordan, p. 121.

Table 5. Central Government Domestic Revenue, Jordan

Item	1951-52[a]		1955-56[b]	
	Amount	Percent	Amount	Percent
Customs	1,826	33.4	2,560	38.5
Import License Fees - Exchange Tax	140	2.6	400	6.0
Excise	190	3.4	226	3.5
Income Tax	320	5.9	300	4.6
Rural Property Tax	95	1.7	75	1.1
Urban Property Tax	105	1.9	175	2.6
Trade License Fees	102	1.9	65	1.0
Animal Tax	108	2.0	100	1.5
Stamp Duty Revenue	77	1.5	100	1.5
Land Registration Fees	66	1.2	89	1.3
Traffic Licenses and Fees	37	0.6	62	0.9
Court Fees	85	1.5	89	1.3
Other Fees	165	3.1	213	3.2
Social Welfare and National Guard Tax	--	--	335	5.0
Aviation Deposit Tax	519	9.6	500	7.5
Post, Telegraph, Telephone	235	4.3	364	5.5
Revenue of State Property	25	0.4	36	0.5
Royalties	377	6.9	360	5.4
Interests, Profits	254	4.6	345	5.2
Various Taxes and Revenues	731	13.5	261	3.9
Total	5,457	100.0	6,655	100.0
Tax Revenue	4,165	76.4	5,443	81.8
Non-Tax Revenue	1,292	23.6	1,212	18.2

(a) Actual.
(b) Budget estimates.

Source: Adapted from International Bank for Reconstruction and
Development, The Economic Development of Jordan, Vol. III,
1956, p. 471.

Table 6. Summary of Central Government Fiscal Operations, Jordan[a]

(JD 1,000)

	1950-51	1951-52	1952-53	1953-54	1954-55[b]	1955-56[c]
Expenditure						
Part I						
Ordinary	2,040	4,359	4,038	4,326	4,923	5,808
Extraordinary	1,318	1,431	1,018	880	1,314	1,270
Part II - Defense	5,295	7,759	7,672	8,950	9,059	8,847
Part III - U.K. Development Loans[d]	489	241	705	1,234	1,338	1,949
Total	9,142	13,790	13,433	15,390	16,634	17,874
Receipts						
Domestic Revenue	4,388	5,459	5,572	5,768	7,495	6,655
U.K. and Other Foreign Grants	4,898	7,200	7,314	9,144	9,102	8,700
Total	9,286	12,659	12,886	14,912	16,597	15,355

continued

Table 6. (continued)

	1950-51	1951-52	1952-53	1953-54	1954-55[b]	1955-56[c]
Budget Surplus or Deficit (-)	144	-1,197[e]	-547	-478	-37	-2,519
Drawing on U.K. Loans	1,000	--	570	1,192	1,246	1,924
Reserve Fund Decrease or Increase (-)	-1,144	1,197	-23	-714[f]	-1,209	595

(a) Part I included nonmilitary expenditures from the first of the British Development Loans (see footnote (d)) and from domestic revenue. "Extraordinary expenditures" include development projects and government participation in industrial ventures. Part II records military expenditures administered by the Arab Legion, now the Jordan Arab Army. Part III indicates the expenditures made by the Jordan Development Board on the basis of loan arrangements with Britain. All three parts of the budget are administered separately.

(b) Provisional.

(c) Estimated.

(d) For the sake of uniformity of presentation IBRD has transferred from Part I the following expenditures from the first U.K. Development Loan: 1950-51, JD 489,000; 1951-52, JD 241,000; 1952-53, JD 135,000; 1953-54, JD 42,000; 1954-55, JD 92,000; 1955-56, JD 25,000.

(e) Including JD 66,000 deficit incurred in West Jordan administration.

(f) Including JD 161,000 receipts from Arab League countries booked "below the line."

Source: Adapted from International Bank for Reconstruction and Development, The Economic Development of Jordan, Vol. III, 1956, p. 468.

Table 7. Major Industries in Jordan, 1954

(employing five or more persons)

Industry	Number of Plants	Employment	Gross Value Output--JD
Food Processing			
Dairy	2	24	11,400
Canning	2	73	123,000
Flour Milling	17	342	2,173,500
Bakeries	16	200	291,000
Confectionery	21	244	180,120
Alimentary Paste	3	29	17,700
Distilling and Beverages			
Alcohol (commercial)	2	27	30,500
Intoxicating Drinks	8	69	73,230
Wine	3	22	17,600
Soft Drinks	17	235	111,120
Cigarettes and Tobacco	5	583	615,188
Weaving and Knitting	26	388	171,678
Wearing Apparel			
Shoemaking	39	---[a]	154,300
Shirts and Pajamas	6	123	77,000
Other Clothing	8	110	23,600
Tent Manufacturing	4	202	93,800
Carpentries	25	322	117,010
Furniture Making	25	445	173,471
Paper and Cardboard Products	8	179	156,000
Printing and Bookbinding	14	351	176,448
Leather Tanning and Products	11	---[a]	55,100
Manufacturing Rubber Products	3	20	40,950
Soap	21	225	293,600
Other Chemical Works (including matches)	6	227	47,962
Tiles, Cement Bricks, and Pipes	27	260	73,650
Marble	1)		(66,000
Cement	1)	576	(750,000
Ironworking	29	360	155,250
Kitchenware	2	32	41,500
Mirrors	4	63	38,600
Glass Blowing	2	21	10,500
Pottery	2	27	3,550
Foundries	18	496	240,000
Bus and Truck Bodies	11	256	84,700
Mother-of-Pearl Work	32	231	66,200
Mining			
Phosphates	1)		
Common Salt	2)	699	174,000

[a] Figure not available.

Table 8. Jordan's Import Trade in 1955

A. Major Suppliers by Country
(in million dollars)

United Kingdom	14.6
United States	7.8
West Germany	6.4
Lebanon (foreign goods)	6.2
(domestic goods)	1.9
Syria	5.0
France	4.5
Iraq	2.1
Other	27.2
Total	$75.7

B. Major Types of Commodities
(in terms of percentage of total)

Foodstuffs, Including Oils and Fats	31.08
Textiles and Clothing	12.98
Fuels	7.27
Building Materials	6.32
Transport Equipment	8.22
Industrial and Agricultural Machinery and Parts	5.59
Metals and Manufacturing Works	2.10
Chemicals and Pharmaceuticals	2.40
Beverages and Tobacco	1.89
Paper and Paper Products	1.55
Other	20.60
Total	100.00

Table 9.   Exports of Principal Commodities, Jordan

(millions of U.S. dollars)

Commodity	1950	1951	1952	1953	1954	1955
Total Exports[a] (excludes re-exports)	4.3	2.9	3.6	5.3	6.8	7.3
Olive Oil	.4	.1	.5	1.8	1.5	1.0
Raw Wool	.6	1.4	.2	.1	.1	.2
Vegetables and Fruits	.6	.6	1.2	2.0	2.1	2.8
Wheat and Barley	1.1	--[b]	.4	--[b]	.6	.1
Phosphate Rock	--[b]	--[c]	.1	.2	.2	1.7
Other	1.6	.8	1.2	1.2	2.3	1.5

[a] Totals not adjusted to date shown in selected annual statistics.
[b] No exports.
[c] Less than $50,000.

Table 10.   Enrollment in Jordanian Schools, 1952-53

	Public	Private Moslem	Private Christian	Total
Primary Schools	95,291	11,870	24,209	131,370
Secondary Schools	5,573	848	1,882	8,303
Vocational Schools	158	--	--	158
Teacher-training Course	46	--	--	46
Total	101,068	12,718	26,091	139,877
Boys	77,382	10,368	14,685	102,435 (63.5%)
Girls	23,686	2,350	11,406	37,442 (36.5%)

Source: Adapted from working papers prepared under contract with the
Human Relations Area Files at Dropsie College under the
direction of Raphael Patai.

RECOMMENDED READING

The following are recommended as additional reading on the basis of quality and general availability.

Baster, James. "The Economic Problems of Jordan," *International Affairs,* XXXI (January 1955), 26–35.

Cragg, Kenneth. *The Call of the Minaret.* New York: Oxford University Press, 1956.

Fisher, Sydney Nettleton (ed.). *Social Forces in the Middle East.* Ithaca, N. Y.: Cornell University Press, 1955.

Gibb, H. A. R. *Mohammedanism.* London, Toronto, and New York: Oxford University Press, 1953.

Glubb, John Bagot. *The Story of the Arab Legion.* London: Hodder & Stoughton, 1948.

Graves, Philip P. (ed.). *Memoirs of King Abdullah of Transjordan.* London: Jonathan Cape, 1950.

Grunebaum, G. E. von. *Muhammedan Festivals.* New York: Henry Schuman, Inc., 1951.

Hourani, A. H. *Minorities in the Arab World.* London, Toronto, and New York: Oxford University Press, 1947.

Hurewitz, J. C. *Diplomacy in the Near and Middle East: A Documentary Record,* 1914–1956. Vol. II. New York: D. Van Nostrand Co., Inc., 1956.

Husseini, Ishaq. "Islam Past and Present," *Atlantic Monthly* (Special Supplement), CXCVIII (October 1956), 169–172.

International Bank for Reconstruction and Development. *The Economic Development of Jordan.* Baltimore: Johns Hopkins Press, 1957.

Jurji, Edward J. *The Middle East: Its Religion and Culture.* Philadelphia: The Westminster Press, 1956.

Khadduri, Majid. "The Juridical Theory of the Islamic State," *The Moslem World,* XLI, No. 2 (July 1951), 181–185.

Khadduri, Majid, and Liebesny, Herbert J. *Law in the Middle East.* Washington, D. C.: Middle East Institute, 1955.

Lenczowski, George. *The Middle East in World Affairs.* Ithaca, N. Y.: Cornell University Press, 1956.

Mogannam, E. Theodore. "Developments in the Legal System of Jordan," *Middle East Journal,* VI, No. 2 (Spring 1952), 194–206.

Phillips, Paul G. *The Hashemite Kingdom of Jordan: Prolegomena to a Technical Assistance Program.* A Dissertation Submitted to the Faculty of the Division of the Social Sciences in Candidacy for the Degree of Doctor of Philosophy. Research paper No. 34. Chicago: University of Chicago Press, 1954.

Shafaq, S. R. "The Clergy in Islam." In Sydney N. Fisher (ed.), *Social Forces in the Middle East.* Ithaca, N. Y.: Cornell University Press, 1955.

Toukan, Baha Uddin. *A Short History of Trans-Jordan.* London: Luzac, 1945.

UNESCO. *Compulsory Education in the Arab States.* Paris, 1956.

Woodsmall, Ruth F. (director). *Study of the Role of Women; Their Activities and Organizations in Lebanon, Egypt, Iraq, Jordan, and Syria, October 1954–August 1955.* New York: The International Federation of Business and Professional Women, 1956.

Wright, Esmond. "Abdallah's Jordan." *Middle East Journal,* V, No. 4 (Autumn 1951), 439–460.

OTHER USEFUL SOURCES

Abdullah, King of Jordan. *My Memoirs Completed.* Ann Arbor, Mich.: J. W. Edwards, Publisher, Inc., 1954.

Arab Public Administration Conference I, Beirut, 1954. Beirut: Kashaf Press, 1954.

Arab Public Administration Conference II, Cairo, 1955. Beirut: Kashaf Press, 1955.

Badre, Dr. "Economic Life and Problems." Pages 63–68 in American University of Beirut, *Summer Seminar on the Middle East,* July 1–August 15, 1953.

Bruhns, Fred C. "A Study of Arab Refugee Attitudes," *Middle East Journal,* IX, No. 2 (Spring 1955), 130–138.

Burns, Norman. *Middle East Economic Problems.* (Course lectures given at the School of Advanced International Studies of the Johns Hopkins University, Washington, D. C., 1952–53; mimeographed.)

Cooke, Hedley V. *Challenge and Response in the Middle East; the Quest for Prosperity 1919–1951.* New York: Harper & Brothers, 1952.

Davis, Helen Miller. *Constitutions, Electoral Laws, Treaties of States in the Near and Middle East.* Durham, North Carolina: Duke University Press, 1947.

Dropsie College. *The Hashemite Kingdom of Jordan.* HRAF Subcontractor's Monograph, 1956.

Fisher, W. B. *The Middle East: A Physical, Social, and Regional Geography.* (2d ed.) New York: E. P. Dutton & Co., Inc., 1952.

Graves, Philip P. (ed.). *Memoirs of King Abdullah of Transjordan.* London: Jonathan Cape, 1950.

International Labour Conference. *Forced Labour, Report and Draft Questionnaire.* Twelfth Session. Geneva: International Labour Office, 1929.

———. *Report of the Ad Hoc Committee on Forced Labour.* Geneva, 1953.

Johansen, O. Lund (ed.). *World Radio Handbook for Listeners; Broadcasting, Television, 1956.* Copenhagen: Johansen, 1957.

Konikoff, A. *Transjordan: An Economic Survey.* Jerusalem: Economic Research Institute of the Jewish Agency for Palestine, "Hauman" Press, 1956.

Kurani, Habib. "Evolution in Education." Pages 3–12 in *Evolution in the Middle East: Reform, Revolt and Change.* Washington, D. C.: Middle East Institute, 1953.

Levy, Reuben. *The Social Structure of Islam.* Cambridge, England: Cambridge University Press, 1957.

Love, Kenneth. In *New York Times,* April 2, 1957.

Mackenzie, Marcus. "Transjordan," *Royal Central Asian Society Journal,* XXXIII (July–October 1946), 260–270.

Matthews, Roderic D., and Akrawi, Matta. *Education in Arab Countries of the Near East.* Washington, D. C.: American Council on Education, 1949.

The Middle East. (4th ed.). London: Europa Publications, 1955.

Morrison, S. A. *Middle East Tensions: Political, Social, and Religious.* New York: Harper & Brothers, 1954.

The New York Times, April and May 1957, *passim.*

Political Handbook of the World, 1956. New York: Harper & Brothers, 1956.

Royal Institute of International Affairs. *The Middle East: A Political and Economy Survey.* (2d ed.) London: Royal Institute of International Affairs, 1954.

Sherwood, Sidney. "Economic Problems in the Middle East," *Middle Eastern Affairs,* II (April 1951), 115–126.

Steinberg, S. H. (ed.). *The Statesman's Yearbook: Statistical and Historical Annual of the States of the World for the Year 1954.* London: The Macmillan Company, 1954.

Tritton, A. S. *Islam Beliefs and Practices.* London: Hutchinson's University Library, 1951.

United Nations. *Middle East Seminar on the Prevention of Crime and the Treatment of Offenders.* (Cairo, December 5–17, 1953.) New York, 1954.

United Nations: Department of Economic and Social Affairs. *Statistical Yearbook 1955.* New York, 1955.

UNESCO. *World Communications: Press, Radio, Film, Television.* (3rd ed.) New York, 1956.

———. *World Survey of Education, Handbook of Educational Organization and Statistics.* Paris, 1955.

United Nations Relief and Works Agency for Palestine Refugees. *Bulletin of Economic Development, No. 14, Special Reports on Jordan.* Beirut, July 1956.

Warriner, Doreen. *Land and Poverty in the Middle East.* New York: Royal Institute of International Affairs, 1948.

Yasin, A. H. "Teacher Training in Jordan," *Institute of International Education News Bulletin* (New York), XXXI, No. 8 (May 1956), 44–46.

Young, Peter. *Bedouin Command.* London: William Kimber, 1956.